SOCIAL CLASSES

SOCIAL CLASSES

M. A. Bagulia

ANMOL PUBLICATIONS PVT. LTD.
NEW DELHI - 110 002 (INDIA)

ANMOL PUBLICATIONS PVT. LTD.
H.O.: 4374/4B, Ansari Road, Darya Ganj,
New Delhi - 110 002 (India)
Ph.: 23278000, 23261597
B.O.: No. 1015, Ist Main Road, BSK IIIrd Stage,
IIIrd Phase, IIIrd Block,
Bangalore - 560 085 (India)
Visit us at: www.anmolpublications.com

Social Classes

First Published, 2007
ISBN 978-81-261-3219-5

PRINTED IN INDIA

Printed at Mehra Offset Press, Delhi.

CONTENTS

PREFACE

Social class is a unit in itself. It comes into being in a natural manner, over the decades and centuries. The class differentiation is the result of backwardness, lack of education and biased treatment by the governing bodies to some extent. But the root cause lies elsewhere. Human actions—good or bad—and efforts can be accounted for playing a significant part in formation of different classes, whereas, fate is the ultimate truth, beyond suspicion.

The system of life is such that all the creatures constitute a sound chain of interdependence. In spite of all the disparities at different levels, the mechanism, at work, is unchallengeable. But, the great fact remains at its place that people get divided into classes, almost automatically. At the social level, violence, injustice, cheating and fraud, exploitation of the weak, oppression of the poor, practising partisanship, ignorance towards the handicapped, etc., are regarded as inhuman. Humanity demands love for all, justice and fair treatment to the oppressed, help to the needy and so on. These are some of the virtues of humanity, irrespective of classes or castes, etc.

This work, *Social Classes* is a sincere attempt to provide all details of, and bring about an awakening, regarding the divided society of ours. The work is worth its salt and deserves accolades. Researchers, scholars, students, academics and the general readers alike, would find it handy and beneficial. Readers' suggestions and comments are anticipated and would be appreciated.

—Editor

1

SOCIAL ORGANISATION

NATURE OF CASTE AND CLASS

A number of points are there, which have so far remained unclarified in regard to the nature of caste and class in India. Some misconceptions are: Caste and class are polar opposites; caste is being replaced by class; caste is a rural phenomenon whereas class is found in urban-industrial settings; caste is an ascriptive system while class is based on the achievement principle; caste is a closed system and does not permit mobility for its members whereas class is an open system and allows mobility for its members; India has/had a caste system, hence a 'caste model' for studying Indian society and the West has/had classes, hence a 'class model' for studying western societies. However, these notions are rooted in the historicity of Indian society and its culture including British and post-independence academic colonialism.

The other points refer to the debate regarding approaches to the study of caste and class in India. The various approaches can be classified as:

(i) interactional versus attributional;

(ii) structural versus cultural; and

(iii) Marxist versus functional. These approaches have been borrowed from the West, and are clearly reflected in the studies of social stratification in India. Rural versus urban stratification, corporate vs. individual mobility, caste versus class relations, and ritual versus secular hierarchy are found as main issues in most of the studies on social stratification.

The studies range from the study of caste or class alone to caste and class, caste and power, class and power, and caste, class and religion. I wish to analyze these issues in view of the available studies on caste and class from the point of theory, method and data. Both caste and class have been analysed in terms of theory, structure and process. Earlier Singh (1974) made this observation about social stratification in India. There is no epistemological apriorism in this sort of exercise. The studies can be seen from the point of their requirements as well as from the point of caste and class relations in India.

IDEAL SETUP

A certain conception of 'model' of traditional Indian society has emerged. This model has/had implications for studying Indian society. The main features of this caste model are:

(i) it is based primarily on the ideas held or expressed by certain sections of society and not on the observed or recorded behaviour of people;

(ii) it attaches a kind of primary and universal significance to caste as this has been conceived in the classical texts;

(iii) the entire system is viewed as being governed by certain more or less explicitly formulated principles or 'rules of the game' ; and (iv) the different castes which are the basic units in the system are conceived as fulfilling complementary functions and their mutual relations as being 'non-antagonistic' (Beteille, 1969).

No doubt, the 'caste model' brings into focus some of the significant features of the traditional Indian society, but it fails on two counts:

(i) when it is made too general it can be applied to almost every society and therefore does not tell us very much about the specific properties of any society; and

(ii) when it is made too specific it fails to take into account certain crucial features of economic and political life (Ibid.). Beteille observes that the model has been more systematically elaborated by Dumont as it is concerned essentially with ideas and values. It has failed, however, in providing a proper place to material interests in social life. Beteille argues a case for the study of material interests along with the study of ideas and values in terms of the dialectical relations between the two.

But Beteille does not offer a 'class analysis' of Indian society as an alternative to the caste model. In fact, Beteille suggests a sort of modification of the caste model by putting an emphasis on the study of economic and political conflict with a certain degree of autonomy for the economic and political activities of inter-caste relations. However, he points out that it would be wrong to consider India as a 'caste society', and the United States as a 'class society', and Europe as an 'estate society'.

Beteille denies the validity of a sociology of values and ideas. He emphasizes the role of material interests in the studies of traditional society and culture in India. Beteille takes a clue from Leach (1960), Bailey (1963), and Dumont (1970), who have offered a 'caste model' of Indian society. The essence of the views of Leach, Bailey and Dumont is that caste is a non-competitive system, the castes are 'non-antagonistic' strata. Leach (1960) writes: "Wherever caste groups are seen to be acting as corporations in competition against like—groups of different castes, then they are acting in defiance of caste principles." Competition refers to class and cooperation refers to caste. This is really a very erroneous view about both class and caste, and more so about the understanding of caste in India.

VIEWPOINT OF CLASS IN WESTERN SOCIETIES

Western scholars (including Leach) look at the caste system from the viewpoint of class in western societies. Leach refers to castes as groups which cooperate and do not compete. Leach finds competition within the 'dominant caste' and not between the dominant caste and other castes. The latter would refer to a class situation, and the former to a class-like situation without affecting the caste system. The idea of non-antagonistic strata has come from Ossowski (1963) who refers to the Polish situation in terms of status gradations and not as classes based on antagonism.

Thus, the western notions of class as well as non-antagonism have been used for analyzing the structure of Indian society. The historicity of Indian society is the real casualty, and reductionism has been the hallmark of 'caste model'. Everything is reduced to the all-pervasive principle of caste hierarchy. However, factually, this was not the situation in ancient, medieval and British India. Migration, mobility and defiance have been reported in historical researches (Thapar, 1974; Panikkar, 1955; Stein, 1968; Habib, 1974; and Desai, 1948). These researches have been ignored by anthropologists and sociologists perhaps due to British colonialism and an overwhelming impact of American and British social science research.

British ethnographers have defined caste in terms of its assumed or real functionality to Indian society and culture. The salient features given by them (including some Indian sociologists) are that a caste has a common name, common descent, and the same hereditary calling and communitarian living (Risley, 1969). Ketkar (1909) mentions hereditary membership and endogamy as the most striking features of the caste system in India. Senart (1930) writes: "A caste system is one whereby a society is divided up into a number of self-contained and completely segregated units (castes), the mutual relations between which are ritually determined in a graded scale."

DEFINITION OF THE CASTE SYSTEM

The uniqueness of the system is prominently emphasized in the above definitions of the caste system. Furnivall (1939), Hutton (1946) and Sherring (1974) observe that the caste system is 'functional' for Indian society. Furnivall applauds the 'pluralism' of the caste system. Hutton speaks of its functions for the individual, community and society as a whole. Sherring refers to cleanliness and order and a bond of union among Hindus promoted by the caste system. Ghurye (1950) refers to six features of the caste system and upholds endogamy as its essence.

Other students of Indian society have also provided a view which either refers to the uniqueness of the caste system or they have viewed it from the viewpoint of their own society. Marx (1945) related the (Asiatic) mode of production to the stability of the caste system in India. Maine (1890) referred to caste as an example of a non-contractual 'status-society'. Senart (1930), Hocart (1950), and Dumont (1970) have emphasized ritual criteria and pollution-purity as the bases of Hindu society. Weber (1947) considered caste as a system of 'status groups' based on the other-worldly doctrines of Hinduism.

Sinha (1974), in a report on caste, notes the following trends:

(i) Speculative theories about the origin of the caste system have practically been given up.

(ii) The bulk of the work on caste is done by the method of social anthropology on the basis of a study of multi-caste villages.

(iii) Considerable interest is shown in these studies on an understanding of the adaptability of the caste system to view situations and forces of changes.

(iv) Study of inter-ethnic status ranking is done through an analysis of data collected through a rigorous methodology.

(v) Literature on social mobility in the caste system has grown in abundance and improved in quality.

(vi) The concept of hierarchy based on the binary polarity of purity-pollution has received much attention.

(vii) There is a felt need for interregional comparison.

(viii) The comparability of caste beyond Indian society has been examined.

(ix) The emergent non-caste phenomena are left unanalyzed because of the obsession with caste.

(x) The number of scholars interested in the study of caste has grown considerably.

CASTE, CLASS AND POWER

Sinha does not reflect upon caste and class polarity, the 'caste, class and power' approach to stratification, and caste as a cultural or structural phenomenon (Sharma, 1977). Sinha also ignores the analysis of the entrenchment of caste into politics, education, industry and ethnicity. A sociology of knowledge perspective would demand an understanding of theory, structure and process of the caste system and this is lacking in Sinha's trend report. Sinha considers caste basically as a cultural phenomenon.

"The cultural system of caste thus naturally promotes an infinite variety of stable crafts and ritual styles" (Sinha, 1967). Sinha further observes: 'The social and cultural systems of caste thus segment the total society into many Jati groups committed to particular britis and styles of life, arranged in a social hierarchy defined in terms of the cultural value of the purity and impurity of these occupations and styles of life" (Ibid.). Sinha's plea for combining structural and cultural perspectives on caste stratification will not stand the test of validity in view of his clear preference for considering caste as a cultural phenomenon.

Thus, the studies on caste aimed at the legitimacy and justification of the caste system itself. Caste was pronounced as an all-inclusive and encompassing functional system. The 'pluralism' of caste was glorified with the intent of establishing British rule on a sounder footing. This was an exercise in befooling the Indian people and the leaders of various castes and even intellectuals. At the same time, the scholars of the West glorified the class system with a view to establishing the superiority of western society and culture (Sharma, 1980). "Class was considered as an open system, the individual was given freedom of movement under the system, and achievement was the essence of the system.

In contrast, the caste system was considered as a closed system, the individual could not move up in the hierarchy, and it was a system based on ascription. Caste and class were polar opposites, caste was considered a feature of an archaic society like India, and class was considered a characteristic feature of the industrially advanced achievement-based western society" (Ibid.). This clearly shows that the western scholars (mainly American and British) tried to establish their hegemony by academic propaganda.

Mac Iver and Page (1967) do not define class strictly in the economic sense. They refer to 'status' as the basis of what they call 'social class'. Marshall (1934), Parsons (1954), Davis and Moore (1945), Bottomore (1964: 148) and Centres (1961: 27) define class either in terms of 'status' or in psychological terms (attitudes and consciousness). The quintessence of the definitions of caste *vis-a-vis* class is that caste is found in India and class is a feature of the western world. The important point is that caste is used as a double-edged weapon, namely, keeping it intact by declaring it as a 'functional' system, and by pronouncing its inferiority or subordination to the class system of the West. Two consequences followed from this academic propaganda:

(i) the indoctrination of social scientists in terms of theorization, methodology and field studies; and

(ii) legitimation of British hegemony and the superiority of their understanding of Indian society. Consequently, social science research in India in the fifties and the sixties was clearly directed by the western social scientists and was patterned in terms of their perspectives.

Literature on caste was produced in abundance in the fifties and sixties. The emphasis was on the overwhelming role of caste in Indian society, caste ranking and mobility in the caste system. Some writings also dealt with class in India. A brief resume is given here. The higher castes revolted against any attempt to challenge their status and power, and the lower castes were content with their lower status, believing that it was due to their *karma* (Prasad, 1957). Srinivas's collection of essays on caste (1962) and his earlier essay on caste (1959), Mathur's book on the role of caste and ritual (1964), Marriott's study of caste and kinship in Central India (1960), and Kothari's edited work on the role of caste in politics (1970) are some of the important studies on the theme.

Dube (1955) writes that the main criteria for the ranking of castes are ritual and not economic. Srinivas's work on religion and society among the Coorgs of South India (1952) is also an attempt towards caste ranking based on the criterion of pollution and purity. Marriott's essay (1959) is on the criteria of caste ranking whether they are 'interactional' or 'attributional' or both. Later on Marriott (1965) has used the concept of 'elaboration' for examining the rigidity and flexibility of the caste system in five regions of India. Mahar (1959) and Hazlthurst (1968) have referred to multiple criteria for caste ranking. Dube (1968) and Gardner (1968) refer to 'levels' of caste dominance and highlight the role of the individual in caste mobility and refute the utility of the concepts of 'dominant caste' and 'sanskritisation' as advocated by Srinivas. There are other studies in which 'structural mobility' has been noted. Sharma (1969,1970,1974,1980) discusses stresses in caste stratification, modernization and rural stratification, and bourgeoisification, proletarianization, downward social mobility and levels of social mobility in village India. He also discusses the crystallization of class relations in the countryside.

STUDIES ON CASTE MOBILITY

A number of studies on caste mobility have been reported by Majumdar (1958), Silverberg (1968), Lynch (1968) and Singer (1968). Silverberg, Singer and Cohn have brought out several studies on caste and mobility in their edited volumes with particular emphasis on the relevance of concepts of reference group and relative deprivation, etc. Saberwal (1976) discusses mobility among the Rampurias of a Punjab town who belonged to the lower stratum but took up trade and commerce as their main occupation. Berreman (1979) has published his essays on caste written over a period of two decades. The emphasis in Berreman's essays is that caste-based inequalities in India are not different from race-based inequalities in the United States of America.

Gough has highlighted the class basis of the caste system in India. She refers to conflicts and litigations between different castes in a Tanjore village (1960) based on economic inequalities. The mix of caste and class in East Bengal (now Bangladesh) is referred to by Ramakrishna Mukherjee (1957). Bose (1967) refers to the class genesis of the caste structure in Bengal. Changes from caste to class are noted by Misra (1960), Beteille

(1969), Miller (1975), and Kolenda (1978). But none of them deny the resurgence of caste in the new situation. A class analysis of Indian society in general and the caste system and village community in particular is found in Desai's edited work on rural sociology (1978) and in his book on Indian nationalism (1948), and in Bettelheim (1968), Harris (1982), and in an edited work by Omvedt (1982).

THE SETUP

Caste is a unique system; it pervades the whole of Hindu society in India; and it is an encompassing system. These are the views upheld by Bougie, Srinivas and Dumont in particular and several others in general. Bougie (1971) writes: "To sum up on these points: hereditary specialization, hierarchical organization, reciprocal repulsion: as far as any social form can realize itself in its purity, the caste system is realized in India. At the very least it penetrates Hindu society to a level unknown elsewhere.

It plays some part in other civilizations but in India it has invaded the whole. It is in this sense that we may speak of the caste system as a phenomenon peculiar to India." Srinivas (1952) following Bougie, notes the preeminence of religious values in the caste system. The religious values among the Hindus centre in the ideas of pollution and purity. Bougie follows Hocart in regard to the role of rituals in the caste hierarchy. However, Hocart (1958) finds that religion encompasses power, hence the priesthood is not 'absolute' in nature. Relations between Brahmin and Kshatriya are defined in terms of a certain reciprocity, namely, the Brahmin represents the 'religious' authority and the Kshatriya enjoys 'political' power.

Srinivas notes various types of purity and impurity among the Coorgs of South India. Ritual impurity, normal ritual status and ritual purity form a hierarchy based on the notion of pollution and purity. Normal ritual status is the one which a person normally enjoys: it is a mild form of impurity. However, Dumont and Pocock (1959) discard the expression of 'normal ritual status'. Hierarchy based on pollution-purity does not include 'mildly impure', it includes only 'pure' and 'impure'. Ephemeral purity or impurity after purification do not guide inter-caste relations. Ritual purification or impurification is a generalized phenomenon among all Hindus.

However, Srinivas feels that the concept is absolutely fundamental to the caste system. Sanskritisation is the only way to remove impurity or to minimize it. While commenting on a book by Srinivas (1976), Parvathamma (1978: 91) writes: "In all the writings of Srinivas, the Brahmin-non-Brahmin values are juxtaposed." Hierarchy based on pollution-purity remains intrinsic to Srinivas's thinking in regard to all aspects of human life, even if it is actually not so pronounced. That sanskritisation can also cause tensions and contradictions manifestly or latently is overlooked by Srinivas. His main emphasis remains on dominance and solidarity. It is not only Srinivas who has heavily endorsed 'Brahminical' sociology, several others including Dumont (1970), Marriott (1955) and Singer (1968) have emphasized disproportionately the phenomenon of caste in Indian society. Pollution-purity, religion and rituals are the central foci of their studies. Today, social structure is not considered beyond the parameters of the notions of pollution-purity, hierarchy and dominance.

Compared to Leach, Dumont and Srinivas, a different view is provided by Bailey (1963). Bailey refers to three types of definitions of caste. These are: (1) the 'rigidity' type; (2) the 'cultural' type, and (3) the 'structural' type. The first type of definition is found inapplicable as it refers to status immobility, hence 'analytic'. The second type is found 'useful' as it refers to religious ideas, namely, opposition based on purity and pollution and hierarchy. The pollution-purity opposition implies

(i) hereditary specialization,

(ii) hierarchy, and

(iii) opposition of parts. Caste as a system based on beliefs and ideas becomes a closed unique system of social stratification. The third type of definition refers to exclusiveness, exhaustiveness and ranking as the 'structural' criteria of the caste system. The 'cultural' criteria limit comparison and the structural ones facilitate cross-cultural comparison.

Thus, according to Bailey, caste is a unique system so far as its cultural criteria are concerned, and it shares certain features with other systems of social stratification so far as structural criteria are concerned. Bailey disapproves Dumont's view about caste as he considers it in terms of 'finality' and 'completeness'. Bailey considers Dumont's definition of caste 'analytic' rather than 'synthetic'. The latter refers to the existence of the caste system at the micro-level. The analytic statement tends to become axiomatic. However, Bailey also accepts the analytic statement of Dumont as the starting point of his analysis. Bailey does not refer to 'class analysis' or inherence of class in caste. Like Leach and Dumont, Bailey's view also refers to 'organicism' ; competition and equality are not found in the caste system. Bailey's attempt at formulating a 'compromised definition' of the caste system is not different from the understanding of the caste system provided by Dumont, Leach and Srinivas.

Thus, ultimately, Bailey also tends to formulate an 'analytic' statement about the caste system, and in effect, not so different from that of Dumont and Srinivas. Bailey fails to recognize the historicity of the caste system which brings to light innumerable adaptations and contradictions faced by it. For Bailey, the caste system is an inviolate system, hence closed and organic in nature. Inviolate systems are found in simple societies, or in relatively insulated enclaves of complex societies. Caste is also seen by Bailey as an organizing principle of competition, and not the one by which politico-economic groups are recruited.

Castes are not corporate or organic political groups, hence caste is a closed segmentary stratification. 'Segmentation' refers to change from organicism.

However, such a conception of change does not explain the change of the caste system. Segmentation does not lead ultimately to equality or castelessness. Bailey's notion of change in caste is thus based on a sort of false consciousness about change (Sharma, 1980). Increasing segmentation does not mean emergence of class-based relations, and the latter do not mean equality or egalitarianism. Singh (1968: 170) observes that Bailey's analysis is based on a static and abstract model of caste, and on the same type of 'analytic' statements as those of Dumont. Beteille's notion of the emergence of 'differentiated structures' (1966) also does not provide a class-view of social stratification or/of the village community.

UPCOMING ORDER

Marriott (1959) was the first to make a reference to the 'interactional' and 'attributional' approaches to the study of the caste system. Later on it was exemplified in great detail by Singh (1974) in a trend report on social stratification. Marriott is the one who has promoted 'culturology' by studying Indian tradition and the interaction between what he calls 'Great Tradition' and 'Little Tradition'. Marriott's study (1955) substantiates the interactional approach to the study of Indian society in terms of the relations between 'Sanskritic' and 'oral' traditions. The study of relations between higher and lower castes in basic to the 'interactional' approach. However, this approach has also been vigorously applied by Marxist scholars to the study of class relations in village India.

Emphasis in the 'attributional' approach is on 'order' rather than 'relation'. The configuration of elements constituting a system of hierarchy is the essence of the attributional approach. The attributes are, for example, income, occupation, education, positions of power, etc. These attributes have sufficient measurability, and they facilitate construction of categories such as upper, middle and lower. Thus, an attempt is made to work out the indicators of status, and the variations are measured on different types of scales and indices. The 'composite status' of individuals is worked out. 'Corporateness' of status is ruled out as the individual's attributes are the basis of constructing the 'order'.

That caste is not an exclusively cultural system is the view held by D' Souza (1967). Caste and class are different forms of social stratification. Groups (caste groups or *jatis)* are ranked in the caste system, whereas positions are ranked in social stratification (particularly with reference to class stratification). The ranking of endogamous groups and not endogamy as the rule of marriage, is the hallmark of the caste system. D' Souza's contention is that changes in the caste system have brought about changes in the properties of individual members. A 'hereditary group' might continue in the caste system as a 'class'. This fact explains the similarity between caste and class. In fact, D' Souza emphasizes the significance of the continuum of the rigidity-fluidity dimensions in regard to both caste and class. Thus, the individual and his properties are the real units of analysis rather than the endogamous groups.

D' Souza decisively concludes that class is replacing caste, and the individual is replacing the group. A certain place for the individual as a unit of status, and a certain level of social mobility at that level are the basic assumptions of D' Souza's formulation. Even if the role of the individual and the fact of social mobility are admitted, class would not take the place of caste inspite of the fact that caste has undergone significant changes. It would be untenable to infer that change is taking place from caste to class, from hierarchy to stratification, from closed to open system, and from an organic to a segmentary system of social stratification (Sharma, 1977; 1980). Singh (1968) rightly points out that a 'prismatic model' of change is suitable where traditional segments of caste and kinship undergo adaptive transformation without completely being 'diffracted' into classes or corporate groups. Thus, class segments operate within the frame of caste categories with a new sense of identity, and they also violate caste norms, hence contradictions. Caste has been a dynamic system full of adaptations, accretions, contradictions and transformations, hence resilience and change.

SOCIAL STRATIFICATION

Having realized that caste alone is not the totality of social stratification and that caste is not being replaced by class as the two are not necessarily antithetical to each other, Beteille (1965), following Weber's trio of 'class, status and party', analyzes patterns of social stratification in a Tanjore village in terms of 'caste, class and power'. Beteille is not quite clear about the phenomenon of class. He says that "classes are categories rather than groups," but he contradicts this statement when he writes that "by class we mean a category of persons occupying a specific position in the system of production" (1965).

The first statement has the overtones of the Weberian notion of class and the second has those of Marx's conception of class. However, Beteille by no means intends to provide a Marxian analysis of social stratification, nor he does justice to Weber's ideas of rationalism and *verste-hen*. Beteille's study, therefore, also falls short of the 'attributional' or 'interactional' criteria of social ranking.

In fact, it is Anil Bhatt (1975) who has done more justice to the attributional approach in studying social stratification. Bhatt's trio comprises 'caste, class and politics.' He observes that social stratification in India has deviated considerably from the traditional caste model. Caste does not encompass economic position and political power. A caste is internally differentiated in terms of class and power of its members. Thus, Bhatt finds status incongruence, relative openness, mobility, and competition as the salient features of the emergent system of social stratification. Bhatt has relied on secondary data and attitudinal responses. It is more of a 'formalistic' approach and does not go into actual details regarding the functioning of institutions related to caste, class and power. Aggrawal (1971) and recently Chauhan (1980) have also followed the viewpoint adopted by Beteille. There is no doubt that Beteille has presented a new approach to the study of social stratification in India, but without realizing the incongruity between the his approach and the method of his study (Sharma, 1980).

Whether caste is a cultural aspect of the Indian tradition or a structural form was discussed in a symposium (Reuck and Knight, 1967) in which Myrdal, Leach, Dumont, Berreman, Sinha, Cohn, Mayer and Tambiah participated along with some others. I have already referred to the view that caste is considered a cultural aspect of the Indian tradition. Dumont, Leach, Srinivas and Marriott consider castes as corporate groups, found exclusively in Indian society, particularly among Hindus. Beteille and Bailey partly agree with this view; however, D' Souza and Bhatt clearly advocate the application of an attributional approach (class approach in a non-Marxian sense). Caste as a cultural phenomenon is seen as a system of values and ideas. Srinivas's (1966) notions of sanskritisation and westernisation are examples of 'intra-systemic' or 'positional changes.'

Caste as a structural phenomenon is considered as a part of the general theory of social stratification. Earth (1960) writes: "If the concept of caste is to be useful in sociological analysis, its definition must be based on structural criteria, and not on particular features of the Hindu philosophical scheme." Barth considers caste in general as a system of social stratification. The principle of status summation seems to be the structural feature of caste stratification. In other words, caste should label not a particular social system but a general social sub-system. Opposition, segmentation and hierarchy are universal criteria of social stratification, and are expressed in different cultural idioms including caste. Berreman (1967) also refers to three universal elements of all castes, namely, stratification, culturalism and interaction. Harper (1968) and Nadel (1957) have expressed the view that caste stratification is one of the various forms of social stratification.

As we have stated earlier that D' Souza (1967) draws a polar distinction between caste and class, but he does not consider caste as an exclusively cultural system. D' Souza's main concern is that changes in the caste system are ultimately brought about by changes in the properties of the individual members. The emphasis in D' Souza's view is on the significance of the continuum of the rigidity-fluidity dimensions to the understanding of both caste and class. Leach (1960) also refers to emergence of 'caste grades' as class-like changes in the caste system.

STRUCTURAL DIMENSIONS

Studies on caste mobility refer to the structural dimension of caste stratification. Thapar (1974), Panikkar (1955) and Stein (1968) refer to caste mobility in spatial and status contexts rather than in the context of rituals. Bailey (1957) and Epstein (1962) also consider economic factors responsible for changing inter-caste relations. Kothari (1970) mentions caste as a variable in politics in independent India. Singh (1974) analyzes caste in terms of cultural and structural factors and considers it as a 'structural-particularistic' type of social stratification.

The essence of the structural approach is that caste should be seen in terms of a system of 'relations' between different castes, and structural factors bring about changes in the vertical and horizontal gradations in the caste system. Mencher (1974) analyzes caste from a Marxist (also structural) point of view.

She considers the exploitation of the low castes and the prevention of the formation of classes as the two main features of the caste system. Thus, caste is, in fact, a system of class relations, and at the same time, its functioning idiom does not allow it to operate as a class system.

THE OUTCOME

Class in India is generally seen as a consequence of change in the caste system and not as a concomitant and coexistent system inseparable from caste. Several questions can be raised about the studies of caste hierarchy and social mobility. For example, why did Srinivas and his associates often study caste structure, positional changes, village community, and family life and kinship; and why did they leave out the studies of class relations, vertical mobility, urban community, industry and formal organizations from their sociological purview? Culturology is given primacy over the structural perspective in the understanding of the caste system in most studies carried out by Srinivas and his followers. Structural changes are visualized only latently and that too due to sanskritisation and westernisation.

Emphasis on the study of social mobility in terms of upward movement in the caste hierarchy further legitimizes the culturological approach to the study of society and culture in India. The concepts of dominant caste and sanskritisation remain central to this view. Corporate mobility and the study of the social and cultural aspects receive greater attention instead of mobility at the level of family and individual and economic and political aspects. Resentment, opposition and conflict in the study of inter-group relations remain inactive notions.

Dube (1976) and Singh (1979) both realize that the concepts of caste and class have been basically 'western', and therefore, ignore the historicity of Indian society in their formulations. Indigenization of social science paradigms would ensure a proper input of historical substance in the concepts and theories related to Indian society. Both Marxist and non-Marxist scholars (Thorner, 1974; Saran, 1962) have pleaded for the use of native concepts and categories, respectively. D.P. Mukerji (1958) has argued vehemently for making the Indian tradition as the sole basis of analyzing social change. Desai (1948) has strongly opposed to the application of the non-Marxist approaches. Srinivas has been blamed for an inappropriate application of British structural-functionalism by Mencher (1974) and Saberwal (1979).

Caste has been taken as synonym with the social formation of Indian society and therefore class is treated as an alternate system to caste. However, the fact is that neither does caste refer to the totality of social formations nor is class the polar opposite of caste. Studies such as caste and class (D' Souza, 1967); caste, class and power (Beteille, 1965); caste, religion and power (Aggrawal, 1971); and caste, class and politics (Bhatt, 1975) do not provide a corrective to the 'caste alone' approach. These studies are rooted in the falsity of the western dichotomy of tradition and modernity and the trio of 'class, status and party' (Weber, 1947). They do not incorporate the experience of Indian society into the concepts of caste, class and power, hence inadequate in rescuing us from these alien concepts and theories.

Class in India has existed along with caste and power. Caste incorporates class and class incorporates caste in the Indian context. Neither the 'caste alone' view nor the 'class alone' perspective can help in a proper and fuller understanding of Indian society. It has been noted that there was never a perfect congruence between caste, class and power. Mobility and migration were quite normal activities in ancient and medieval India. However, Bailey, Beteille and Bhatt give the impression that a congruence prevailed between caste, class and power in the pre-independent India, and land reforms and politicization have brought about incongruities and caste-free areas.

Historians of the Marxist disposition have realized that there is an intertwining of caste and class in India, but they prefer to look at caste from a class point of view. Koshambi (1956) makes a class analysis of the Aryans after the Rig Veda. Thapar (1974), Habib (1974), and Desai (1948) have also done a class analysis of Indian society. According to Desai, caste inheres in an under-developed but potentially explosive class character. In another study, Desai (1975) has analyzed the Indian State from a class (Marxist) point of view. But class does not necessarily mean openness, mobility and a combination of certain attributes as generally perceived by western social scientists and their followers in India. Castes have been functioning as classes for all practical considerations. Class relations are as old as caste relations or even older than caste relations. Lamb (1975) reports the prevalence of class relations as early as 600 B.C. in India. Material and cultural traditions existed with a sort of congruity, and class transformation had been a vital fact in the form of new kingdoms, settled agriculture, trade, cities and banking and guild organizations.

CLASSES IN INDIA

The non-Marxist scholars in general have relied on analytical abstractions in the form of statistical-mathematical indicators or analytical topologies (Singh, 1981). D' Souza (1975) treats class as a conceptually abstracted category. Class does not exist as a community like caste. Class is defined operationally in terms of certain indices. D' Souza applies the attributional approach to class purely in terms of constructing an 'order' comprising upper, middle and lower class categories. The following points have been made about classes in India:

(1) Classes are not found as a system of stratification in the same way as castes are rooted in the Indian society.

(2) Class is not a universalistic phenomenon of social stratification.

(3) There are no objective criteria of class identification.

(4) It is not clear whether class is a category or a concrete unit of interaction with other units.

One could affirm that these points have been put forth in order to prevent a class analysis of Indian society. Caste has created numerous problems of a class nature related to economic domination and subjugation, privileges and deprivations, 'conspicuous waste' and bare survival. However, these problems have not been taken up as central concerns of social research. Pollution-purity and the encompassing power of caste have been taken up as a positive dimension of the caste system. The usual pretension is that class antagonism, class consciousness and class unity are not found as Karl Marx had seen, hence no class analysis. However, this is not true. Caste is a system of harmonic relations from a particular perspective only, it is also a system of opposition and antagonism from another perspective, and the latter has not been taken up seriously.

The mode of production and class contradictions are essential features of the Marxian approach to social stratification. Gough (1980) considers the mode of production as a social formation in which she finds interconnections of caste, kinship, family, marriage and even rituals with the forces of production and production relations. Gough's study of Thanjavur explains the emergence of a new bourgeoisie, the polarization of the peasantry, and the pau-perization of the working class due to historical transformations in the mode of production. The totality of contradictions in social stratification can be seen through the contradictions in the mode of production. Marxist ideologists like Namboodaripad (1979) and Ranadive (1979) consider class relationships as a domain assumption in the treatment of caste and kinship in India.

Even *varna* and the *jajmani* system can be explained in terms of class relations as they are embedded in the mode of production (Meillassoux, 1973). Others who have used the mode of production as the framework for analysis of class relations in village India are: Djurfeldt and Lind-berg (1975), Heera Singh (1979), Thorner (1969), Saith and Tanakha (1972), and Bhardwaj and Das (1975).

The main classes today in India are:

(i) agrarian,

(ii) industrial,

(iii) business and mercantile, and

(iv) professional. Contradictions can be found between various classes in terms of continuance of the old classes and the emergence of new ones at the same time. Industrial, business and professional classes characterize urban India, and landowners, tenants, sharecroppers and agricultural labourers are found in the countryside. These classifications have ideological overtones. The classification comprising landowners, moneylenders and labourers does not refer necessarily to class antagonism. But the other classification comprising the bourgeoisie, capitalist-type landowners, rich peasants, landless peasantry and agricultural labourers necessarily refers to class interaction, dependence-independence and conflict as the basic elements of class structure.

OBSERVATIONAL EFFECTS

Approaches to the concepts of caste and class bear ideological contents. The methodology and data used in the studies of caste and class provided legitimacy to these approaches. Caste was treated not as a 'social formation', but as an encompassing institution which encompassed all other aspects of Hindu society. However, caste, in fact, was more than a 'ritualistic' mechanism, and it could face a variety of forces and constraints due to its all-inclusive character. If it were simply a ritualistic arrangement, it would have crumbled down long ago due to its very cumbersome nature. The social formation of Indian society comprises class, ethnicity, power, religion and economy along with caste. All these aspects of the social formation are incorporated into each other. They provide an understanding of the historicity of Indian society including that of caste and class. Indigenization of the concepts of caste and class must come from the realization of such a formation and the totality of its historicity.

The approaches such as the functional, dialectical, psychological and structuralist are inadequate for explaining the historicity of the Indian situation as they are rooted in the experience of the situations that are unfamiliar with India's historicity. Issues relating to caste and class were raised and debated elsewhere and subsequently passed on to Indian scholars through the mechanism of the academic hegemony of western scholars. Whether caste is a cultural phenomenon or a structural aspect, whether it should be studied by participant observation or by using survey method, whether it should be treated as the sole representative institution or class, power and religion should also be studied, whether 'caste alone' should be studied—have been raised by western scholars and later on taken up by their Indian counterparts with the tacit understanding of promoting certain ideas upheld by them.

We must examine carefully why structural-functionalism has become so popular, why participant observation is regarded as a sacrosanct technique of research, why Redfield's notions of 'little community' and 'peasant society' or Marriott's notions of Little and Great Traditions and parochialization and universalization have gained currency. One view is that the Brahminocentric sociology produced by Srinivas is due to such indoctrination by these academic forces.

In an earlier study, Singh (1974) provides a paradigm of social stratification in the light of cultural versus structural and particular versus universal characteristics. The types that emerge from these criteria are:

(i) cultural-universalistic;

(ii) cultural-particularistic;

(iii) structural-universalistic; and

(iv) structural-particularistic.

This paradigm is based on Parson's analysis of social structure. Singh's analysis shows relevance of the structural-particularistic type for analyzing social stratification in India. However, Singh does not provide reasons for the suitability of such a classification. Nomology is the obvious reason for Singh's scientism. However, in a recent study, Singh (1981) provides another classification of the studies on social stratification carried out in the 1970s. The main theoretic concerns are:

(i) structural-functional;

(ii) structuralist;

(iii) structural-historical; and

(iv) historical-materialist or Marxist.

I have already referred to some of the studies which have been analyzed under the rubric of these approaches. Caste is the central concern of all the researchers including the Marxists.

Caste is an all-inclusive institution and it subsumes class relations. Any departure from caste is treated as incongruence between caste, status, wealth and power, hence the emergence of class relations. Such a view is known as the structural-functional. Change within the caste (sanskritisation), resilience and consensus are the hallmarks of structural-functionalism. Dumont is the most well known proponent of structuralism. The pivotal notions of this approach are reflected in *Dumont's Homo Hierarchicus* (1970). Singh (1981) points out ideology, dialectics, transformational relationship and comparison as the salient features of Dumont's study of caste. For Dumont, hierarchy is ideology, and hierarchy implies ranking based on the notion of purity-impurity.

The opposition between pure and impure refers to binary tension or dialectics. Pure and impure imply exclusion as well as inclusion in regard to caste hierarchy. Hierarchy also refers to the relationship of the 'encompassing' and the 'encompassed'. The 'pure' encompasses the 'less pure' and so on. This applies to all the sections and aspects of society. Thus, change is in the society and not of the society.

Dumont's view falls short of all those points which have been indicated in regard to structural-functionalism. In addition to these points, Singh (1981) comments that Dumont's structuralism suffers both theoretically and substantively. Gould's notion of 'contra priest' (1967) also negates the dichotomy or binary opposition between the pure and impure. The lower caste men also function as priests, hence they become pure. But they remain impure being lower in the caste hierarchy.

STRUCTURALIST'S TREATMENT

The implication of Dumont's treatment of caste is that caste and class are in binary opposition. Singh's (1981) comments on structuralism are as follows: "The structuralist's treatment of dialectics is dissociated from history. History, indeed, links essence to existence, form to content, superstructure to infrastructure and theory to practice. Devoid of such a sense of historical conjecture structuralism amounts to a set of conceptual schema, devoid of a basis in evolutionary changes in society. Its transformational relationships being a historical abound in tautologies."

In a study, Klass (1980) has raised the question of origin of caste. Klass projects a paradigm of the possible development of the caste system. The main idea is that clans exchange women, whereas the caste system exchanges goods without exchanging women. The explanation given by Klass is that India has developed ecosystems in which people have different modes of life, and the various human groups (corporate groups) would have a minimum of intercourse and not exchange women with outside groups. Thus, corporate groups form marriage circles. Klass relates caste with physical force and economic power. However, the corporateness of caste groups is equated with their egalitarian character, and this might be historically and substantively incorrect.

The understanding of caste and class demands an approach which has such as:

(i) dialects,

(ii) history,

(iii) culture, and

(iv) structure.

Dialectics refers to the effective notions which bring about contradictions and highlight relations between unequal segments and men and women. Thus, it does not simply mean binary fission in the cognitive structure of Indian society as perceived by structuralists in terms of pure and impure. History provides a substantial account of the conditions of human existence. It is not a conjectural construction based on mythology, scriptures and ideations.

Culture defines the rules of the game, the nature of relations between the haves and the have-nots. Thus culture does not include only cultural practices, rituals, *rites de passage,* etc. Structure is a product of dialectical contradictions, historical forces, and a certain 'formation'. Once it has emerged, it becomes a sort of force in determining the course of history, the nature of contradictions and the evaluational standards. Thus, structure refers to relations between social segments at a point of time as a historical product and as an existent reality.

Dialectics, history, culture and structure refer to a combination of theory, structure and process about the social formation (both caste and class) of Indian society. Together they explain the historicity of Indian society from the point of its genesis.

The debates today are: whether changes in caste and class are 'transformational' or they are 'replacements', whether caste is 'closed' and class is 'open' ; whether caste is 'organic' and whether class is 'segmentary' ; and whether caste is replaced by class. These are questions which have come up quite often as the idea of 'social formation' has not gained currency in our understanding of caste and class.

The obsession of considering caste and class as polar opposites has prevented us from thinking of caste and class as dimensions of the historicity of India's social formation.

Several scholars have denied the 'congruence' version about caste, class and power in the ancient India. They have conclusively established that social mobility existed in ancient and medieval India. The *jajmani* system was never completely 'organic' in practice. The idea of the contrapriest exposes the hollowness of the concepts of hierarchy and pollution-purity. In the place of sanskritisation, westernisation and dominant caste etc., it is necessary to study downward mobility and proletarianization, upward mobility and embourgeoisiement, urban incomes for the rural people and the migration of the rural rich to towns, and rural non-agricultural income and mobility etc.

Caste has inhered in class and class has inhered in caste for centuries in the Indian context, and Indian society continues to have this inseparable mix even today. Role of caste and class in elections is an evidence of this mix. However, caste operates as a 'marriage circle' in a different way from the way it functions in other arenas.

Hypergamy explains the role of status and wealth within caste. Class-like distinctions within caste and caste-like styles within a class are part of the people's life situations.

'Class' has been an inbuilt mechanism within caste, and therefore, caste cannot be seen simply as a 'ritualistic' system, and class cannot be seen as an open system as it has often been influenced by the institution of caste. In order to go deep into such a phenomenon the structural-historical perspective becomes inescapable.

2

CASTE ELEMENTS

LITERARY TRACES OF CASTE SYSTEM

The first literary traces of the caste system are to be found in the *Rig-Veda,* where three groups are mentioned: *Brahman* (Priests), *Kshatriya* (Kings or Rulers), and *Vaisya* (common people). The *Purusukta* hymn, however, speaks of four classes originating from four parts of the body of the creator. These classes, *Brahmana, Rajanya, Vaisya* and *Sudra,* are referred to in later literature as *Chaturvarna.* The term *varna* does not seem to have been applied to these classes in the earliest literature, except to contrast the fair *Arya* with the dark *Dasa.* The initial distinction of people into two *varnas* later developed into three *(Brahman, Kshatriya,* and *Vaisya)* and finally into four.

The occupations of the first two *varnas* are clearly stated to be priesthood, and administrative and military duties, respectively. But the duties of the Vaisya and Sudra are not very clear. The village headman was usually a Vaisya, and Sudras were servants. The *Vaisya* cate-gories do not, however, exhaust the various occupations practised in Vedic India. The *Rig-Veda,* for instance, mentions several occupa-tions by name—chariot-builder, goldsmith, barber, physician, leather-worker, potter, merchant and others. The question arises whether these occupations referred to endogamous *jatis* as we know them today. It is not known how they fitted into the *vaisya* framework.

POST-VEDIC PERIOD

The post-Vedic period saw the growth and consolidation of the power of the Brahmins. Brahmin writers continually discussed and defined the duties and rights of each caste and its place in the hierarchy. The relation which these writings bore to the empirical reality is not clear) Justifications and rationalizations of the hierarchy were also produced during this period. In the *Bhagavad-Gita,* for instance, the caste system is sought to be justified on the basis of the ideas of *gyhna, karma* and *dharma.*

The 6th century B.C. saw the rise of Buddhism, which is believed to have questioned the basis of the caste system itself. Some scholars, however, have said that Buddhism on its social and political side was chiefly a Ksatriya movement against Brahminical supremacy.

Post-Vedic Brahminical writers continued their attempts to systematize and codify inter-caste relations. The idea of pollution was elaborated to define the distance separating the castes. Violations of caste rules were punished either by the village panchayat or the panchayat of the locally dominant caste or by the king.

The Bhakti movement with its long history contained elements which ran counter to caste ideology. The Bhakti saints came from all castes, including the Harijans. It appears as though the path of *Bhakti* offered a way out of the tyrannies of the caste system, and as the Bhakti saints commanded respect from everyone, the movement itself served to stress the worth of an individual irrespective of his caste affiliations. The origins of the Bhakti movement are traced to the Krsna-Vasudeva cult in the first century B.C. The Saiva (Nayanar) and Vaisnava (Alvar) saints of the Tamil country, the Haridasa and Lingayat saints of Karnataka, Vallabhacarya and his followers in Gujarat, Chaitanya in Bengal, and Tulasidas, Surdas, Kabir and Radim in the North, were all representatives of the Bhakti movement. The movement was more or less continuous in Indian history, and it spread right across the sub-continent. It may not be too fanciful to regard it as a protest, in the realm of religion, against the division of human beings into high and low castes.

The Lingayat movement, which came into existence in Karnataka in the 12th century A.D., rejected many ideas of traditional Hinduism, including *karma,* ritualism and caste. It also emphasized the necessity as well as the dignity of labour. The movement attracted converts from all castes including Harijans, but over the centuries it became a congeries of small, endogamous *Jatis.* The followers of Kablr (Kabirpanthi) also became a caste. Caste even survived conversion to Christianity and Islam. During the last century there came into existence the Arya Samaj in Punjab and the Brahmo Samaj in Bengal. These movements, as well as the Ramakrishna Mission, represented a shift towards the liberalization of caste.

IMPORTANT ELEMENTS

We shall now consider the main features of caste before it was deeply affected by recent changes. Those changes, which present a quite different picture of the Indian social structure today are discussed in the last pages of this chapter.

The features of caste prevailing through the past centuries may be described under nine heads: hierarchy; endogamy and hypergamy; occupational association; restriction on food, drink and smoking; distinction in custom, dress and speech; pollution; ritual and other privileges and disabilities; caste organization and caste mobility.

The essence of caste is the arrangement of hereditary groups in a hierarchy. The popular impression of the hierarchy is a clear-cut one, derived from the idea of *varna,* with Brahmins at the top and Harijans at the bottom. But, as a matter of fact, only the two opposite ends of the hierarchy are relatively fixed; in between, and especially in the middle regions, there is considerable room for debate regulating mutual position.

In a dispute over rank each caste would cite as evidence of its superiority the items of its dietary, the other caste groups from which it accepted or refused to accept cooked food and water, the ritual it performed and the customs it observed, its traditional privileges and disabilities, and the myth of its origin. The fact that mutual position is arguable, if not vague, over great areas of the hierarchy permits social mobi-lity. Mobility, it may be noted, is not a recent phenomenon.

Even in the traditional system it was possible for a caste to move up. The Raj Gonds of Central India, for instance, successfully claimed for themselves the rank of Ksatriyas on the basis of their acquisition of political power. At the coronation of Shivaji, Brahmin priests declared him a Ksatriya. Not infrequently the claim of a caste to a higher rank is not conceded. Thus, the Smith group of castes in South India have claimed to be a twice-born caste and call themselves Visvakarma Brahmin. The other castes resent this and even the Harijans do not accept drinking water from a Smith. The Lingayats consider themselves superior to the Brahmins but others do not accept their claim.

Disputes regarding mutual position occur even at either extremes of the hierarchy. In Kerala, Nambudris consider themselves superior to Tamil Brahmins, and among the Nambudris those who have a hereditary right to study the Vedas claim supe-riority over the others. Again, there are very low groups among the Brahmins. No caste, including the Harijan, will accept cooked food or water from the Marka Brahmins of

Mysore. Likewise, the Vatima Brahmins in the Tamil country and the Tapodhan Brahmins in Gujarat are considered as inferior.

All Caste Hindus regard Harijans as being at the bottom rung of the ladder. But the category of Harijans is not homogeneous. In each linguistic area there are a few Harijan castes which form a hierarchy. The leather-working Chamar in Uttar Pradesh considers himself superior to the Bhangi, a sweeper. The Kannada Holera places himself above the Madiga; he proudly stresses the fact that he does not accept even water or betel leaf from either the Smith or the Marka Brahmin.

Islam proclaims the idea of equality of all those who profess the faith, but in India it has been characterized by caste. Muslim caste differs in some respects from the Hindu caste system; there are no ethico-religious ideas justifying the hierarchy or regulating inter-caste relations through ideas of purity and pollution; there are no *varna* categories. What we have is a hierarchy formed by several *jatis*.

In Uttar Pradesh, *Muslims* who have a tradition of foreign ancestry (Iran, Arabia) are called Shurafa or Ashraf and are considered to be the highest. After them come converts from high-caste Hindus, such as Rajputs. Next come occupational castes such as the Weaver (Julaha), Barber (Nai), Cotton Carder (Dhuniya), Potter (Kumhar) and Oilman (Teli). Last come the Sweepers. Among the Ashraf, the Syeds rank as the highest.

The Moplah (Mappilla) *Muslims* of Kerala are also divided into castes. The Thangals, claiming descent from the Prophet's daughter, Fatima, are at the top; next to them are the Arabs, descendants of immigrants from Arabia. The Pusalars, said to be recent converts from the Fisherman caste, occupy the third position while the Ossans, who are barbers, are at the bottom.

Equality is a tenet of Sikhism also, but that has not prevented the existence of castes, including Brahmins, among Sikhs. Sikhs are broadly divided into Sardars and Mazhabis, the former consisting of higher castes and the latter of Sweepers. The Sardars include Jar and Kamboh (landowners), Tarkhan (Carpenter). Kumhar (Potter), Mehra (Water-carrier), and Cimba (Washer man). The first two castes regard themselves as superior to the others. The Mazhabis, not only came from a low caste but Were converted to Sikhism later than the higher caste groups. In some parts of Punjab there exist the Sansi (Shepherd) who were for merly included among the "Criminal Tribes"; Sansi converts to Sikhism rank even lower than Mazhabis.

There are three divisions among Indian Jews: Beni-Israel, Cochin Jews and Baghdadi Jews. The Beni-Israel are to be found principally in Mumbai. They are divided into groups, *Gora* (White) and *Kala* (Black), the former being considered higher in rank. The Cochin Jews are divided into similar White and Black groups, and there is a third division called Meshurarim comprising the descendants of Cochin Jews and their slave concubines; the Meshurarim, who are decended from a White Cochin Jew, claim superiority over those descended from a Black Cochin Jew. The third Jewist- group, the Baghdadi, are later immigrants, and are found in Mumbai and Calcutta.

Caste divisions occur among Indian Christians, Catholics as well as Protestants. The Syrian Christians of Kerala, the earliest converts to Christianity in India, claim to have been recruited originally from Nambudri Brahmins and Nayars, and caste distinctions are conspicuous among them. Caste restrictions are rigidly observed among the Christians of the West Coast. A Catho-lic Brahmin from Maharashtra would marry none other than a Catholic Brahmin. Some West Coast Christians have migrated to East Africa and their descendants try to marry within their particular sub-caste.

Conversion does, however, weaken pollution ideas, and social life among Christian converts is more free than among

Hindus. Again, all over India, caste restrictions are far less meticulously observed today than they were a few decades ago. Social institutions are changing, and this affects all social groups, though in varying degrees.

OCCUPATIONAL SEGMENTS

The hereditary association of a caste with an occupation has been so striking that it has occasionally been argued that caste is nothing more than the systematization of occupational differen-tiation. Even though a caste is not only associated with an occupa-tion but has a limited kind of monopoly over it, it is not true to say that every member of the caste practises that occupation exclusively. This kind of association is suggested when, for instance, the term Kumhar is translated as Potter, and Dhobi as Washerman.

But, generally speaking, most castes also practise agriculture in addition to their traditional occupation. A Kumhar may be an agriculturist in the monsoon months, and a trader in grain for a brief period after the harvest. Often, the artisan and servicing castes do not have an adequate income from their tradi-tional occupations and they therefore work on land, either as tenants or as casual labourers. It could be argued that, in the context of a growing population, the occupational aspect of the caste system would have broken down completely if the surplus in the artisan, trading and servicing castes had not been either absorbed in agriculture or able to migrate to other areas.

Traditionally, agriculture (used broadly to include even mere landownership) was a common occupation for all castes. The profession of arms was also practised occasionally by the non-Ksatriya castes, including Brahmins and the locally dominant peasant groups.

To associate a caste invariably with a single occupation is an oversimplification. Even "agriculture" can mean a variety of things: landownership, tenancy and labour. Each may be practised exclu-sively or in combination with the others. Sometimes cultivation includes processing the grown crop into a sale able commodity. Thus, the cultivation of sugarcane, except when grown for a factory, includes the processing of cane into jaggery and its sale to a middleman. Again, different members of a family may have different occupations. All Women cook and they may also take some part in agriculture. Women of the artisan castes may in addition participate in the caste craft.

Occupations are also classified into high and low, those practised by the high castes being regarded as high. Manual labour is looked upon as low, and certain occupations like swine herding and butchery are considered to be polluting.

Among Muslims, only artisan castes such as the Teli, Darzi, and Julaha are associated with traditional occupations. Priests tend to come more from the Syed and Shaikh castes than from the others. Among the Sikhs, the traditiODaIoccupation is often practised along with agriculture. Jats are generally landowners, while the Mazhabis are agricultural labourers. Sikh Tarkhans are Carpenters. An occupation which is indispensable every where except among the Sikhs is hair-cutting. But the Sikh Nai renders other services: he clips the nails of his patrons; he carries news of birth, marriage and death. He is also a masseur.

CASTE BASED SOCIETY

An individual in a caste society lives in a hierarchical world. It is not only the people who are divided into higher and lower groups, but also the food they eat, the dress and ornaments they wear, and the customs and manners they practise. In India's dietetic hierarchy the highest castes are usually vegetarians and teetotallers. Even in meat there is a hierarchy. The highest non-vegetarian castes eschew chicken, pork and beef. Wild pork is superior to domestic pork, since the village pig is a scavenger. Eating beef in rural India means eating carrion and it comes accordingly under a double ban. Liquor is prohibited to the high castes.

Elaborate rules govern the acceptance of cooked food and water from another caste. Food cooked with ghee, milk or butter is called *pakkii* food and may be accepted from inferior castes. (Higher castes buy sweets from the *Halwai* because he is supposed to be cooking them with ghee.) *Kaccii* food, on the other hand, is food cooked with water and it may be accepted normally only from one's own or equivalent or superior castes. When two castes are contending for superiority, they stop accepting cooked food and water from each other. Sometimes, a very low caste refuses cooked food or water from a high caste. We have already men-tioned the instance of the Kannada Holeya. The explanation of these usages lies in the history of inter-caste relations in the area in question, and in particular, in the attempts of individual castes to raise themselves up.

There are exceptions to the general restrictions on the accep-tance of food and water. Food or drink which has been sanctified by being offered to a deity in a temple may not be refused, even though the cook is from a low caste. The cooks in the famous Jagannath temple at Puri are Barbers by caste. Significant regional variations also occur. Further, women tend to observe restrictions more strictly than men, and the old more strictly than the young. Among the highly westernised sections in the big cities, such restrictions are minimal.

In North India, *hukka* smoking offers an index of castc-status. Castes which may share, *on* occasions, a single *hukka* are equals. Thus Jats and Ahirs may smoke from the same *hukkii*. Sometimes the Lobar (Blacksmith) and Khan (Carpenter) are allowed to smoke from the same *hukka* as the Jat and Ahir. The Nais (Barber) like many other castes, have their own *hukka*.

Muslim castes freely accept cooked food and water from

one another. Such restrictions regarding food and drink as obtai-ned among Muslims are common to them all. As for the Sikhs, Sardars have reservations about *kaccii* food cooked by Mazhabis, but accept liquor brewed by them.

Each caste has a culture which is to some extent autonomous: there are differences in dress, speech, manners, ritual and ways of life. The higher castes wear fine clothes and gold ornaments while the lower castes wear coarse material and silver ornaments. The speech of the higher castes is refined while that of the lower castes is rugged. Traditionally, the lower castes were prohibited from taking on the dress, ornaments and customs of the higher, and the offenders were punished by the village panchayat.

The concept of pollution plays a crucial part in maintaining the required distance between different castes. A high caste man may not touch a low caste man, let alone accept cooked food and water from him. Where the two castes involved belong to either extreme of the hierarchy, the lower caste man may be required to keep a minimum distance between himself and the high caste man. In Kerala, a Nayadi had to keep 22 m. away from a Nambudri and 13 m. from a Tiyan, who himself had to keep 10 m. away from a Nambudri. A few decades ago, in most areas of South India, there were rules which laid down what parts of a high caste man's house the others could enter. The rules of pollution, at least so far as inter-caste relations were concerned, were more clearly elaborated in South than in North India.

There is a broad line between Caste Hindus and Harijans in the matter of pollution. The village barber and washerman will not serve Harijans, and the latrer have to provide for these services from among themselves. Harijans have to take water from a lower end of a river canal than the high castes and they may not use the Caste Hindu well.

The breaking of pollution rules results in the higher castes becoming "impure", and the latter have to perform certain purifi-catory rites *to* regain their normal status. Where the breach of the rule is serious, as when a high caste person eats food cooked by a Harijan or a high caste woman has sex relations with a Harijan, the offender may be thrown out of caste irrevocably.

The idea of pollution is present among the Sikhs. The Mazhabis have a well of their own everywhere, and in rural areas they may not be allowed to enter the houses of Sikh high castes beyond the cattle-yard.

The culture of each caste is to some extent peculiar to itself, and this is related to the fact that the lower castes are barred, at least in theory, from taking over the customs and rituals of the higher castes. Only the "twice-born" castes are entitled to study the Vedas and perform rituals in which Vedic mantras are chanted. Traditionally, the Brahmin was exempt from capital punishment and his land was assessed at a lower rate. These restrictions and disabilities operate fully against the Harijans they may not use Caste Hindu wells or enter temples and teashops. In some parts of the country they were prohibited from entering the high caste streets. The high castes also kept away from the Harijan ward of the village.

Among the Sikhs, Mazhabi wedding parties are not acco-mmodated in gurdwaras as they are regarded as impure. Among Muslims, however, lower caste groups are not Subjected to dis- abilities. The Christians on the west coast of India observe caste restrictions: there are separate pews for the Brahmins and the Harijans in some churches, and very rarely, even a separate church for the Harijans.

Villagers are subject to the two-fold control of caste and village panchayats, (Caste panchayats, however, are not well developed among Brahmins.) When the disputes concern law and order in the village, for example, setting fire to someone's hayrick, grazing cattle on another's land, stealing fuel or vegetable-it is reported to village elders who may levy a fine on the offender or subject him to corporal punishment or declare a boycott against him. In a marital dispute the council of the concerned caste is the proper body to adjudicate. But the village council may take a hand in the dispute. Where a man is accused of having sex or commensal relations with a member of a lower caste, his own caste or the council of the locally dominant caste, or the village council might be called upon to adjudicate. Punishment may include a fine, temporary outcasting and fine, or permanent outcasting. Re-admission to caste requires that the offender undergo purificatory ritual, express his regret to the caste assembly, and give avdinner to the caste. Occasionally an offender may be re-admitted to caste after having been outcasted for a decade or two.

Many Muslim castes, excepting the *Ashraf* and *Shaikh,* have councils like Hindu castes. Generally, a caste council deals with all questions concerning trade, morals and religion. Sometimes a caste may not permit its members to take up an occupation considered less honourable than its traditional one.

VILLAGE LIFE

We have given a brief description of the genetal features of the caste system and we shall now show how it actually functions in the context of the village community. Inter-caste relations at the village level constitute "vertical" ties. They may be classified into economic, ritual, political and civic ties.

The castes living in a village, or a group of neighbouring villages are bound together by economic ties. Generally, peasant castes are numerically preponderant in villages and they need the Carpenter, Blacksmith and Leather-worker castes to perform agricultural work. Servicing castes such as Priest (Brahmin as well as non-Brahmin), Barber, Washerman and Water-carrier cater to the needs of everyone except Harijans. Artisan castes produce goods which are wanted by everyone. Most Indian villages do not have more than a few of the essential castes and depend on neighbouring villages for certain services, skills and goods.

In rural India, with its largely subsistence and not fully monetized economy, the relationship between the different caste' groups in a village takes a particular form. The essential artisan and servicing castes are paid annually in grain at harvest. In some parts of India, the artisan and servicing castes are also provided with free food, clothing, fodder and a residential site. On such occasions as birth, marriage and death these castes perform extra duties for which they are paid a customary sum of money and some gifts in kind.

This type of relationship is found allover India and is called by different names: *jajrnani* in the North, *bara balute* in Maharashtra, *mirasi* in Chennai and *adade* in Mysore. The relationship between a *jajrnan* and his *kamin* is unequal, since the latter is regarded as inferior. Though primarily an economic or ritual tie, it has a tendency to spread to other fields and become a patron-client relationship.

The relationship is generally stable, and usually inherited. The right to serve is hereditary, transferable, saleable, mortgaable and partible. Thus, for instance, the right to officiate as priest to high castes living in some sixty villages in the Mysore district is shared among the different branches of a single Brahmin lineage in Bannur.

JAJMANI SYSTEM

The *jajmani* system bound together the different castes living in a village or a group of neighbouring villages. The caste-wise division of labour and the consequent linking up of different castes in enduring and pervasive relationships provided a pattern of alliances which cut across the ties of caste. The modern "caste problem" is to some extent the result of the weakening, in the last fifty years or more, of these vertical and local ties and the consequent strengthening of horizontal ties over wide areas.

Caste was related to the exercise of differential rights in land. At the top were the castes who were either absentee or non-cultivating owners. Next came the cultivating tenants (not infre-quently owning a little land as well), and at the bottom of the hierarchy came the landless labourers. There was regional variation in this matter. Kerala, for instance, had a chain of intermediaries between the owner and the actual cultivator.

There was more or less perfect congruence between caste hierarchy and differential rights in land in Kerala. At the top of the hierarchy were the Nambudri Brahmins who were non-cultivating owners *(jenmi)*. The "high" Nayar castes were the non-cultivating lessees of Nambudri land on twelve-year leases *(karzam)*. The agricultural labourers, both tied and free, came from the lower castes like Ceruman and Pulayan and from the Panan tribes.

In Punjab, however, there was a lack of coherence between the agricultural and caste hierarchies, Brahmins being the cultivating tenants of Jat landowners. But, in both areas, agricultural labourers came from the Harijan castes. In some parts of Punjab and Uttar Pradesh, only a few castes snowed a direct concern with land and agriculture, the owner cultivators being either Jats, Ahirs and Rajputs (Thakurs) or Gujars, while the agricultural labourers were mostly Chamars.

The existence of a high degree of congruence between caste and agricultural hierarchy meant that the stratification ran deep, economic stratification strengthened ritual stratification and *vice versa*. This enabled the landowners to exploit the tenants as much as they could-rack-renting, eviction and forced labour were usual features of rural life. But where the tenants' caste was higher than that of the landowner, and particularly when a tenant was also the landowner's priest (as was sometimes the case with the Brahmin tenant of a Rajput landowner), exploitation had to be much less extreme.

In pre-British India, in many parts of the country, the lower castes were serfs or slaves, either attached to the land and liable to be transferred along with it, or attached to the landowner and liable to be sold by him. The economic forces released under British rule (*e.g.*, the starting of tea and coffee plantations, and of factories and railways) enabled the law abolishing slavery to be translated into reality. But even now the agricultural hierarchy have been mixed up in different ways and degrees with the caste hierarchy in several parts of India.

THE RELATIONSHIP

The relationship between master and servant is another type of bond which often cuts across caste, and more rarely, even religion. The terms and conditions of this bond vary from region to region. A common form is the advance by the master of a loan which is worked off by the servant in the course of two or three years in the master's house.

Frequently, before the expiry of the period, the servant takes another loan which results in prolonging his servitude. It is not unusual to come across families linked with each other for generations by ties of master and servant. In some parts of the country, like Mysore, there was until recently a traditional bond as of master and servant between the landowning castes and the local Harijans. The obligations involved were only a few duties on occasions such as marriage and death. The payments were also traditionally fixed. The relationship between landowner and tenant, master and servant, creditor and debtor, may all be subsumed under a single category-patron and client. This relationship is widespread and crucial to the understanding of rural India. Voting at elections, local and general, is influenced by the patron-client tie.

Ritual occasions, e.g., life-cycle ceremonies, festivals and fairs, require the co-operation of several castes. Life-cycle ceremonies are somewhat more elaborate for the "twice-born", especially the Brahmin castes. Certain rituals which are common for all the castes occur at birth, a girl's puberty, marriage and death. Thus when a son is born to an Abu or Thakur, a Bhaksorin (Harijan) woman helps in the delivery and a Bhangi beats a drum before the house in which the birth occurred. A Brahmin casts a horo-scope, while the village barber acts as a messenger and also serves food at the feast.

These services are paid for by gifts in cash as well as kind. In Kerala, the Washerwoman gives freshly-washed clothes to her high caste patrons after the termination of birth, menstrual and death pollution. In rural Mysore there is a saying that eighteen castes have to come together at a wedding: the Harijan servants cut the wood, whitewash the house and clean the grain; the Barber not only shaves the groom but provides the wedding band; the Washerman supplies the washed cloth for the bridal pair to walk on; the Potter provides the utensils and ritual pots, the Carpenter puts up the wedding *pandal;* the Goldsmith makes the ornaments; the Oilman supplies the oil; the Brahmin acts as priest; the dancing girl threads the *tali,* the trader supplies several articles; the Shepherd provides a woollen thread which is tied as *Kankan* round the wrists of the bridal pair, and so on.

SEVERAL CASTES

Several castes are also required to cooperate in the performance of calendrical festivals, and festivals of village deities. In the case of the latter, the castes may come from more than one village. Thus, Bannas from Malabar dance at the festivals of some Coorg village deities. The festival of a village deity always involves the co-operation of several castes, and frequently a few of these castes come from neighbouring villages.

The temple organization itself needs the coming together of several castes. In Kerala, for instance, the head priest of a Sanskritic, vegetarian and teetotal deity is a Nambudri Brahmin. A few Nayar castes have the task of washing the vessels and cleaning the temple. The Ambalavasis perform a variety of tasks and they make gar-lands, assist the chief priest, provide music. There is a caste of story-tellers attached to the temple. In temples to non-vegetarian deities, a member of the Pidarar caste is the priest. Low caste dancers get possessed by the deities, and sing and dance in that state.

It may be taken as axiomatic that all the local castes are involved in the festival of a village deity. Even the Harijans have important duties, such as beating the drum, carrying messages, and removing the leaves on which the villagers have dined.

In many parts of India, villagers believe (or at least believed until recently) that the goddesses Mari, Kali and Sitala presided over epidemic diseases such as smallpox, plague and cholera. An outbreak of one of these diseases was attributed to the wrath of the village goddesses and their propitiation followed. The priest was usually a member of a non-Brahmin caste and occasionally even a Harijan. Members of all castes including the Brahmin sent their contributions in cash as well as in kind to the ritual propitiation. The fact that occasionally a Harijan or other low caste priest catered to the religious needs of all, including the highest castes, affected the quality of inter-caste relations.

Sometimes the ties of ritual stretch even across religious cleavages. A Sikh farmer may go to a Brahmin priest to find out an auspicious hour for starting ploughing operations. Until *forty* years ago, Brahmin priests officiated a life-cycle ritual in Sikh homes. In recent years the Akali Movement has enjoined religious self-sufficiency on the Sikhs, and the Sikh Granthi is increasingly acting as priest at Sikh weddings. The Sikh priest may come from any caste except Mazhabi. Sikhs and Hindus attend festivals in honour of Pirs (Muslim saints). In Mysore a Muslim peasant may vow to Madesvara that he will give a money-offering if his cow calves, or if it is cured of a disease. However, the tendency to religious and even sectarian self-sufficiency has gained strength in recent years.

The functioning of the village as a political and social entity brought together members from different castes. First, there was the traditional village panchayat which, though run by the locally dominant caste, usually included a few representatives from the other castes. The available historical evidence points to the existence of vigorous communities in South India in the pancha-yats of which members of every caste took part.

Every village had a headman usually belonging to the dominant caste. The accountant was always a Brahmin in South India. Every village had a watchman and messengers and town-criers. In irrigated areas, there was always a man to look after and regulate the flow of water in the canals feeding the fields. The headman and accountant collected the land taxes with the aid of the Harijan village servants.

The village council performed a variety of tasks, including the maintenance of law and order, settling of disputes, celebration of,. festivals and construction of roads, bridges and tanks.

In many parts of rural India there exist castes which are locally numerically preponderant, own the bulk of the arable land, occupy a fairly high position in the ritual hierarchy, and wield power over the other castes. Examples of such castes are Jats, Ahirs and Rajputs in the North, Patidars in Central Gujarat, Marathas in Maharashtra, Kamma and Reddi in Andhra Pradesh, Limgayat and Okkaliga (Vakkaliga) in Mysore, Vellala and Gounder in Chennai and Nayar in Kerala. Sometimes the dominance of a caste is decisive, all types of power being concentrated in it. At other times, however, the different elements of dominance may be distributed among several castes. In the first instance, the dominant caste wields great power over the others, while in the second there is likely to be a balance of power among the powerful castes.

It should be noted in this connection that the maintenance of law and order in rural areas even now depends to some extent upon the leaders of the dominant caste. They are the people who can punish errant individuals and ensure the maintenance of the caste codes. When a caste is politically or economically dominant, its religious position tends to fall in line with its secular position.

The Sikhs as a whole are dominant in many parts of Punjab and Sikh Jats are dominant among the Sikhs. Similarly, in parts of Kerala, the Syrian Christians and Moplahs are dominant. In Mallhabad Tahsil in the Lucknow district there are villages in which Pathans are dominant.

VILLAGE COMMUNITY

The village community consisted of hierarchical groups, each with its own rights, duties and privileges. The castes at the top had power and privileges which were denied to the lower castes. The lower castes were tenants, servants, landless labourers, debtors and clients of the higher castes. There was competition among the former to be clients of the rich and powerful patrons while the latter wanted to have as many clients as possible.

The patrons had duties towards clients and vice versa. The caste system together with the inequalities of landownership produced a deeply stratified society, but that did not prevent the village from functioning as a community. Conflict and co-operation went together. There was economic conflict between masters and servants, landowners and tenants, and competition between members of the same caste. The struggle for higher status between structurally neighbouring castes also produced conflict. And in recent years the lower castes have shown an increasing desire to free themselves from the control of the locally dominant caste. This has been assisted by political forces operating from higher levels.

SOCIAL SANCTIONS

By a social sanction is meant here, broadly, any institution a consequence of which is to incline persons occupying certain roles to conform to the norms and expectations associated with those roles. Now it is considered that the sanctioning aspect of social institutions in relation not only to political authorities, but to all the members of a community.

As mentioned earlier individual self-interest may often incite to behaviour which is incompatible with the common good. This implies that any social system must provide some institutionalized means of constraining individuals to at least some degree of conformity to accepted norms.

We have distinguished above between norms and sanctions; that is, between institutionalized ways of doing things which themselves have certain implications for the maintenance of peace and good order in a society, and the consequences, themselves more or less institutionalized, which may follow from breaches of approved, normative behaviour. Consistently with the distinction between social institutions seen as systems of ideas and beliefs, and social institutions regarded as components of systems of action, sanctions themselves may be regarded from two different viewpoints.

First they may be seen, at least in some degree, as the members of the society being studied themselves see them, that is, as the possible or likely consequences of deviance from socially-approved norms. This is the sense in which they may be said to be (more or less) effective in preventing people from breaking the rules. It can be presumed that people will generally tend to avoid behaviour which they believe will entail painful consequences for themselves.

So what is preventive is an idea, and this is so whether their belief is founded in past experience, either direct or vicarious, or on culturally-dictated representations about the activities of gods, ghosts or witches, ideas which are less susceptible of empirical verification. To understand social sensations we have to conceive the social and cultural situations in which they operate as far as possible as these are conceived by the people concerned. Whether their conceptions are scientifically 'true' or not is irrelevant from this point of view.

Second and no less important, though calling for somewhat different methods of investigation, is the question what actually happens when norms are breached. As Llewelyn and Hoebel remark in their study of law in an American Indian tribe, 'it is the case of trouble which makes, breaks, twists or flatly establishes a rule, an institution, an authority'.

What new social activities (whether fully institutionalized or not—and we must remember that institutionalization is a matter of degree) are brought into play in such cases, and what consequences do these activities have ? We shall see that sometimes these consequences are not foreseen or even thought of by the members of the societies concerned; none-the-less they may be very important. So the understanding of social sanctions, like the understanding of other social and cultural phenomena, requires analysis on two quite distinct levels. Sometimes these levels may overlap, but they do not always do so.

Although evidently social sanctions can only affect individual people, we are not here concerned with questions of personality or of psychological conditioning. Problems of education and 'acculturation' are evidently of very great importance, and the considerations which we classify as sanctions no doubt affect different people in different ways.

But we assume that there is in general a normal, customary way of reacting within a given culture, and we are chiefly interested in the social and cultural institutions characteristic of that culture, rather than in the component individuals *qua* individuals. Of course the actual behaviour of individual people is our basic material, as it is of all the social sciences.

But all scientists have to select, in the light of their particular interests, from the multiplicity of data presented to them. And the central interest of social anthropologists is in social and cultural institutions, and in the implications of these for one another. Individual case histories have an important part to play in social anthropology, but their importance lies less in their individuality and uniqueness than in the light they throw on the institutions, values and beliefs which all or most of the members of a community have in common, and on the social implications of these.

The question, then, is this: what are the kinds of social and cultural institutions which tend to prevent breaches of norms, and in terms of which action is taken when norms are breached? The first thing to be considered is how we are to phrase our problem. Is it useful to speak of this field as 'law' and to regard all such institutions as legal ? Or is it better to speak of the whole field as that of sanctions, 'law' being merely one part of this field ?

The question is more than merely verbal, for by using terms which have well-known (if not always very exact) meanings in our own culture we may fall into what might be called the pathetic fallacy of social anthropology, the mistake of uncritically assimilating unfamiliar institutions to our own. When we speak in the Western world of law in its juridical sense, at least if we are speaking at all precisely, we imply the existence of rules which have been enacted by some authorized rule-making body or legislature, and we further imply that these laws are or can be enforced by the State (both through its judiciary and through a body of law-enforcement officers). Thus the jurist Roscoe Pound suggests that the term 'law' is best restricted to 'social control through the systematic application of the force of politically-organized society'.

But this is not much help in the case of many of the societies studied by social anthropologists. When we speak of the blood feud, for example, or of the likelihood that peasants will withdraw economic services from an oppressive chief, we are certainly not speaking of anything that could be called law in this sense. In many such contexts, the familiar distinction between criminal and civil law is even less appropriate.

Thus among the Nuer, there is nothing remotely resembling a central judiciary, so that all wrongs are wrongs against particular people or groups of people, not against the 'state' or against the 'law' as a formal body of enacted rules. In such societies people help themselves; they do not appeal to judges or lawgivers. Here any distinction between criminal and civil law would be meaningless. Even where there are chiefs and courts, often offences against individuals and offences which affect the whole community are not explicitly distinguished, For sometimes the same offence may have both aspects.

Many delicts (to use the term adopted by Radcliffe-Brown) have both public and private aspects, so that any distinction based on the opposition between criminal and civil law cannot usefully be applied to them. Sometimes too, as we shall see later, the primary aim of proceedings which we should classify as judicial is not to punish an offender, or even to recompense an injured party, but rather to restore good relations by re-establishing a disrupted social harmony.

Where it is necessary to distinguish between offences which concern the whole community and those which are only the concern of individuals or groups within the community, we shall do better to follow Radcliffe-Brown in distinguishing between public and private wrongs or delicts. In this way we shall avoid bringing into our discussion of the maintenance of social control in other societies values and preconceptions which are appropriate only to more highly-developed and complex legal systems.

CRIME AND CUSTOM IN SAVAGE SOCIETY

In the study of social control in simpler societies, the contributions of Malinowski and Radcliffe-Brown have been particularly important. In his *Crime and Custom in Savage Society* (it was still customary forty years ago to speak of the simpler, smaller-scale societies as 'savage'). Malinowski discussed the maintenance of social order among the Trobriand Islanders. Although he tended to regard all factors of social control equally as 'law', an approach which leaves us with no sound way of distinguishing custom and convention from law, his intimate knowledge of the people he studied, combined with an easy and vivid style, bring home to us the reality of everyday life for these islanders.

More than the figures in many anthropological monographs, they are real flesh and blood people. Malinowski's principal theme is that the chief foundation of social order, among so-called 'savages' as among ourselves, is the principle of reciprocity. Like other people, a Trobriand islander conforms to the rules which govern social relationships because he knows that if he obliges others they are more likely to oblige him.

Putting it negatively, if you do not do what is expected of you in regard to other people, you are likely to find that others will not do as you expect and wish them to do in regard to you. This is the adage 'do as you would be done by' raised to a sociological principle. Malinowski illustrates it by reference to such Trobriand institutions as the mutual and obligatory exchange of fish and vegetables between coastal and inland Trobrianders, and the argument of his book is that primitive people are not constrained by blind obedience to conformity with custom and tradition, but that, like everyone else, they are moved rather by pragmatic considerations of self-interest and expediency.

Now there is no doubt that in most societies reciprocity, or the possibility of its withdrawal, is a very important social sanction. But it is only one of a number of sanctions (Malinowski himself discusses the importance of sorcery and of religious belief in ensuring conformity), and the author of *Crime and Custom* has been legitimately criticized for somewhat exaggerating its significance. He did this partly, perhaps, because reciprocal relations do seem to have been particularly important for the Trobrianders, especially in economic matters.

But by erecting his Trobriand findings into a general principle he exposed himself to the criticism that he has illicitly drawn from this one field generalizations which he has then applied to all 'primitive' societies, a fallacy to which anthropologists, especially those whose main fieldwork has been in one culture only, are particularly prone. But, more importantly, Malinowski's emphasis was a reaction against the widely-held view, still current at his time, that simpler peoples or 'savages' were kept in a state of slavish, almost automatic, obedience to tradition and custom, through fear of public opinion or supernatural punishment.

This view of the maintenance of order in simpler or 'earlier' forms of society had had a long and respectable history, and we are much indebted to Malinowski for exposing its inadequacy. The great Victorian historian Sir Henry Maine thought that unlike modern, 'civilized' societies, the earliest kinds of societies (which modern 'primitive' ones were supposed to resemble) were based on status relationships rather than on relationships of contract.

He meant that in such societies people conformed to the rules because they occupied particular positions, usually hereditary, and not because they saw, as civilized people do, that a complex social system can only be maintained when different people base their inter-relationships upon agreements mutually arrived at. Durkheim used the same idea in his book *The Division of Labour.* In the earliest (and simplest) societies everybody did much the same kinds of things and produced much the same kinds of goods. Order was maintained through common submission to universally-accepted rules, which Durkheim compared to the enactments of the criminal law in European culture.

More advanced societies, on the other hand, are marked by increased specialization, so that different people do different things, and everyone depends upon very many other people for the necessities of life. So interpersonal relations are not determined by common obedience to a rigid code of law, but rather by the necessity for the mutual exchange of goods and services. These exchanges involve relationships of a contractual kind, and so they are amenable to something analogous to the civil law of civilized society.

Malinowski's point, and it was a good one, was that reciprocity and mutual interdependence are important in 'primitive' societies as well as in advanced ones, so that to represent the 'savage' as blindly subservient to custom backed by ritual and magic is to travesty the facts. But he went too far to the other extreme. There is no doubt that for the most part the members of simpler societies are more inclined than most modern. Westerners are unquestioningly to accept customary rules and beliefs just because they are there and are prescribed by tradition.

There is not, as there is in Western culture, a tradition of philosophic and scientific enquiry more than two thousand years old (even though not all Westerners partake fully in this tradition). So, in most simpler societies, there is little room for scepticism or dissent in regard to established usages. After all, peasant agricultural communities are notoriously conservative in all countries. Of course it does not mean that an analytical and critical temper is universal or even common in modern societies; it is plain enough that it is not. Still it is unlikely that custom is never breached nor tradition criticized in simpler societies. But in simple as in advanced societies conformity is ensured (in so far as it is ensured) by a variety of means other than the need for reciprocity, and Malinowski's somewhat one-sided approach tends to obscure this fact.

Also, his rather imprecise use of the term 'law', and especially his application of the ideas of criminal and civil law to Trobriand society, means that his account, vivid though it is, lacks analytic usefulness and cannot readily be applied in other contexts.

Malinowski was the more brilliant fieldworker, but Radcliffe-Brown was the clearer and more systematic thinker, though he was sometimes wrong. His analyses of social sanctions and of primitive law have proved more useful than Malinowski's ideas in dealing with the very much wider range of sociological field material which has become available in the half-century since Malinowski carried out his field work.

Radcliffe-Brown defines a social sanction as 'a reaction on the part of a society or of a considerable number of its members to a mode of behaviour which is thereby approved or disapproved' (he does not say how a society could react otherwise than through its members). If a mode of behaviour is approved then the sanction is positive; if it is disapproved it is negative.

Examples of positive sanctions are prizes, titles, fame, decorations for public service, and the good opinion of one's neighbours. They underline what one should do. Negative sanctions, on the other hand, underline what one should not do. And they always entail the idea that something unpleasant will happen, such as the imposition of a penalty of some kind, if one does what one ought not.

Positive sanctions are sometimes important incentives to

approved behaviour; but it seems that on the whole people are inclined to behave as they should rather because the consequences will be unpleasant if they do not, than because they will be rewarded if they do. At any rate, even though the same sanction may have positive and negative aspects (as the prospect of an examination may inspire in a student hope of success as well as fear of failure), in most societies the stress is on the negative rather than on the positive aspect. So in what follows we shall be chiefly concerned with negative sanctions.

Following Radcliffe-Brown, negative sanctions may be usefully distinguished as organized and diffuse. Organized sanctions are definite, regulated and recognized procedures directed against persons whose behaviour is socially disapproved: diffuse sanctions are spontaneous and unorganized, usually expressing the general disapproval of the community or of a significant part of it. Like so many sociological distinctions the difference is very much one of degree.

For example it is not easy to say how the blood feud among the Nuer should be regarded. It is organized in so far as a recognized procedure is involved, diffuse in so far as there is no formal mechanism for each step in the procedures involved. But even if there are borderline cases, the distinction is important and useful. In modern societies the most important organized negative sanctions are those comprised in the criminal law. Where we have organized negative sanctions backed by a constituted authority with the power to enforce its decisions, we have legal sanctions, or 'law' in the strict sense.

This is a much more useful way of employing the term 'law' than to distribute it over all, or most, social sanctions, as Malinowski did. Strictly, then, there is law only when there are courts, and where there is an organization for carrying out the court's decisions. The American jurist Seagle wrote: 'In human societies there exists one institution which is conceded authority over all other institutions in that society. This speaks as the whole community, and its commands are recognized as law'. But what when no such institution exists, as it does not in many societies? Strictly, such societies have no law. But, paradoxically, this is not to say that they are wholly 'lawless'. They have systems of social sanctions, and Radcliffe-Brown offers us a way of analysing and classifying these.

There are other organized negative sanctions besides law. Bodies which do not represent the whole community but only particular associations within it, for example, such as churches, clubs and professional groups, may have organized ways of dealing with breaches of accepted rules, and these may form effective social sanctions. For a doctor to be struck off the Medical Register, or a solicitor from the Rolls, may be a far severer penalty than a court conviction. Also, often in simpler societies there are tribunals or 'courts' which although they do not command the backing of physical force, nevertheless do express the consensus of a community.

Their decisions may be more or less effectively backed by diffuse sanctions expressing public opinion. Sometimes, (as in many ex-colonial African territories) these tribunals co-exist with legally established courts, operating at the lower, 'face-to-face' level of community relations. Thus in Bunyoro disputes between fellow-villagers are often settled by an informal group of neighbours, who have the traditional right to impose a penalty on the party judged to be in the wrong, but lack any formal means of enforcing their judgments.

The penalty imposed is always a payment of meat and beer, which must be brought to the successful litigant's house on an appointed day. There it is consumed by both parties to the dispute, as well as by those neighbours who were concerned in the settlement (and anyone else who happens to drop in). It is plain that the object of this procedure—which does not always work, though it often does—is not so much to punish a wrongdoer as to reconcile the disputants and to restore a disrupted village harmony.

There are a great many negative sanctions which are more or less unorganized or 'diffuse', in the sense that even though they involve more or less institutionalised patterns of behaviour they do not imply action by officially constituted bodies or authorities. Almost always they are expressions of the public opinion of the community. Ostracism and house-burning are types of diffuse negative sanctions.

There are numerous borderline cases, where there is some degree of organization. Thus the Kamba of Kenya used to have a custom, called *king'ole,* whereby with the approval of the elders an incorrigible thief or sorcerer might be put to death by a group of fellow-villagers assembled for the occasion. By all acting together the possibility that the death might give rise to a blood feud was avoided, for responsibility was shared by the whole village, and not attached only to a particular clan or lineage within it.

There is an old (southern) Spanish custom called the *vito;* similar customs exist in other Mediterranean countries. This is a way of bringing home to a person who has offended against the standards of the community the public opprobrium in which he is held. A party of villagers visit his house at night, make a great din and shout abusive songs, and submit their victim to other annoyances, to such an extent that often a culprit finds it expedient to leave the area.

Here what Radcliffe-Brown calls the 'satirical sanction' may come into play. The fear of being laughed at, and especially of being subjected to public mockery, is a powerful social sanction, especially where honour and shame are important values, as they are in most Mediterranean cultures, and also, in one form or another, in many other societies.

Witchcraft and sorcery beliefs often act as powerful diffuse negative sanctions. For a disagreeable and anti-social sort of person is likely to invite the enmity of others, and it is believed in many cultures that this may be expressed in reprisal by witchcraft or sorcery. Also, a surly and bad-tempered man is likely himself to incur the suspicion of being a witch or a sorcerer, with possibly most unpleasant consequences. Sometimes the negative force of public opinion is expressed symbolically.

The Nyakyusa people of southern Tanzania, described by Monica Wilson, have a concept which they call 'the breath of men'. This is thought to be a power which although it is associated with witchcraft is not in itself evil, and it is believed that people who have it (who generally include the headman and other important members of the community) can cause a person whose behaviour is generally disapproved to become ill.

CEREMONIAL SANCTIONS

This brings us into the field of what Radcliffe-Brown calls 'ritual sanctions'. Strictly speaking, these are not 'social sanctions in the sense that the other sanctions which have been discussed. Although, like them, they depend for their efficacy on the ideas that people have of the likely consequences of their actions, in their case the consequences which are foreseen are not reactions by other living people, by 'society', but instead the action of ghosts, spirits, and other non-human forces and powers.

So while the sanctions hitherto considered act both on the level of idea and, in the case of breach, on the level of action, ritual and religious sanctions owe their effectiveness mainly to the systems of belief in which they are incorporated. Thus, the belief that certain kinds of disapproved behaviour may cause ancestral ghosts to injure the delinquent is a ritual sanction; for it is the belief, and not the actually experienced activities of ghosts, that tends to ensure conformity. On the other hand, the belief that anti-social manners may cause others to suspect one of being a witch or a sorcerer is not a ritual sanction. For such suspicion may, and often does, entail social action of a very vigorous and (for the suspect) painful kind, as the social history of Europe and America—to look no further afield—amply shows.

So understood, ritual sanctions include the many forms of religious belief, whether these imply reference to a god or gods with the power to punish, either in this life or after it, or to the power of ancestral or other ghosts which may visit injury on living persons who act in disapproved ways. Among many African people the ghosts of dead lineage ancestors are believed to attach high importance to the maintenance of good relations among the living members of the lineage.

In such societies illness is often diagnosed as being due to the failure of brothers to live near one another as they ought, or to lineage members neglecting to assemble at appropriate intervals for sacrifice to the ancestors. Almost always it is believed to be a condition of successful sacrifice that the participants should be on good terms with one another, and that none should be harbouring feelings of hostility or resentment. In this way joint participation in sacrificial ritual may be an important ritual sanction for good mutual relations between the members of a lineage group.

Radcliffe-Brown suggests a further division of social sanctions, cutting across the organized—diffuse dichotomy, into primary and secondary ones. Though the terms are a little misleading, it is hard to think of better ones. Primary sanctions are those which involve action by the whole community (whether the action is 'organized' or not) or by its authorized representatives.

They thus include the sanctions of the criminal law. Secondary sanctions are those which involve only the action of a particular person or group of people in regard to another person or group of people, within a society. But though this action is in a sense private, since it is primarily the concern of the persons or groups concerned, it is nevertheless carried out with the general approval and concurrence of the community as a whole. For everyone recognizes that the action taken is appropriate and correct in the circumstances. So these sanctions no less than primary ones involve the moral approval of the community, but only in a secondary sense, for they are primarily the business of the individuals or groups concerned, who may initiate action without regard to higher authority.

The civil law, as this is understood in Western societies, is a secondary sanction, for a civil case is not usually initiated by the community or its official representative (the State); primary action is taken by the injured party. But he can only do so with the State's agreement. And, in Western countries, the State can if necessary bring certain primary sanctions to bear on a defendant, such as distraint or imprisonment.

LOCAL DELICTS

So secondary sanctions are concerned with private rather than public delicts. Societies differ greatly in respect of which delicts they regard as 'private' and which as 'public', or rather—since the same wrong may be of both private and public concern—in respect of the emphasis they give to the private and public aspects of delicts. Where there is no centralized authority, and specialized political and judicial offices are lacking, most wrongs have to be treated as private delicts and dealt with by the injured party without reference to higher authority.

In the last chapter that homicide affords a test case has been noted. In fully centralized states like those of Western countries homicide is entirely a public or state concern; it is treated as a public and not as a private delict. But in some traditional states in Africa and elsewhere homicide has been regarded as having both aspects. Thus in pre-European Buganda a group which had suffered the loss of one of its members through homicide by a member of another group could undertake a blood feud against the group which had injured it, but it could only do so with the chief's permission, and if compensation were agreed to, a part of this would have to be paid to him. Even in recent years, the members of many African communities have regarded it as strange and unreasonable that European administrators should take away a homicide and kill or imprison him, without concerning itself at all about the matter of compensation for the group which has lost a member.

To deprive of another member a community which has already lost one member by death seems to them the reverse of common sense. For them homicide is still pre-eminently a private delict, even though it is of public concern.

PROLONGED MUTUAL HOSTILITY

The blood feud is a characteristic secondary sanction. The danger that a man may involve his kin in unwanted hostilities may serve to restrain him from homicide, and, if it fails to restrain him, institutionalized action will ensue to restore the *status quo.* The principle which the blood feud expresses is the *lex talionis,* the law of like for like.

Only one life should be taken for one life, and in some societies, such as that of the Berbers of North Africa, the requirement of exact equivalence demands that the person killed in revenge must be of the same standing as the original victim. So if a man in one group kills a woman in another, the object of the injured group will be not to kill the murderer, but to kill a woman on their opponent's side.

It is evident that what is sought in the blood feud is not to punish a guilty individual, but rather to restore a disrupted balance. In the Berber case just quoted the actual killer is technically immune from revenge (though of course outraged feelings may lead to attempts against him). It is consistent with this that the first killer's intentions are irrelevant; in some societies an accidental homicide no less than a deliberate one may lead to the reciprocal killing involved by the feud. But almost always there are institutionalized means for settling the dispute without recourse to a further homicide, even though these means may not always or even often be adopted. Among the Nuer a feud may be settled by the payment of compensation, through the mediation of a ritual authority called a leopard-skin chief.

It is this institutionalized provision for settlement, together with the strict adherence to the *lex talionis,* that distinguishes the blood feud from war (involving hostilities between societies or within a whole society) and vendetta (involving hostilities between two groups within a society), for in these types of conflict there are no, or fewer, rules, and there is usually no socially acceptable means for final settlement. When, in the blood feud, the injured party accepts some form of compensation, it often does so with some show of reluctance, for it is usually held to be ignominious to agree tamely to accept property in lieu of a further life. Hence the importance of face-saving intermediaries in such contexts, like the Nuer leopard-skin chief.

Where compensation is accepted it may assume various forms. In some societies another person is handed over to replace the one who was killed; a man for a man, a woman for a woman, and a child for a child. Sometimes a woman is handed over, to bear children for the bereaved group to replace the person lost. Where there is movable wealth in the form of livestock, as among the Nuer and the Bedouin, payment of a prescribed number of cattle or camels may be acceptable. This may be thought of as a means to obtain a wife and child-bearer for the group which has lost a member.

As we have seen, the blood feud relationship is always between groups rather than between individuals' as such, and always its object is not punishment, but the restoration of a disrupted equilibrium. It may be an important social sanction in those societies which have a strong group organization but are incompletely or not at all centralized; indeed it is characteristic of such societies.

Other secondary sanctions which involve or may involve the use of physical force by private parties are the duel, once a familiar institution in Western society, and what has been called the expiatory encounter, engaged in by certain aboriginal Australian tribes.

This provides that a person against whom an offence has been committed may throw spears at the offender until he succeeds in wounding him, after which the matter is supposed to be closed. Secondary sanctions which do not entail recourse to physical force include the 'singing duel' of the Eskimos, among whom a dispute may be settled by the parties publicly singing abusive songs about one another, the one whose abuse is the most potent and convincing being adjudged the winner.

Among the Trobriand Islanders, described by Malinowski, a person who believes himself to have been injured by another may shout out his accusations and his contempt for the offender from within his house in the middle of the night, so that the whole village hears his complaint. A person thus charged would be unlikely to stay in the village unless he were very sure of his own rights in the matter, and Malinowski records several cases of suicide arising from the feeling of shame thus engendered.

Whether the satirical sanction is invoked by an injured party or, as a primary sanction, by the community at large (as in the case of the public obloquy to which people who have earned the community's disapproval are subjected in some societies), it can be a very potent one, especially, as noted above, where honour, and shame when honour is breached, are important.

Economic reciprocity, much stressed by Malinowski, is

undoubtedly a very important secondary sanction. In the conditions of most small-scale societies mutual cooperation is an essential condition of survival, so the possibility that cooperation may be withdrawn is a powerful inducement to conformity.

Malinowski was right in claiming high importance for this sanction, although, as we saw, in his anxiety to prove that 'savages' are not slaves of custom he rather overdid it. In its very broadest sense, indeed, 'reciprocity' expresses the fact that men are dependent on one another and that no one can live for himself alone. The possibility that reciprocity may be withdrawn is an important inducement to good behaviour in a wide range of social relationships is stressed here.

This summary account of some kinds of social sanctions shows that many social institutions, not all of which may usefully be called law, may contribute to the maintenance of social order. We are especially indebted to Malinowski for having shown that social order is not maintained only by the repressive force of an embryonic criminal law, and we are indebted to Radcliffe-Brown for seeing clearly that the categories of Western jurisprudence are inapplicable to the institutions of simpler societies, and that only confusion can result from their indiscriminate application to them.

TYPOLOGY OF MODES OF SOCIAL CONTROL

We also owe to him a typology of modes of social control, based on foundations laid by earlier thinkers. Even if this typology is less than perfect, it does enable us to classify and distinguish with reasonable clarity the kinds of social control which have been described by ethnographers, as well as by historians and sociologists in Western cultures. Here, as elsewhere, Malinowski's and Radcliffe-Brown's contributions to social anthropology are complementary rather than antagonistic. The brilliant fieldwork of the one, combined with the analytical skills of the other, provide an indispensable framework for a comprehensive, comparative approach to problems of social control in small-scale societies.

It has been stressed here that our understanding of the institutions of other cultures has often been obscured by over-facile interpretation of them in terms of our own institutions. This is especially so in the study of breaches of norms, or delicts. Westerners, with their emphasis on the individual and on personal moral responsibility, tend to think of a large range of delicts in terms of sin and guilt. Simpler cultures are by no means without these concepts or ones analogous to them, but often they apply in very different kinds of contexts is noted above that the blood feud, for example, is not directed only (sometimes not at all) to the punishment of a guilty individual, but to quite other ends.

And the aim of many apparently judicial activities, often too readily identified with Western court procedures, is not primarily to convict and punish a wrongdoer; it is rather to restore good relations when these have been disrupted. Certainly many non-Western societies have had written or unwritten criminal codes, and have imposed punishments on offenders, often very severe ones.

But almost always these have been in centralized and relatively advanced societies. When the first Europeans reached the court of the king of Buganda, for example, they were shocked at the savage penalties meted out for what appeared to be trivial offences; death and mutilation were commonplace occurrences.

It may seem odd that such punishments are not found in the simplest and most 'primitive' societies, but only in more 'advanced' ones, with organized systems of government. But evidently punishments like these cannot be inflicted unless there is some person or group of persons with the physical power to inflict them, and there is no such power in most simpler, uncentralized societies.

Also, and most important, punishment may be said to be, among other things, a means of expressing the whole community's reprobation of certain types of behaviour. As Westermarck wrote: 'the immediate aim of punishment has always been to give expression to the righteous moral indignation of the society which inflicts it.' And such expression, if it is to be organized, requires the existence of authorized representatives who can act punitively.

This expressive aspect of punishment, which Radcliffe-Brown also stressed, is crucial. Nowadays we tend to think of punishment as primarily instrumental: thus we may represent it as deterrent (though modern evidence suggests that it is less so than is commonly supposed), and as reformative (though regarded solely in this aspect it can hardly be called punishment). Almost always it expresses the sense of outrage and indignation felt by the community (or part of it) in the face of behaviour which conflicts with its most cherished values.

The primacy of this expressive aspect is plain from the punishments which our ancestors solemnly imposed on animals and even on inanimate objects, for it cannot be supposed that these were aimed at deterrence or reformation. Like other rituals, the rite of punishment expresses a value which, often, the people who hold have neither the desire nor, sometimes, the capacity to express in analytical, rational terms.

When this is realized it is possible to understand why certain sections of modern Western opinion still strongly support such penalties as flogging and hanging, although there is no evidence that such punishments are either more deterrent or more reformative than less brutal ones would be.

What Punishment ? : The importance of regarding punishment as an expression of the moral opprobrium of the whole community or a significant part of it becomes plain when we consider how such crimes as sorcery, witchcraft and incest are regarded and dealt with in many societies. All of these offences have themselves, it may be noted, a ritual or symbolic component, and all of them are thought to be injurious not only to particular individuals, but to everyone in the social group concerned. Thus often in such cases the whole community or its representatives take action against an offender, while homicide and theft, for example (unless habitual) are taken to be the concern of particular individuals or groups, and are often settled by private vengeance or by compensation.

The public concern is also especially manifest when offences against the ruler or state (where such exists) are in issue. Treason is always regarded as especially heinous, and is punished with particular rigour. For in a sense the king is the state; usually he embodies the central values of the whole community, so that an injury to him is seen as an injury to all.

It seems that in all cultures delicts which are regarded as in some way injurious to the community as a whole are thought of as involving a real change for the worse in the person or persons concerned. This is not necessarily a matter of personal morality, though it may be; a man may enter unwittingly into such a state, and if he does special ritual may have to be performed in order to restore him to normality. Here let us mark the important difference between (in our terms) crime and sin.

A crime is an offence against a man-made law, but it need not involve the deterioration in ritual status that the term 'sin' implies. Thus in the modern world it is a crime to fail to submit a correct return of income to the Income Tax Commissioners, but not all of us would regard it as a sin. On the other hand, fornication is not a crime in European countries (provided that it is between consenting adults), but many people regard it as a sin.

So sin, unlike delicts which although wrong are not sinful, is thought to involve a change in the actual condition of the sinner; it is believed that he has suffered a decline in what Radcliffe-Brown called his ritual status. In very many cultures this condition is represented not only negatively (as implying a loss or diminution of such status) but positively, as implying the presence of an actual quantity or 'thing'. We have noted before this universal human propensity to turn qualities and relations into real things. Sometimes this may be personified as an evil spirit or 'devil', which can be exorcised by appropriate ritual.

This idea is common in many cultures (including Western ones), and spirit mediumship cults to deal with such 'devils' are found in many parts of the world. Sometimes it is conceived rather as a kind of diffused substance, a sort of contagion which may spread and infect others if it is not controlled. In this sense it merges with the ubiquitous purity-impurity dichotomy. The Hebraic institution of the scapegoat provided one way of getting rid of this contagion.

Often the idea of expiation is involved, and sacrifice is required, with its implication of symbolically yielding up a part of oneself to a god or gods conceived to be offended. In any case, the persistence of this condition is believed to imply a continuing danger, and ritual action to end it is obligatory.

Although we may not recognize the identity, notions similar to these survive in the rite of punishment in Western society. We have noted above that in so far as punishment is aimed neither at deterrence nor at reformation but is regarded as justifiable for its own sake, its significance is expressive rather than instrumental.

And when we think of 'guilt' as a kind of existent, and of the guilty as somehow deserving of punishment regardless of consequences, we are reifying what is not a thing but an aspect of social relations no less than simpler peoples are, with their devils and scapegoats. It is partly because in modern Western societies the deterioration in moral status involved in wrongdoing is conceived in terms of guilt rather than in terms of spirits or of ritual pollution that punishment is still so strongly institutionalized in them. But there are contributory factors.

One has already been mentioned; it is that where societies are organized in strongly-centralized political communities, as is necessarily the case in complex modern states, the principle of self help must give way to centralized control. This means that most delicts tend to become public delicts or 'crimes', to be dealt with by the community through its constituted judicial organs, and not directly by the injured parties. Thus the state punishes, where the individual or local group might have rather sought redress or the restoration of good relations. A second factor is the development of the notion of individual as opposed to group responsibility.

Although today men are more dependent on their fellow men than ever before, this dependence is now often at many removes. We are no longer, like the Australian aborigines, dependent for our very existence on the constant support of a small group of people with whom we live all our lives in close, face-to-face relations of mutual interdependence. If we were, we too would identify ourselves closely with the group we belonged to. But where every man is for himself, then he, not a group with which he is closely identified, must accept responsibility for his actions, and he and not the group must suffer if he breaks the rules.

And, thirdly, the promulgation of the universalistic systems of ethics associated with the great religions, and in particular with Christianity, has broadened the sphere of personal responsibility and so of potential culpability. When it is claimed that interpersonal obligation extends beyond the family, the kin, the tribe and even the nation, to humanity as a whole, then moral obligation becomes (in principle at least) universal, and involves all human relationships. This is so notwithstanding that the final step is still a long way from being taken.

Here such large themes as these can only be touched upon. In this chapter an attempt is made to show that conformity to approved norms may be achieved (in so far as it is achieved) through a variety of social and cultural institutions, and that only a few of these can properly be regarded as consciously and explicitly directed towards social control.

It has been suggested that when we are considering the maintenance of social order we are thinking primarily on the level of action, rather than on the level of ideas and beliefs (though the theme of the last few pages makes it plain that we cannot deal adequately with either level without taking the other into account). Our central interest in this chapter has been in the consequences of people's behaviour, whether these consequences are foreseen or not.

We have been mainly concerned with what Merton called latent functions rather than with manifest ones. It was not said that Nuer practise the blood feud because they believe that to do so will ensure some degree of conformity to the necessary conditions of a common life, nor that Trobriand islanders attach high importance to reciprocity because they see it to be a condition of orderly social existence, nor that the Azande believe in witchcraft because an effect of their ideas about witches is, in some contexts, to constrain them to socially approved behaviour.

Sometimes people appreciate the social implications of their institutions, but more often they do not, and even where they do not these institutions may have major social significance. The central question here was 'how is social order maintained?' not 'how do people think that social order is maintained, if they think about the matter at all ?' It would be yet another example of the pathetic fallacy in social anthropology to suppose that all of the institutions which have been discussed in this chapter are aimed, like the criminal law of Western society, at suppressing crime by punishing offenders. Often they are aimed at very different ends.

3

ROLE OF CASTEISM

CASTE SYSTEM

A study of caste system in its various dimensions is imperative for a proper understanding of Indian society. The word 'caste' is derived from the Portuguese term *casta.* Its equivalent in Sanskrit is jati.

Caste is a fundamental institution of Indian society. It is also an unique institution of India. Systems similar to caste are said to exist in other parts of the world such as Japan, Indo-China, Indonesia, and in countries situated to the north of India like Afganistan and Baluchistan. Though the systems found in some of these countries have a semblance of the caste system, they do not in any way completely resemble caste. Therefore it would not be wrong to say that caste is an unique institution of Indian society.

Theories of Origin : Caste pervades the entire gamut of Indian social organisation; there is hardly any aspect of Indian society which is not influenced by caste. Therefore it would perhaps not be an exaggeration, if we say of caste in India what

Kingsley Davis said of folkways in all societies. Caste is the be-all and end-all of Indian society. It is the alpha and omega of human life in India. It guides the destiny of a Hindu right, from womb to tomb and from cradle to grave and even beyond. It determines, for example, whom he will marry, how he will marry, where he will live, how he will live, what he will eat, how he will eat, where he will work, how he will work, how and where he may possibly die, where he will be buried (or cremated), how he will be buried, and also what will happen to him after death. In short, caste determines every aspect of life in India.

THE HISTORY

Caste has a long and hoary history. Historians, Indologists and other social scientists are not agreed on the whys and where-fors of its origins. However, they seem to agree that caste, in one form or the other, in a rudimentary or highly developed form, has always been associated with Indian society. The relation between caste and Indian society has been so long and so intimate that many have viewed caste and Indian society as coeval. In fact scholars like Srinivas have wondered whether it would be possible to visualise Indian society without caste.

A cursory reading of the history of caste brings to our notice yet another striking feature of the caste system, namely, its tenacity or resilience. Caste has withstood the test of time and has surmounted many an onslaught on it. Right from the very early times of Indian history vigorous efforts have been made by kings and emperors, saints and seers, revolutionaries and reformers, to eradicate caste. But all these efforts have been infructuous.

We can here cite a few examples of the efforts made to eradicate caste. The great Gautama Buddha was perhaps one of the early religious leaders who waged a war against caste. The influence of his teachings was very much evident during his lifetime and even after. During the Buddhist period, it seemed as though the caste system would disappear. But the subsequent events disproved such a notion. As soon as the early proselytising missionary zeal of the reformers ebbed away, the caste system slowly reasserted itself. Not only did the caste system make its inroads into the new religion itself, but soon the followers, also of the new Buddhist religion were divided into different caste groups within the framework of the new religion.

After the Buddha there were several others who tried to eradicate caste through their efforts in different parts of India. For instance, there were Sant Jnaneswar and Namdev in Maharashtra, Narsi Mehta in Gujarat, Chaitanya Mahaprabhu in Bengal, Mahatma Kabir in Uttar Pradesh, Vallabhacharya in Andhra, Basaveshwara and Akka Mahadevi in Karnataka, who attempted to establish a casteless society. But as we look at their attempts in restrospect we come to the irreversible conclusion that these were all in vain.

Panikkar commenting on these reformatory movements makes a very significant remark. These reformation movements which aimed at the eradication of caste utterly failed in their mission. The reformers who set out to eradicate caste not only failed in their mission but also ultimately ended up in adding one more caste to the long list of castes in India.

Even during the early years of the twentieth century efforts to eradicate caste were not altogether absent. Raja Rammohan Roy and his followers made yet another effort to abolish caste, but their well-meaning efforts did not bear much fruit, deep-rooted as the caste-system was and limited as their appeal was to mainly urban and semi-rural areas.

The Brahmos (the members of the Brahmo Samaj, established by Roy) have now become a caste by themselves. Historians like Panikkar postulated whether, after all, democracy, which is the very antithesis of caste, would sound the death knell of caste in India. He hoped that democracy would prove to be the greatest *sangathana* movement of all times and would end the caste system forever. But even this prophecy has been falsified. The caste system has taken democracy in its stride and has even given a new twist to democracy, as is practised today in India. Swami Vivekananda prophesied that caste would disappear like a mist before the sun in the face of economic competition. The unfortunate fact is that it has not been so.

Caste is an extremely complex institution, kaleidoscopic, with many facets and dimensions. As such it does not lend itself to easy comprehension and much less to easy theorisation.

VARIOUS ASPECTS

Many have tried to define caste, but these definitions are not adequate enough to cover the several aspects. However, Srinivas has been able to highlight these various aspects in the following definition: "...a hereditary, endagamous, usually localised group, having an association with a hereditary occupation, and a particular position in the local hierarchy of castes." According to this definition the following are the important characteristics of caste.

Caste is a hereditary group that is, ideally speaking, one is born in a caste and not converted into a caste. One has to be a Brahmin, a Kshatriya, a Vaisya or an untouchable by birth. Hinduism, unlike other world religions like Islam, Christianity and Buddhism, is not a proselytising religion. Such of the conversion movements which we hear about these days (known as the *suddhi samskam*—purification ceremony by which a Christian or Muslim convert is reconverted and taken back into Hindu fold) are of recent origin.

Endogamy is another important feature of caste, as inter-caste marriages are strictly forbidden. Those who enter into inter-caste marriages are liable to severe punishment including excommunication. According to strict caste rules both commensal and connubial—that is inter-dining and inter-marriage—relations are forbidden. More than anything else inter-caste marriage is very much dis-favoured, as in a strict caste system, *jati-sankara* (intermixture of castes) is viewed as a serious crime.

However, in exceptional circumstances a high caste man is permitted to marry a low caste girl. Such marriages known as *Anuloma* (hypergamy) marriages, though not totally favoured, are tolerated. But the other type, namely, the high caste girl marrying a low caste man, i.e., *Pratiloma* (hypogamy) is strictly forbidden.

Caste is not only a social group but it is also a spatial group. That is, every caste has its own territory, in the sense that generally members of a particular caste inhabit a particular territory. The territorial spread of castes can be seen in each and every village, from the smallest to the largest. The territorial phenomenon of caste can also be seen by taking the entire India into our purview.

It will be observed that different castes are concentrated in different regions of the Indian subcontinent. For instance, we find the concentration of Namboodiris and Nayars in Kerala; Nadars and Kallas in Tamil Nadu; Kammas and Reddis in Andhra Pradesh; Lingayats and Vokkaligas in Karnataka; Mahars, Marathas and Rajputs in Maharashtra; Baniyas and Katis in Gujarat, etc. However, the two castes, namely, the Brahmin and Shudra can be considered, the all-India castes as they are found all over India.

REGIONAL BASE

The localisation of castes in different parts is a fact which is to be noted even today, both in the rural and urban areas. Harold Isaacs makes note of this fact even in cosmopolitan cities like Bombay, Bangalore, etc. In a recent study made by

Chandrasekhariah it was found that nearly 85 per cent of the untouchables in urban areas and nearly hundred per cent in the rural areas live in their own localities.

Ideally, every caste has its own hereditary occupation. The son of a carpenter becomes a carpenter, a son of a Caste is not only a social group but it is also a spatial group blacksmith becomes a blacksmith. The hereditary nature of occupation in the caste system is to be observed even in modern India. Industrialisation and the consequent changes seem to have had very little impact on the caste-based occupational structure of Indian society. For instance, in a study conducted by Chandrasekhariah it was found that among the Scheduled Castes nearly 70 per cent in the urban area and nearly 85 per cent in the rural areas have been pursuing their traditional occupations.

Castes are always arranged in a hierarchy. Majumdar has aptly described the caste-based social structure as pyramidal. Generally the apex of the caste pyramid is occupied by the Brahmins and other twice-born castes and at the bottom of the pyramid are the untouchables. However, the middle zone of the pyramid is occupied by different caste groups in different regions of India.

A number of theories about the origin of caste have been given by Indologists, historians and other social scientists. Hutton, in his well-known book, *Caste in India,* has reviewed a number of theories put forth from time to time. But he seems to feel that no one has so far succeeded in giving a satisfactory theory of the origin of caste. The very dynamic nature of caste seems to elude all efforts to theories or generalise about the system. Against this background some of the important theories of caste can be briefly discussed.

ORIGIN OF CASTE SYSTEM

According to mythology, the origin of the caste system is

explained thus. Brahma, the lord of creation, created human beings from different limbs: the Brahmins from his mouth, and thus the Brahmins, who were to be the intellectuals, were assigned the highest position in society and their occupation was priesthood. The Kshatriyas sprung from the arm of Brahma, and were given the second position in society, that of warriors signified by the use of arms. The Vaishyas, at the third position, were created from the thigh of Brahma, and became traders by occupation. Shudras were sprung from Brahma's feet, and occupied the fourth position in society, their lot being that of manual workers.

These four classes were known as the *Varnas*, the colour groups. The first three groups were known as the *Dwija* or the twice-born castes because it was believed that they have two births, the physical and the spiritual. Only the twice-born Varnas were allowed to wear the holy thread.

In addition to these four classes there was one more class which occupied the lowest rung of the hierarchy. In fact this group was not given the *Varna* or caste status at all, and was known by different names like Antyaja, Panchama, Chandala, Pariah, etc.

SOME VIEWS ON CASTE

The early European Indologists like Abbe Dubois and others regarded caste as the artificial creation of the clever priesthood of the Brahmins for the permanent division and subjugation of the masses. He observes that the caste system was made by Brahmins for the Brahmins. But this theory has been criticised by Hutton and others who say that it is impossible to accept such a view. An institution which has penetrated so deeply and pervades so largely the entire Indian society, could hardly have been imposed by a single group, however brilliant and powerful. Hutton believes that the caste system is more organic than artificial.

Dahlmann and Nesfield maintain that originally Indian society was organised on the bases of three natural groups based on three important functions, namely, religion, politics, and economic organisation. This threefold classification of society is seen elsewhere in the world also. But later history of India shows that these three classes were organised into a number of corporations, and these corporations later on were divided into professional guilds like those of traders and handworkers, etc. Thus the community interest of these guilds gave rise to community sentiments, and as a result the guilds developed into castes.

This view also has been criticised. It has been pointed out that guilds were not unique to Indian society. Guilds of different kinds were also seen in other countries like Germany. But the guild systems in Germany did not have any ban on commensal and connubial relations (inter-dining and inter-marriage) of their members. Therefore there is no reason to believe why these commensal and connubial prejudices which led to the emergence of caste should develop only in India and not elsewhere.

Sir Herbert Risley, basing his theory on race and hypergamy, maintains that caste is mainly due to colour consciousness and practice of hypergamy resulting therefrom. He makes a hypothetical point to support the existence of hypergamy. The early wave of Aryan invaders consisted of young men who, after subjecting the Dravidians, married the dark Dravidian girls. Once they had enough wives, they closed their ranks and forbade any further intermarriages. In this way the castes developed. This theory of race consciousness and hypergamy put forth by Risley is supported by a number of Indologists and historians among whom Dutta is one. However, Dutta maintains that besides these factors, the code of Manu also had an important role to play in the development of caste system.

Blunt follows both Dhalmann and Risley. He says that caste originated in the peculiar circumstances of complex society—a society of classes with cross division of guilds. The classes were largely a matter of colour which resulted in the division of society into a number of groups based on colour. But guilds, which were primarily economic groups, recruited their members from different colour-based classes. Thus, within the same guild a number of small groups with acute class-consciousness and prejudice were found.

So each guild became an endogamous caste, with endogamous sub-castes within it. In support of this theory, Blunt points out that the exogamous *gotra* are found only among functional castes like the Brahmins, Kayastha, Sonar, Lohar, etc.; whereas, they are not found in non-functional castes of Rajput, Khatri, Jat and Bhat. These castes are made up of exogamous sections instead of endogamous groups.

The criticism levelled against this theory is that it is erroneous to maintain that exogamous *gotra* are found only among the functional castes; they are as common among non-functional castes as among the functional castes.

Both Rao and Ghurye regard caste as having risen largely due to racial differences. The latter emphasises particularly the factor of priestly manipulation by the Brahmins attempting to maintain the purity of the Aryan race. He writes! "Caste in India is a Brahmanic child of the Indo-Aryan culture cradled in the land of the Ganga and Jamuna and thence transferred to other parts of the country." But it should be remembered that the priestly manipulation in bringing about such a far-reaching and complicated system was possible because some rudimentary form of caste system was already present. The priestly class only systematised it.

Ibbetson, like Ghurye, has also emphasised the exploitation of the masses by the Brahmin priests, who, through the caste-system degraded all castes except their own and that of their patrons of the ruling caste. Slater combines both the functional and racial factors to explain the origin of caste system. He emphasises the fact that caste is actually stronger in South India than in North India, and suggests that, caste arose in India well before the advent of the Aryans.

The pre-Aryans developed caste because the occupations became hereditary and intergroup marriages were forbidden with a view to preserve the trade secrets within a group. The Aryan impact was that it strengthened caste and also systematised it. This view is supported by Dutta and Ghurye who maintain that the occupational prejudice and preservation of trade secret was mainly responsible for development of caste in pre-Aryan India.

Sarat Chandra Roy feels that, the belief in *mana* and "soul substance" has contributed to the development of caste. He opines that caste is the outcome of the interaction between the Indo-Aryan *varna* system on the one hand, and the tribal system of the pre-Dravidians on the other. These groups were cemented into a caste system by the Indo-Aryan concept of *karma, mana* and "soul substance."

Max Weber, on the other hand maintains that, mere occupational stratification *per se* could not give birth to such sharp segregation like caste. The origin of the castes in a liturgical guild organisation is neither demonstrable nor probable. Occupational differences alone cannot also answer this question.

So ethnic status and economic factors were responsible for the origin of caste system, and the belief in clan charisma especially played an important role in the development of caste. In India the development of the principle of clan charisma far surpassed what is usual elsewhere in the world. Thus he maintains that, the belief in India that an entire clan enjoyed a particular charismatic power which was retained in the clan generation after generation led to the establishment of caste system in India.

By way of conclusion, Hutton says that, it is extremely difficult to say which theory is the best. The various theories contain some facts about the subject, but, none of them explains the phenomenon of caste in its entirety. Therefore he deduces that the Indian caste system is the natural result of the interaction of a number of geographical, social, political, religious and economic factors, not elsewhere found in conjunction.

The caste system has given rise to a number of misconceptions. One of these is that the stratification of Indian society based on caste is rigid, in the sense that the positions of different castes in the hierarchy is immutably fixed. But nothing can be farther from the truth.

The stratification of Indian society based on caste has never been rigid or static. The positions of different castes in the hierarchy have not been the same. The fortunes of castes have changed from time to time and from place to place. In view of this fact, it would be interesting to examine in brief the various periods of Indian history and study the various changes that have taken place from time to time.

EVOLUTION OF CASTE STRUCTURE

At the very outset a word of caution should be said about the nature of historical records in India. Such records as are available regarding ancient India are primarily religious writings. The interest of their authors in society and the social organisation was incidental and secondary. Hence, such of the information that we glean from these records is, more often than not, hazy and unclear.

Manu Bhashya was the administrative guide book of all the Hindu kings of ancient India. According to *Manu Bhashya* (II, 23), a barbarian territory becomes ritually pure when the king establishes the four *varnas* and reduces the indigenous barbarians to the position of Chandalas who are beyond the pale of Hindu social organisation. Therefore the foremost task of a Hindu king after the conquest of a new territory was to establish a four-fold social order, relegating the vanquished natives to the lowest position.

The recorded history of India is said to commence in the sixth century b.c. when the Magadha kings ruled supreme over the land. Like all the true Hindu kings, the Magadha rulers also had established a four-fold society of Brahmins, Kshatriyas, Vaishyas and Shudras, with the indigenous population occupying the lowest position. In this social organisation, the Brahmins were the priests and royal advisers, the Kshatriyas were the rulers and warriors, the Vaishyas were the traders, and the Shudras provided the labour force.

It was believed that the Brahmins and the Kshatriyas were complementary castes, and as such, one without the other was incomplete. A Kshatriya king without a Brahmin *purohita* could hardly be a full king and a Brahmin. However, in spite of the complementary nature of these two *varnas,* there was always a constant rivalry between these two groups hinged on who occupied the highest position in the hierarchy.

The Brahmins claimed superiority over all others including the Kshatriyas on the ground that they were the representatives of gods on earth *(Bliusuras)* and hence superior to all the earthlings. According to the *Mahabharata,* Brahmins are the only *varna,* other *varnas* being merely its modifications. Vashistha writes that the Kshatriya king attains Moksha only if he offers sacrifices through a Brahmin, as an offering made through the Brahmin is far better than an Agnihotra.

In fact, Brahmin is the first husband of the earth. Just as a widow marries the brother of her husband after his death, similarly, the earth resorts to Kshatriya in the absence of Brahmin. Gautama writes that, when a Kshatriya king and a Brahmin pass along the same road, the king should step aside and make way for the Brahmin because the road belongs to the Brahmin and not to the king. Between a hundred-year-old Kshatriya and a ten-year-old Brahmin the latter is superior as the scriptures say that, the ten-year-old Brahmin is like the father of the hundred-year-old Kshatriya.

Indeed, Vishnu goes still further to stress the supremacy of the Brahmins. He writes that the Brahmins are the intermediaries between man and God, and thus, in a way, are equal to the gods; indeed, they are the masters of the gods because it is by the favour of the Brahmins that the gods reside in heaven!

However, the Kshatriyas who were the rulers and who wielded enormous political power did not concede this claim of superiority of the Brahmins. Thus, in all the periods of Indian history we find this rivalry between Brahmins and Kshatriya priests representing sacerdotal power and secular power, respectively.

However, the ascent of the Guptas to power in India brought an important change in the hierarchical organisation of castes in India. The great Gupta rulers of India, during whose reign India is said to have witnessed its golden age, were neither Brahmins nor Kshatriyas. The Guptas were Shudras who occupied the lowly fourth position in the traditional hierarchy.

It is significant that the Brahmanical writers of this period should sarcastically refer to this period of the Gupta rule as the *Kali-yuga* (black-era). It is but natural that the political ascent of the Shudras should touch off serious repercussions in the social order based on caste. During the Gupta rule, the Shudras enjoyed a position which was equal to those of the other higher groups.

BUDDHISM AND CASTE

The next important change in the traditional hierarchy of castes was witnessed during the Buddhist rule. The political supremacy of the Buddhist rulers affected the caste system in more than one way. Firstly, as is well known, Buddhism was opposed to Brahmanical supremacy and also to the social order based on the four-fold system. Thus, during the Buddhist rule, the Brahmins were relegated to the background and their place was taken by the new priesthood of the Buddhists. Besides the Brahmins, Buddhist rule adversely affected the Shudras also. Traditionally Shudras were the agriculturists, but this occupation was not very much favoured because it was opposed to the cardinal doctrine of Buddhism namely *ahimsa*.

An agriculturist while tilling the land caused, though unintentionally, death to a number of worms and insects, and thus committed *lumsa*. Therefore, the Shudras whose occupation was not favoured by the new religion occupied an inferior position. Max Weber writes, "...with the development of the principle of *ahimsa* preached by these religions [Buddhism and Jainism], the peasant who destroys worms and insects while ploughing was not only declassed but degraded."

With the decline of Buddhist rule, the old social order based on the classical caste system was re-established, where the Brahmins and Kshatriyas occupied the high position and the Vaishyas and Shudras the lower positions.

ISLAM AND CASTE

The next important period in Indian history wherein a change was witnessed in the caste order was the Muslim period. The Muslim rulers in general held the non-believing Hindu in contempt. However, the Muslims took care not to interfere unduly in the affairs of the people.

It was their avowed policy to rule their Hindu subjects according to their traditional customs and usages. With this view in mind they appointed Brahmins as advisers. The belief was that the Brahmins, who were a priestly class and who were the custodians of the ancient custom and traditions, would help them to rule the masses according to their traditions. The Kshatriyas on the contrary, who constituted the political rivals of the Muslims, were deprived of their positions and were even exiled from the capital centres.

The strategy of the Muslims had important repercussions on the caste system in India. A number of scholars of Indian society like Maine, Powell, Weber and others have opined that it was during the Muslim rule that Brahmins enjoyed unparalleled and unrivalled social supremacy. In the absence of their traditional rivals, the Kshatriyas, who were now in exile, and with their superior position as the royal advisers, Brahmins enjoyed the highest position.

Here we can note what Max Weber has to say regarding the supremacy of the Brahmins during the Muslim rule.

"The invasion and domination of foreign conquerors benefited the power monopoly of Brahmins. The foreign conquerors divested the most important competitors of Brahmins of all power because it conceived them to be politically dangerous. ... The power of the Brahmins on the other hand grew during the time of the conquerors. After a period of fanatical iconoclasm and Islamic propaganda, the conqueror resigned himself to accept the continued existence of Hindu culture. Indeed, priestly power under foreign domination always serves as a refuge for the conquered and as a tool of domestication for foreign overlords."

At this juncture it is interesting to go into the views of Maine and Max Weber about the impact of Muslim rule on the caste system. Both seem to maintain that the caste system did not very much affect the Indian social organisation prior to the advent of the Muslims. It was confined to the centres of political capitals and affected only the higher strata of society. It was only with the advent of the Muslims and the ascendence of the Brahmins to the highest position of kingly advisers and the exile of the Kshatriyas, that the caste system permeated deep into the rural areas and hence affected the social organisation. Maine writes:

> "The belief that Indian society is divided into a number of horizontal strata, each representing a caste, is an entire mistake. It is extremely doubtful, whether the Brahminical theory of caste was ever true except of the two highest castes; and it is even likely that more importance has been attached to it in modern than ever in ancient time. The real India contains one priestly caste, which in a certain, though a very limited sense, is the highest of all, and there are besides, some princely houses and a certain number of tribes, village communities and guilds, which still in our day advance a claim, considered by many good authorities extremely doubtful to belong to the second or third of the caste recognised by the Brahminical writers. But otherwise, caste is merely a name for trade or occupation, and the sole tangible effect of Brahminical theory is that what is really a primitive and natural distribution of class. The true view of India is that, as a whole, it is divided into a vast number of independent, self-acting organised social groups—trading, manufacturing, cultivating."

Max Weber and Ibbetson seem to have similar views. With regard to the impact of Muslim rule on the caste system, Max Weber writes,

"The Islamic conquest smashed the politico-military power of the Kshatriya but sustained the Brahmans as an instrument of social control. The pretensions of the Brahmins in classical literature and law books were then stereotyped."

Similarly, Ibbetson says that the Mughal conquest deprived the Hindus of their natural leaders, the Rajputs (the Kshatriyas), and this led to the strengthening of caste rather than weaken it, by leaving the matters in the hands of the Brahmins and of caste councils acting under them.

The next important historical period in which changes were witnessed in the caste system was the British period. Like their predecessors, the Muslims, the British also wanted to rule the Indians according to their age-old customs and traditions. Therefore, they retained the Brahmins as their advisers. This was in a way inevitable because the alert and intelligent Brahmins were the first group in India who quickly imbibed Western education.

They equipped themselves adequately to share the task of administration with the British. Thus, as partner in administration, during the early decades of British rule, the Brahmins enjoyed a very high position in India. And always this civil position was utilised by them to enhance their social supremacy.

During the middle of the nineteenth century, relations between the British and the Brahmins seemed to deteriorate with slow rivalry building up between them. It appeared as if the old traditional rivalry between the rulers and the priests was revived. But only this time the rulers were the British. The Brahmin intellectuals soon imbibed the spirit of individualism and democracy, through their Western education. Animated by these new ideals they started a movement aimed at establishing a democratic government in India. This movement naturally was not favoured by the British who thereafter started viewing the Brahmins with suspicion. Therefore, from that period onwards the British launched a systematic programme to suppress the Brahmins.

BRITISH POLICY

To achieve this goal, the British followed their notorious policy of "divide et Impera" (Divide and Rule). They did not crush the Brahmins outright, but instead, they stoked the fire of rivalry between the Brahmins and the non-Brahmins. They encouraged the non-Brahmins in the field of education and opened a number of educational institutions where various facilities were made available for higher education. Similarly, special seats were reserved for non-Brahmins in civil services.

In this way, with an ulterior motive of instigating the non-Brahmins and setting them against the Brahmins, the British encouraged the former in various ways. Thus, the seeds of disruption and rivalry were laid by the British.

The intentions and efforts of the British administrators to curb the Brahmanical supremacy was aided and abetted by foreign missionaries. The Christian missionaries who were engaged in conversion activities realised that it was extremely difficult to make any headway unless the hold of the Brahmins over the masses was broken. Therefore the missionaries readily supported the movement to suppress the Brahmins.

The showdown, however, came in the year 1857 when the first serious effort to oust the British was made by the Indian militia. The British parliament was deeply shocked and taken aback by the suddenness and severity of the upheaval. The uprising was squashed at a great cost in money and human lives.

A special commission was appointed by the parliament to go into the causes and consequences of the revolution. One of the important findings was that the Bengal army where the first sparks of revolution were seen comprised more than 50 per cent of Brahmins.

Therefore, the commission recommended that efforts should be made to purge the Indian army of the Brahmanical elements. Inevitably, in further recruitment to the services, the non-Brahmins were given preference over the Brahmins. So on the eve of 1947 when the British left India, the seedling of caste rivalry, planted and watered by the British, had found its roots firmly established on the Indian soil.

CASTE AND CASTE DYNAMICS

Recent researchers have shown keen interest in studying caste and its dynamics in modern India. The empirical researches of these scholars have yielded very fruitful results. All of them seem to be agreed on the view that the caste system is still very strong in India despite the popular belief that it is disappearing.

They have adequately proved this contention by indicating the role that caste plays in social, economic, political, educational and other aspects of Indian society. Happily for modern scholars and students, unlike classical historians and Indologists who have given a rather sketchy outline of caste, the recent researches have probed deep into the subject and have highlighted some of the very intricate aspects of caste dynamics.

Thanks to their painstaking efforts, much of the mystery and misunderstanding that surrounded the caste system is largely cleared, and now we are in a position to view caste and its dynamics in a dispassionate and objective manner. In the following paragraphs an attempt is made to review in brief some of the important works on caste by various scholars who have studied at length the intricacies of the caste system.

Perhaps one of the more significant contributions of Srinivas to the study of the caste system is the concepts of dominant caste, Sanskritisation and Westernisation, which have been very useful in studying the dynamics of caste system.

The concept of dominant caste was first introduced by him in his study of Rampur village near Mysore. Srinivas discovered that, contrary to the popular notion, Brahmins do not always occupy the highest position in the local hierarchy of castes. This powerful position, be it in the form of economic wealth, political power or even social prestige, is quite often enjoyed by other castes. For instance, in Rampur the caste which enjoys a high position, higher even than that of the Brahmins, is of the Vokkaligas, who are the peasants.

According to Srinivas, a dominant caste possesses three characteristics, namely, a sizeable representation in the village, wealth and political power. Sizeable number does not imply weight of numbers, it means adequate representation in the population. Wealth, especially in the form of land holding, contributes considerably to the dominance of a particular caste. Besides these, the position of the caste in the hierarchy is also important. Generally, it is noted that a dominant caste belongs to the upper reaches of the hierarchy.

Srinivas points out that nowhere in India is an untouchable caste accorded the dominant position. With regard to the third characteristic, political power, generally the dominant caste belongs to a caste group which is politically dominant in that particular state or region and thus has political contacts beyond the immediate territory of the village. As the name signifies, the dominant caste enjoys a preponderant position in the village. Other castes in the village are almost subservient to it.

Srinivas' concepts of Sanskritisation and Westernisation have also proved very useful in the analysis of mobility in the caste system. Caste system was never a rigid or static system. Mobility in the caste system has always been there. However, social mobility in caste society is different from mobility in other societies.

The unit of social mobility in caste is neither the individual nor the family, but the entire caste group. It is impossible in a caste system for an individual or for a family either to rise up or sink down in the hierarchy. In a caste system an individual is not judged according to his individual merit, but he is judged as a member belonging to a particular group which has a specific status in the traditional status system. Mobility in a caste system is a group phenomenon.

SOCIAL AND CULTURAL MOBILITY

While discussing this phenomenon, Sorokin,' in his book,

Social and Cultural Mobility, discusses various theories. He is of the opinion that mobility stems from the demographic vacuum caused in the upper strata due to the lower fertility of the upper classes. He writes that mobility occurs due to dissimilarity between parents and children, that is, highly talented parents who have reached the acme of achievement somehow beget children who are unworthy of them and who lack talent and ability to retain the high position achieved by their parents.

Thus they slide down the hierarchical scale. On the contrary, very ordinary parents who have lived as ordinary people all their lives have highly talented and gifted children. Thus these gifted children rise up in the social hierarchy. Yet another theory stresses the role of social selection machinery in social mobility.

The function of the machinery, present in all societies, is to see that the various social positions in the society are filled and manned by appropriate people. The machinery ensures sifting, selection and gradation of people according to merits and deficiencies. Thus, as a result of all these factors in every society, we find incessant vertical and horizontal mobility. In India, however, due to the unique nature of the caste system we cannot say that mobility occurs as a result of these various factors.

Demographic vacuum, for instance, does not have a significant role in mobility, because it has been found that the high caste people who occupy the higher strata are as prolific as the members of the low castes. Demographic vacuum does not occur at the top layers of the caste system due to low fertility, and even if such a vacuum is caused, it is highly doubtful whether people of the lower rungs would be recruited to fill the vacuum.

In India, it is also very difficult to say how for the theory of dissimilarity of parents and children can be applied to study social mobility. Even if there is dissimilarity between the parents and children in respect of talent and ability, caste system being what it is, may not lead to mobility. Nor can we say that the social selection machinery in India is functioning so efficiently as to give rise to mobility; in a caste society, the status of an individual is fixed by birth, it is ascribed and not achieved. The function of the social machinery in India is thus, at best, limited.

According to Srinivas, mobility in the caste system in India occurs mainly due to Sanskritisation. The term 'Sanskritisation' refers to a process wherein the lower castes attempt to improve their status, and rise up in the caste hierarchy, by emulating the ways of the higher castes like the Brahmins and other ritually superior castes. This emulation may take different forms.

A non-vegetarian lower caste might give up meat-eating and take to pure vegetarianism: it may give up alcoholism, give up certain social practices like child marriage, widow remarriage, dedication of women to temples, imitating the Brahmins in such things as seeking the help of a Brahmin priest to officiate at rituals, using Sanskritic *shlokas* and *mantras* in prayers, etc. Thus, all these attempts are made to imitate the high castes with the belief that to be similar to the Brahmins is to be nearer the Brahmins and to be nearer the Brahmins is to be higher up in the hierarchy of castes. We can here cite the case of the

Nadavars of North Kanara district in Karnataka State. Some of the changes that one observes in the ritual practices of the Nadavars closely resemble the Sanskritisation process explained by Srinivas. Nadavars are a non-vegetarian caste. But now partly due to the impact of Brahmanical culture and also perhaps due to the aspiration of the Nadavars to rise up in the hierarchy of castes, they are slowly giving up non-vegetarian food. For instance, items of non-vegetarian food are a taboo for them on festival days, and even a separate kitchen is constructed in the garden and separate utensils are used for cooking non-vegetarian food. In fact the non-vegetarian food is referred to as *holasu* which in Kannada means dirt.

This phenomenon of lower castes or other non-Hindu tribal groups, imitating the higher castes has been noted by Max Weber also. He observes that the emulation of the higher castes has been a patent method of spread of Hinduism from the very early times. He writes:

> "Ordinarily, the propagation of Hinduism occurs in approximately the following way. The ruling stratum of an 'Animistic' tribal territory begins to imitate specific Hindu customs in something like the following order: abstention from meat, particularly beef; the absolute refusal to butcher cows; total abstinence from intoxicating drinks. To these certain other purification practices of good Hindu castes may be added. The ruling stratum gives up marriage practices that may deviate from Hindu customs and organises itself into exogamous sibs forbidding the marriage of their daughters to men of socially inferior strata. The assumption of additional Hindu customs follows rapidly; restrictions are placed upon contact and table community; widows are forced into celibacy; daughters are given into marriage before puberty without being asked; the dead are cremated rather than buried, ancestral death sacrifices (Shradha) are arranged; and native deities are rechristened with the names of Hindu gods and goddesses. Finally, tribal priests are eliminated and some Brahman is requested to provide and take charge of ritual concerns and thereby also to convince himself and provide testimony to the fact that they—the rulers of the tribe-were of ancient, only

> temporarily forgotten, knightly (Kshatriya) blood. Or under favourable circumstances the tribal priests borrow the Brahman's way of life, acquire some knowledge of the Vedas and maintain that they are themselves Brahmans of some special Veda school and members of an ancient well-know Brahman sib *(gotra)* going back to such and such sage."

Almost similar views are expressed by Baden Powell who writes :

> "When once it became a mark of respectability to be in 'Hindu' caste, the highest families, as we so constantly find, would employ Brahman family priests and become strict observers of caste rules. Their ruling chiefs take Hindu names, and in time their real origin being forgotten they are received into 'Rajput' rank, and after a few generations they are allowed to marry into the best houses. Mythical heroic ancestors are easily provided for them by court bards; and everything is traced back to Hindu deity, or some miraculous occurrence in Puranic books."

Thus mobility in the caste through emulation is a phenomenon which has been noted from the early times in Hinduism.

Another process of mobility which is linked with Sanskritisation is Westernisation. Sanskritisation and Westernisation are processes which are concomitant; the former specifically refers to mobility within the caste system as also the way in which the tribal groups enter into the Hindu fold. But Westernisation, on the other hand, implies mobility outside the framework of caste.

PROCEDURE OF WESTERNISATION

The process of Westernisation can be said to have

commenced in the 19th century when British rule was firmly established in India and when various attempts were made by the British administrators like Bentinck to end some of the evil practices in India. Westernisation in simple terms means imitation by the Brahmins the customs and way of life of the Westerners, in this case the British.

The imitation of the Western way of life began with the educated and secularised Brahmins. The Westernisation of these educated Brahmins was seen in various ways. There was a change in their appearance and dress. The traditional dresses were replaced by Western clothes and shoes. Gone were such of the traditional practices like wearing sacred thread, tuft, shaving of the heads of the widows, wearing of white *sari* by the widows, avoidance of a woman during menstruation and childbirth, etc. There was a noticeable change in dietary also.

Some of the food items which were formerly forbidden such as onion, potato, radish carrot and beetroot were slowly introduced in the dietary list. Many started consuming eggs on health ground, and also were introduced to other non-vegetarian items like cod-liver oil, etc. Similarly, as a result of Westernisation, Brahmins did not mind taking to certain occupations like the one involving manual work in factories and industries. In this way slow but profound changes were brought about in the way of life of the Brahmins.

However, the Westernisation process did not in any way demean the position of the Brahmins as the process was not confined to the Brahmins only; it was a widespread phenomenon involving all the castes. But the proximity of the Brahmins to the British made it possible for them to adopt the Western way of life more rapidly than other castes. In fact, the proximity of the Brahmins to the British was important because even in this process of Westernisation they became the leaders. They became the filters through which Westernisation reached the rest of the castes.

Thus, a dual process has been witnessed in the caste system ever since the 19th century. The castes in the lower reaches of the hierarchy are attempting to improve their status by imitating the higher castes like the Brahmins. Thus, they are becoming increasingly rigid in their ritual practices. At the same time, the Brahmins (and other higher castes) are becoming relaxed in their caste practices and increasingly adopting the Western way of life.

The theory of Sanskritisation and Westernisation put forth by Srinivas to explain the dynamics of caste has been criticised by some. Commenting on the concept of Sanskritisation as a tool of analysis, Majumdar writes, "the usefulness of Sanskritisation as a tool of analysis of Indian society is greatly limited by the complexity of the concept as well as its looseness." However, the main criticism of Majumdar is that in a caste system vertical mobility is not possible.

Only horizontal mobility on the same social plane can be possible. The process of Sanskritisation, "a process in which a lower caste is able in a generation or two to rise to a higher position in hierarchy" is only a theoretic possibility. But in concrete cases it is hardly done.

The emulation of the Brahmanical ways by the lower castes may only lead to horizontal mobility— castes on the same social plane moving closer to one another. For a Brahmin, a Chamar is a Chamar whether he imitates his way of life or not. The higher castes have never tolerated the vertical mobility of the lower castes and they have in fact, ruthlessly suppressed such attempts.

However, they have looked with indifference if not disconcern the horizontal mobility of the castes as this is characteristic not only of the lower castes but of the higher castes also. But the horizontal mobility of castes at higher levels is achieved through gradual dropping of rituals, customs and practices which can be called the de-ritualisation or de-Sanskritisation process, whereas, the horizontal mobility at the lower reaches of the caste hierarchy is achieved through Sanskritisation, that is accepting and practicing more and more of the Brahmanical way of life.

In support of this view we can cite the example of the changes that are occurring in the caste structure of the Voddas of Kalyanipura. About fifty years ago this community was divided into three distinct subcastes, namely, the Kallu Vodda (stone dressers), Mannu Vodda (earth diggers) and Bandi Vodda (cart workers).

There were certain ritual nuances which separated these subcastes. Inter-dining and intermarriage was strictly forbidden. But now these ritual differences are being given up, and as a result the subcaste barriers are fast disappearing. This has led to the virtual coalescence of these three subcastes into a single caste of the Voddas.

HIGHER AND LOWER CASTES

Writing about Westernisation, Majumdar says that it stands for ideological as well as technological change which have affected both the higher and lower castes. Therefore there need not be any unilinear progress such as from detribalisation to Sanskritisation and then to Westernisation. These stages need not be evolutionary or sequential.

Thus, he finally writes : "To conclude we are not very happy about the tool that we have used to describe the process of cultural change... Sanskritisation connotes a group of concepts and at best is a loose one, devoid of any special merit."

However, in fairness to Srinivas it must be said that in the absence of other tools of analysis his concepts of Sanskritisation and Westernisation are very helpful in understanding the changes in caste system. As for their imperfectibility, Srinivas himself has candidly stated that these concepts may not be perfect:

> "It is necessary to underline the fact that Sanskritisation is an extremely complex and heterogeneous concept. It is even possible that it would be more profitable to treat it as a bundle of concepts than as a single concept. The important thing to remember is that it is only a name for a widespread social and cultural process, and our main task is to understand the nature of these processes. The moment it is discovered that the term is more a hindrance than a help in analysis, it should be discarded quickly and without regret."

Beteille's contributions to the study of stratification based on the caste system are very significant. On the data collected by him in a village in Tamil Nadu, Beteille' has drawn our attention to the very significant changes now taking place in the social system based on caste.

The traditional structure based on caste was relatively a closed society where there was not much of a mobility. But the process of modernisation which has been impinging on Indian society ever since the consolidation of British rule in India, has been precipitating profound changes in the traditional structure of Indian society. In his book he has tried to prove that in the traditional structure of Indian society there was inter-correlation of caste, class, and power, that is, generally all the three, namely wealth, power, and social prestige were concentrated in a single group, that of the Brahmins.

In other words, in the traditional social order Brahmins were highest in the caste ladder (social power), they were the landlords (economic power), and they also occupied important offices in the village (political power). But this is no longer the case at present. Due to various factors of modernisation the social system has acquired a much more complex and dynamic character, and as a result there is a tendency for the cleavage to cut across one another.

In the traditional order both class system and the distribution of power were to a large extent subsumed under caste. But today class and power positions have a greater measure of autonomy in relation to caste. If it is the introduction of cash nexus and development of market mechanism which has brought about differentiation in the class system, it is the introduction of *panchayats* and adult franchise which has been the instrument of change in political power. A major portion of the village land which once belonged to the Brahmins has now been taken away from them by the non-Brahmins.

Similarly, the old bases of power, such as birth and ritual status, are being supplanted by new ones such as numerical support, party membership, and contact with officials. Here again the Brahmins have been the prime losers. Now the power has been shifted decisively from the traditional elites of the village (Brahmins) into the hands of the new popular non-Brahmin leaders.

Thus, in this way Beteille has proved how the changes have been occurring in the traditional social system with regard to caste, class and power.

FUTURE OF THE CASTE SYSTEM

About the future of caste system in India many have chosen to remain non-committal because a number of predictions and prophecies about caste and its future have been falsified by the unforeseen changes in caste. There are others like Srinivas who think that caste is an inextricable part of the Hindu social organisation and as such it is difficult to visualise Hindu society without caste. There are yet others who consider that the caste system has now outlived its usefulness and has become a drag on Indian society. In view of this fact they advocate that the sooner the caste system is got rid of the better will it be for

Indian society as a whole. G.S. Ghurye belongs to this group of thinkers.

He writes: "Every educated and progressive Hindu leader ought to ignore caste. He must not only denounce the institution on the platform and in the press, but must show by his way of living that his professions are sincere." To those who maintain that so deep-rooted a system as caste in India would defy any attempt to root it out, he says that it is not impossible. He has great faith in the ability of Indians to achieve seemingly impossible things. Indians who were once passionate eaters of flesh and drinkers of intoxicating beverages, abjured their coveted food and drink and voluntarily accepted abstinence from all stimulants.

This, he says, is a moral triumph unparalleled in human history. "The same people, now called upon to throw off caste would rise to the occasion and achieve a still greater triumph." Ghurye has even suggested certain measures to eradicate caste, such as inter-caste marriage, common priesthood and establishment of a central organisation to impart training in priesthood, etc.

At the same time there are others who vociferously defend caste with bell, book, and candle. They find nothing wrong with the classification of population into hierarchical groups of high and low status, and accept with chilling equanimity the discriminatory practices arising out of the caste system. The Jagadguru of Puri, for instance, vehemently defended the basic principles underlying the caste system and maintained that there is nothing in the caste system about which Hindus have to be apologetic or ashamed. Others like Swami Vivekananda, and Gandhi tried to cleanse the caste system of its unsavoury aspects by advocating egalitarianism within the framework of caste. Swami Vivekananda thought that such egalitarianism would ensue if all became Brahmins, whereas Gandhi thought that this goal could be achieved if all undertook menial work.

4

CASTE BASED SOCIETY

INDIAN SOCIETY

Indian society was based on a sort of realistic idealism. The practice of life was made to agree with its philosophy, there was no partition wall in the Indian mind between the secular and the spiritual, which were peculiarly blended into a harmonious whole. In his relation to the rest of society, the individual, according to the Indian scheme, lays stress upon his duties—his dharma by which he is to secure his own advancement, and thus may be distinguished from the European, who emphasized his rights. The most salient feature of Indian social tradition is its long and unbroken continuity.

THE HISTORY

India has received peoples from outside for thousands of years, but this age long contact of varied cultures has never resulted in a conflict so severe that one culture attained survival by the complete annihilation of the others. A cultural compromise was always effected between the old and indigenous on the one hand, and the new and foreign on the other, so that elements of all the cultures have survived in the resulted tradition. This process was helped by an attitude of tolerance towards other Gods, creeds and customs.

The peculiarities of the cultural process in India are responsible for the relative importance which different social institutions have for the life of the individuals. Due to infinite variety in the patterns of social institutions, the institutions of the family have been strengthened beyond all others, and the sentiments relating to family life have become all powerful. By the family is generally meant the extended family, where kinship is reckoned through the blood-bond and martial connection. The most striking peculiarities of Indian society are represented by the Hindu caste system and the Hindu joint family system.

Other peculiarities of the Indian social system are the Hindu laws of inheritance, the Purdah system, the profoundly religious attitude towards the problem of marriage and of begetting children, the religious and spiritualists outlook, prejudice against female education and other social ceremonies. But the religious attitude, pervades every sphere of life, and tends to engender rigid traditionalism and conservatism.

Many religions are represented in India, but Hinduism and Mohammedanism, together with several sects closely allied to Hinduism, which have given its peculiar characteristics to Indian social organization and have led to the overwhelming emphasis upon the spiritual side of life. Indian culture finds its foundation in religion i.e. Dharma. Dharma is the most important concept of Indian society. Dharma is a comprehensive doctrine of the duties and rights of an individual in an ideal society. Dharma binds the Indian way of life.

Eighteenth century is an inglorious period in the history of India. Gradual disintegration and ultimate collapse of Mughal imperial authority and debased character of the mobility marred in that period all progressive forces and subjected the country to dreadful political turmon, social disorder.

In Indian social evolution the family has always meant the joint family made-up of many generations of collateral relatives living under one roof and sharing a common heritage. The typical joint family consists of father, his sons and grandsons, together with the corresponding women folk until some of them are married off and enter into other joint families. Jointness is the normal condition of Hindu society.

In the words of I.P. Desai: "We call that house a joint family which has greater generation depth, than under family and the members of which are selected to one another by property, income and the mental rights and obligations": No separation or particularization of accommodation is unthinkable in the joint families. Sir Henry Maine opines that joint family is a group, constitutes of known ancestors and adopted sons and relatives related to these sons through marriage.

The earning of all the members are put in a common pool out of which the needs of every member are met. The senior most member of the family controls and conducts affairs with the advice of others but his voice is final. The joint family is generally supposed to be a characteristic peculiar to the Hindus. As a matter of fact, it seems to be general in India, as it is found among, many communities, non-Hindu as well as Hindu. The joint family and caste as usually described as the basis on which social life among the Hindus, is organized. These two institutions, the caste and the joint family are in practise interlocked to an extend which makes them in effect a common institution.

SEVERAL GENERATIONS

Thus, it seems that the joint family was a group of agnatically related males of several generations, their unmarried sisters, daughters. There was common worship and common kitchen. It was the duty and right of the eldest male member to fix individual responsibility for various tasks on all other members. The head rules the family lâying more emphasis on love and persuasion. Besides, the members of the family jointly undertake production and consumption and are joint owners of the wealth of the family. Because of its joint ownership and presence of cooperation among the member it has been called a cooperative institution. Accumulated capital pays for contingent expenditure on such occasions as marriage, deaths and litigation.

According to Kapadia "The whole history of the Hindu family unfolds one significant fact that even when the trends towards individualism were recognized and attempts were being made to harmonize them with the interest of the joint family, the family constitution was unequivocally declared to be, and maintained as joint and agnatic". The trend towards individualism became strengthened with the passage of time. Specific decisions by British courts may be cited to show how their administration of Hindu family law dealt serious blows to the joint family.

The joint family system guarantees economic security to all. The joint family system acts as a social insurance company for the old, and the sick. It promotes the spirit of cooperation and unselfish service. It avoids fragmentation of holdings and evils inherent there in. At the same time, the main defects of the system are as follows. Namely it encourages litigation, beads to quarrels, loss of privacy and not favourable for capital accumulation.

But the joint family system Is disintegrating rapidly due to the increase of population and the spread of Western culture. As a consequence of economic changes and legislative measures, the Hindu joint family has suffered in size, and internal cohesion and solidarity. Further, due to industrialization, extension of communications and transport, decline of agricultural and village trade and impact of the West are solely responsible for the disintegration of the Hindu joint family. Yet, the Indian people still keep intact the family attachment and live their traditional morality. The joint family is a cooperative institution where every member does his duty under the guidance of the eldest member.

One of the oldest institutions in Indian society is caste system. The caste system was the steel frame of Hinduism. A caste or sub-caste is an endogamous social group. One has to view the caste as an extension of the family, the principle of grouping appears to be the blood-bond and relationship through marriage. Birth determines irrevocably the whole course of a man's social and domestic relations and he must throughout life eat, drink, dress, marry and give in marriage in accordance with the usages into which he was born.

Ghurye list the following features as characteristic of Hindu caste system, segmental division of society, hierarchical arrangement of castes, restrictions on feeding and social intercourse, civil and religious disabilities and privileges of the different castes, lock of unrestricted choice of occupation and restrictions on marriage.

According to M.N. Srinivas:

> "Caste is undoubtedly an all-India phenomenon in the sense that there are everywhere hereditary, endogamous groups which forms a hierarchy and that each of these groups has a traditional association with one or two occupations. Everywhere there are Brahmins, untouchables, and peasants, artisans, trading, and service castes,... certain Hindu theological ideas such as Karma and Dharma are woven into the caste system, but it is not known whether awareness of these concepts is universal or confined only to certain sections of hierarchy. This depends on the degree to which an area is sanskritized.

But the existence of some universal features should not

lead us to ignore the significant regional differences... All the Brahmins in India do not form a single endogamous group. There may be a dozen endogamous groups among them.... There are hundreds of Jatis or endogamous groups in each of the linguistic area of modern India. The four or five varnas represent only broad all-India categories into which the innumerable jatis can be grouped for some limited purposes. According to a varna model, the Harijans or untouchable are outside the caste system and contact with Harijans pollutes members of the other four varnas".

Liche writes "Caste, in my view, denotes a particular species of structural organization indissolubly linked with what... is a Pan India civilization." Risley has defined caste as a collection of families or group of families bearing a common name, claiming a common descent from a mythical ancestor... In the words of Rapson the caste system now divides the great majority of the inhabitants of Northern and Southern India into hundreds of self-contained groups. A man is obliged to marry outside his family, but within the caste. A family consists of persons reputed to be descended from a common ancestor, and between whom marriage is prohibited.

The cardinal principle which underlies this system of caste is the preservation of purity of descent, and purity of religious belief and ceremonial usage, Ghurye writes caste is a Brahmanic child of Indo-Aryan culture cradled in the land of the Ganges and thence transferred to other parts of India by Brahmin prospectors.

James Mill believes that caste system developed as a result of the need for division of labour. Many mentioned four caste functions as teaching and preaching, administration and protection, agriculture and commerce, and service and manual labour. Their corresponding names are the Brahman, the Kshtriya, the Vaisya, and the Shudras. In the beginning, movement from one to the other was possible, but gradually the caste system became rigid and hereditary.

SPREAD OF BRAHMANISM

The institution of caste is essentially Brahmanical, and has spread with the spread of Brahmanism. The uniqueness of caste system did not consist in that it was based on differences of Functions. Its specifications lay in the fact that it made birth the basis of social grouping. It implies not only the negation of equality but the organization of inequality exclusively on the basis of inheritance.

Differences there will be in any imaginable society, differences of function at all events. It is not in recognizing their inevitability that caste is peculiar, it is in the method it adopts to systematize and control them. Further, the caste system was sanctified by the sanction of religion.

Its very genesis was attributed to Brahman. Religion forfeited the hold of the caste over its members. The caste system thrived for many centuries primarily because of the low level of economic existence of the Indian people. The precapitalist economy on which it rested was primarily because of the low level of economic existence of the Indian people. The hierarchic construction of the caste gave rise to inequalities among the peoples.

Even in matter of residence, the lower castes were segregated from the higher ones. Even the untouchables were forbidden from using the public wells and tanks. Their mere sight contaminated and an unapproachable who, wittingly or unwittingly, happened to come within the ocular vision of the holy Brahmin, was often meted out most brutal punishment.

The caste system is based on two main principles, i.e. the doctrine of Karma, and religious unity of the family. The doctrine of Karma lays it down that a man is born into that position which he has earned in a former incarnation. The principle of religious unity of the family is largely responsible for the emphasis laid on community feeling, as opposed to individualism. It also accounts for the joint Hindu family system, many features of the marriage system, and the position of women in the society.

The Mohammedan invasion and rule were to leave village life fundamentally unaffected and simply to increase the insecurity of life and property. The day when the government attempts to interfere with any of the more important religious and civil usages of the Hindus will be the last of its existence as a political power.

The main principles of the government remained unchanged throughout the ages. The Mughal rule did not succeed in welding the population into a unified whole. Rather, the presence of foreign rulers caused the Hindus to tighten up their social organization in self-defence. Of course, the Hindu adopted the Purdah system of the conquerors.

The caste system was not at all weakened by the foreign invasion rather it influenced the foreigners (Muslims) to such an extent that they themselves have tended to form exclusive classes, and the resulting fabric of society has thus become far more resistant to external influences, and consistently conservative. There was perfect freedom of worship in the Hindu society. It was the freedom of worship which had sustained the power of assimilation, and also maintain the continuity in the society.

The Mohammedans themselves tended to become a caste, instead of helping to break-up the caste system, and the very contact which might have been expected to induce social progress became a factor helping to crystallize the status quo. Thus, the peoples of India are divided into a number of religious and social sects, classes and castes, each of which keeps itself to, maintained purity of descent and its own social ideals and customs and belief of its fellow members.

Thus social stratification has become an apparently irremovable fetter on material progress. But on account of the economic and administrative changes in India since the middle of the 18th century, there was some laxity in professional specialization on caste basis. All proper Hindus regret that in these days no caste adheres to its proper duties, but many persons, in order to procure a subsistence, be take themselves to professions for which they were not ordinarily intended. The rigid rule of caste forcing its every member to follow the hereditary occupation.

The caste system was one of the root causes which obstructed social reform in other fields of social life also. Later on in the 19th and 20th century the social reformers attacked heredity as the basis of distinctions, and the law of Karma which supplied the religio-philosophic defence of the undemocratic authoritarian caste institution. However, endogamy, the formidable pillar which sustained the caste structure, remained almost unshaken.

In a society which lacked central or political organization, social security dependent very largely in the first instance on the prosperity of the joint family, and on the strength and solidarity of the caste group. The scattering of cultural entities, the lack of a strong central power, and the resulting isolation and stagnation have preserved the Hindu social organization in spite of the powerful attacks of Christianity and Mohammedanism.

Muslims were no less divided by considerations of caste, race, tribe and status, even though there religion enjoined social equality. The Shia and Sunni nobles were sometimes at loggerheads on account of their religious differences. A large number of Hindus converted to Islam carried their caste into the new religion and observed its distinctions, though not as rigidly as before. Moreover, the sharif Muslims consisting of nobles, scholars, priests, looked down upon the ajlaf Muslims or the lower class Muslims in a manner similar to that adopted by the higher caste Hindus towards the lower caste Hindus.

SOME PRIMITIVE COMMUNITIES

Family system was mainly patriarchal in character, except in Malabar and among some primitive communities in backward areas. The senior most member of a family was its head. In case of a joint family the mistress of the house had a dignified position. It is true to say that the Hindu marriage is not a contract but a religious sacrament and spiritual bond.

Hindu marriage binds the wife and husband to undertake the dharma, to procreate and to discharge other duties concerning physical, social and spiritual requirements. According to Hindu beliefs male offspring are necessary for the performance of the religious ceremonies that will secure salvation. Caste rules, make marriage obligatory. Although marriage is usually contracted at a very early age amongst Hindus, as a rule marital relations do not begin until puberty is attained to quote Mandelbaum:

> "Two kinds of rules are followed in marriage negotiations, explicit structural rules such as those of endogamy and exogamy, and the implicit rules of the game of maneuvring for family advantage. The structural rules require that the couple belong to the same endogamous group, the jati, and also that each spouse come from a different exogamous category within the jati. Each jati defines these categories in its own way and there are myriad elaborations on these rules, but in fundamental outline they are quite similar throughout land. Exogamy means that husband and wife may not be related to each other before marriage in ways that are prohibited...
>
> The tabooed relationships are those of kin, position of kin grouping, and in some of the Northern regions of locality two people in certain specific

kin position are forbidden to marry, as for example, a man and his mother's sister. Prohibited also are the unions within kin groupings, such as between two who are paternally descended from the same real or mythical ancestors.

In jati which follow Sanskritic usage, the prohibited kin positions are collectively known as Sapinda relations are traced through both father and mother". Amongst Mohammedans, marriage usually occurs at adolescence, but although the evils of pre-puberty marriage are thus avoided. The universality and early age of marriage, together with the intense desire for male offspring, tends to increase the birth-rate. Frequent, motherhood saps the vitality of Indian women, and tends to increase both maternal and infant mortality.

The physical strain on the young wives is aggravated by excessive sexual indulgence. These evils are accentuated by the frequent disparity in age between husband and wife. Considering the physical immaturity and ignorance of the young mothers, the insanitary surroundings, the lack of care for female infants, and malnutrition which necessarily are found in large families belonging to the poorer classes, it is little wonder that a large proportion of the babies born die in infancy. But society in general had feelings of reverence for its womenfolk. A Hindu woman can go anywhere alone, even in the most crowded places .... A house inhabited solely by women is a sanctuary which the most shameless libertine would not dream of violating. Purdah or seclusion of women in houses was observed in Hindu and Muslim families.

In Indian village life, Purdah is the hall mark of the

lady. The Rajput women cannot even draw water from the well, and being a lady must have servants to help her in her domestic tasks. The purdah system and pride of caste withdraw many women from productive employment, and prevent them from assisting their men-folk even at busy seasons.

Succession among Hindus is governed by the Mitakshara and Dayabhaga school of law. Under the Mitakshara system the ancestral property is owned and enjoyed by all members of the family as a body. The head of the family is only a manager for the time being. He has no right to dispose of any property without the consent of the male members. In case of a member's death there is no succession to his share.

The family remains joint till there is a partition of ancestral property. On the other hand in case of Dayabhaga the head of the family is an absolute owner of the entire property during his life time and he can dispose of the property as and when he likes. Under this law there is no succession even in joint property and a dead members share goes to his heir. Under both systems of law, woman have no right to ancestral property.

On the other hand, Islamic law gives a share of the property to both males as well as females though not on an equal basis. But in actual practice, customary Hindu law is followed by Muslims. 17th and 18th centuries law of succession leads to a number of evils. Land gets subdivided into smaller pieces, till it is uneconomic to cultivate. The laws encourage litigation which wastes time and money and it also discourage large-scale enterprise.

Untouchability was prevalent in society. The untouchables were the out-castes of the Hindu society. For centuries, untouchability persisted in the Hindu society. Historically, untouchability was the social fruit of the Aryan conquest of India. Hallowed with tradition and sanctified by religion, it continued to exist in all its barbarous vigour for centuries. In the Hindu society, the hereditary untouchables were assigned such low functions as those of scavengers, of removers of dead cattle, and others. History has known hierarchically graded societies were based on social privileges and inequalities.

The mere physical touch of an untouchable was a sin. The Hindu state enacted draconic laws to punish those untouchables who rebelled against their intolerable conditions. They had to reside in a separate area in the village or town and had no freedom to use public wells and tanks which the caste Hindus used.

The social oppression of the untouchables had religious sanction. The outraging of human reached its high watermark under it. But the extent of untouchability varied from place to place. The depressed classes were demarcated from the upper caste Hindus by certain fundamental social oppression and disabilities common to them. Above all, untouchability had basically economic foundation and the untouchables were the most poverty stricken section of the Indian people. Their low social position accentuated their economic exploitation and their economic conditions tended to stabilize their low status.

Among the upper classes, the evil customs of incurring heavy expenses on marriages and of giving dowry to the bride prevailed. Ordinarily dowry is the property which a man receives when he marries, either from his wife or his family. Dowry is the amount received by the grooms party and the chief evil of this system lies in the compulsion that is employed to extract these things from brides party, much against to their capacity, willingness and desire.

Besides, ordinarily there was no polygamy. Dubios note significantly "polygamy is tolerated amongst persons of high rank. None-the less plurality of wives amongst the great is looked upon as an infraction of law and custom, in fact, as an abuse.. I know only of one case in which a man can legally marry a second wife, his first wife being still alive, and that is when, after he has lived for a long time with his wife, she is certified to be barren, or if she has borne only female children.." But polygamy had become a regular and notorious practice among those who were regarded as kulins in Bengal.

Among the kulins family pedigree was like a marketable commodity. At the same time polyandry was exceptionally practised in Indian society. Buchanan writes that polyandry prevailed among the Tiyahs in Malabar. Similarly as early as in 200 A.D. widow remarriage was prohibited for being a sin against the departed soul of husband.

But widow remarriage was widely prevalent among the non-Brahmins of Maharashtra. Even the Peshwa collected a tax called patdam on the remarriage of widow. In the 19th century many social reformers fought for widow remarriage notable among them was Ishwar Chandra Vidyasagar with whose efforts saw the enactment of Hindu widow remarriage act in 1856. To quote Altekar in this context, for nearly 2,000 years from 200 B.C. to 1800 A.D. the position of women steadily deteriorated.

The prohibition of remarriage, the spread of purdah and the greater prevalence of polygamy made her position very bad." The great social changes which took place after 300 B.C. led to a degradation in the status of women. One shocking practice rampant in certain parts of India was sati, that is women burning themselves on the funeral pyre of their husband. It was mostly prevalent in Rajputana, Bengal and other parts of Northern India.

In the 18th century it was widely prevalent. The lot of the Hindu widow was pitiable, and there were all sorts of restriction on her diet, clothing and movement. Such is the influence of customs and sense of shame that women of highest birth will undergo, this awful sacrifice with as much compassion as ever were exhibited by any philosopher of antiquity. Ideologically women were considered a completely inferior species, having no significance, no personality, socially, she was kept in a state of utter subjection, denied by polygamy, the Purdah, early marriage, self-immolation of widows or a state of permanent widowhood, all these contribute to the smoothening of the free development of women.

Slavery prevailed in the country during the 18th century. There were two types of slavery in India, domestic slaves and slaves tied to the land. The serfs attached to lands were considered to be property of their masters, and when lands were transferred from one master to another they had also to change masters.

A poor man sold himself under perpetual bondage to a rich man and he even sold his children as slaves or servants in lieu of money. Of course slaves are treated by the Hindus with great indulgence, and if they conduct themselves well are considered rather as hereditary servants of the family than as menials. However, the foreign companies carried on traffic in slaves and even there was a slave market in Kolkata.

Friendly relations between Hindu and Muslims were a very healthy feature of the 18th century. In fact there was little religious intolerance in the country. The evolution of a composite Hindu-Muslim culture continued unchecked. In religious sphere, the mutual influence and respect that had been developing in the last few centuries as a result of the Bhakti movement among Hindus and Sufism among Muslims, continued to grow. The development of Urdu language and literature provided a new meeting ground between Hindus and Muslims.

IMPORTANCE OF RELIGION

Hinduism was characterized by an attitude of toleration towards other faiths and adaptation to new environments. The general body of the Hindu population were followers of the old forms and practices of religious worship. Religious performance filled the days of the Hindu. In the words of Forbes:

> "In its simplicity, Hinduism taught that was one supreme ruler of the universe who was styled Brahma, the great one, this supreme intelligence consisted of a triple divinity expressed by the mystic word OM, and distinguished by the name Brahma, Vishnu and Mahesh.. Images of these attributes were placed in temples and worshipped daily."

In course of time, this sublime religion had been, supplanted by a system of polytheism and idolatry. There were many followers of the cult of Shiva and Vishnu and their sub-cults which appeared in course of time and spread in different parts of the country. Besides the old religious sects, new ones appeared during the 18th century. A few of the latter were either of an eclectic or monotheistic nature, and the rest were Vaishnava sects. The founders of these sects were mostly non-Brahminical castes, and Guru worship was a common feature of all of them. The founders of these sects directed their energy against rituals, ceremonies, Brahminical supremacy, religious persecution etc. The birth of these sects were simply a protest movement.

The Bhakti movement of the middle ages was a protest against the ritual of Brahmanism and the superstition of the masses. The supremacy of one God was the first creed with everyone of the saints. But in spite of the existence of numerous reformist sects, the majority of the Hindus followed the traditional ways of performing religious rites and ceremonies. Idol worship was very common. Along with idol worship many irrational practices had crept into the Hindu religion in the form of ceremonies and sacrifices. By giving much importance to the observance of rituals and ceremonies, they promoted the priesthood in society. But some new religious sects appeared during the 18th century, and the founder of these sects raised voices of protest against certain prevailing abuses which had crept into the religious system in course of centuries.

Ghasi Das the founder of the Satnami sect of Chhatisgarh was a chamar, Balarama, the founder of Balarami sect, was a Hari whose social position is about the same as that of a chamara, Ramasarana Pala, the real founder of the Kartabhaja sect was a Sadgopa. They have been influenced by a desire for social betterment for which orthodox Hinduism holds out no prospect, is evident from the fact that they nearly all abrogate caste if not altogether, at least in their religious houses and at their festivals. Whether the sects profess vaishnavism, monotheism, or eclecticism, there is one feature common to nearly all of them - viz. Guru worship.

Amongst Hindus, the Guru or spiritual guide from the remotest antiquity has been held in the highest respect. But the guru of the sects is something more than a spiritual guide. The founders of several sects like the Kabirpanthis and the Satnamis taught the unity of the God head, and abjured idolatory.

The Charan Dasis Sect was founded by Charan Das about the year 1758. He preached the worship of Krishna and Radha. Like most other Vaishnavas, the Charandasis regard their guru as divine. According to Wilson:

> "They affirm that originally they differed from other sects of Vaishnavas in worshipping no sensible representations of the deity, and in excluding even the Tulsi plant and Salagrama stone from their devotion, they have, however, recently adopted them, in order to maintain a friendly intercourse with the followers of Ramananda... Their moral code, which they seem to have borrowed from the Madhwas, consists of ten prohibitions. They are not to tell lie, not to revile, not to speak harshly,

> not to discourse idly, not to steal, not to commit adultery, not to offer violence to any living being, not to imagine evil, not to cherish hatred, and not to indulge in pride."

The Bhagavata Purana and Bhagavat Gita are the recognized scriptures of the sect.

Sahajananda Swami, who became famous as Swami Narayan, was the founder of Swami Narayan Sect. He was born near Oudh in 1780-81 A.D. His guru was one Ramananda and when he settled down at Ahmedabad, the orthodox Brahmana made his stay there so uncomfortable that he had to retire to Wartal. He erected there a temple of Lakshmi-Narayan. He preached the worship of Krishna and Radha, and directed his effort to the abolition of bloody sacrifices, Sati, infanticide. In fact this sect arose as a protest against the voluptuousness of the Vallabhacharis. He held the tenth book of the Bhagavata Purana as the supreme authority.

The Paltu Dasi sect came into existence during the last part of the 18th century. Paltu Das after whom the sect is called was a disciple of an ascetic called Gobind Sahab. Paltu gadi is still in existence in Oudh, where a great annual fair is held on the Ram Navami day. The Paltu Dasis salute each other by saying Satya Rama (Rama is true). They worship Rama and mostly found in Oudh and Nepal.

There are two distinct sects bearing the same name Satnami, one in Northern India and the other in Central province. During the last part of 18th century an inhabitant of Oudh named Jagajiban Das was the founder of Satnami sect in Northern India. He was the author of several works in the Hindi language. The creed of the Satnamis is a form of Pantheism. They address God as the true name (Satnam). Caste distinctions are observed by the Grihastha members of this sect, but not by the ascetics. On the other hand, the Chamars form the largest caste in Chhatisgarh. They mostly belonged to the Satnami sect. They are agriculturists, rather tenacious of their rights, and as they are untied, quite capable of holding their own against the Hindus who look down upon them with great contempt. They also call themselves Rai Dasas after Rai Das, a chamar reformer and disciple of Ramanand who lived in the 15th century A.D.

The modem Satnami creed is a revival of the doctrines of Raidas Preached by Ghasi Das. Ghasi Das an unlettered but thoughtful charms was deeply impressed with the degraded condition of his community, who were deeply addicted to drink and other bad habits. He gradually acquired considerable influence by his wisdom and high moral character. He spread the message that there is only one true God, the Satnam, that all man are equal, that the idols of the Hindus are false, and that meat, intoxicating liquors and smoking are interdicted.

Ghasi Das became the Guru of the Chamars. The dissemination of the Satnami doctrines infused new life into the Chamars, and they rose to positions of comparative influence and respectability, which apparently made them an eyesore to their Hindu neighbours, to whom the veiy name of chamars is a byword for all that is degraded.

The lower strata of the Hindu society in Bengal, Bihar and Orissa worshipped strange creatures like Kallo Rai, the patron saint of tigers, Rama Thakur, a ghost, the cult of Baro Bhaiya, twelve demons, the son of Vana Durga, a tree goddess, came into vogue in the 18th century. This village cult was affiliated to tantricism and Sanskrit mantras came to be used in its worship. There arose a number of saintly reformers amongst the depressed classes. Garib Das, a Jat by birth founded a small sect, the followers of which worship God in the name of Rama, Hari and Allah. He advised his followers to adhere to the path of love and devotion.

Sadhu Shanti Das founded the Ramasanehi sect. He asked his followers to avoid image worship. He prescribed the offering of prayers in the morning, noon and in the evening. He enjoined strict moral discipline. His followers do not observe Hindu festivals. Madhavgar, a Kanbi farmer of Nadiad in Gujrat founded a sect and raised his voice against the worship of images, condemned caste distinction and did away with the practice of untouchability.

SOCIAL REFORMS

The Kartabhajas sect was founded by an ascetic named Aulechand. Tradition has it, that he was picked up in a field by one Mahadeva of the Barui caste, in the village of Ula in the district of Nadiya. After leaving for Mahadev's house for sometime, he left it to travel and preach in various parts of Bengal. He had some disciples and all belonging to low castes. Among these disciples was Ramsaran Pal of the Sadgopa caste an inhabitant of Ghosphara near Naihati. This sect acknowledge the authority of Gurus from the non-Brahman community. They were far in advance of the orthodox community in matters relating to social reform.

The Kartabhafes disregard caste distinctions, at least in religious celebrations. They encouraged the remarriage of widows. The majority of the sect belonged to the Sudra order. A sect known as Spastadayaka is said to have been founded by Rupram Kaviraj. The date of its foundation in unknown. The Vaishnavas belonging to it do not recognize the divinity of the Guru.

The members of the sect sing and dance together, overpowered by love for Chaitanya and Krishna. The female of this sect shave their heads and keeping only a slender tress. Admission into the sect is made without distinction of caste. Siva Narayan, a Rajput of the Uttar Pradesh founded a sect in the first half of the 18th century. He was a pure monist and he did not admit the validity of Image worship.

The followers of this sect are forbidden to use any animal

food or intoxicant. Baldeva Vidyabhusana, a leader of the Vaishnav community in Orissa wrote a commentary on the Brahmasutra. He undertook the task because the followers of Ramanuja, Nimbarka tauntingly said that while each of the older Vaishnav sects had their special Bhashyas on Venta, the followers of Chaitanya had none. He thus made a significant departure from the philosophical tent; preached by the earlier teachers of the sect.

The founder of the Balarami sect was Balarama Hari, an inhabitant of the village Meherpur in the district of Nadia. He was a man of great natural parts and succeed in gathering round him a few disciple. The Balarami ridicule idolatry, and recognize no distinction of caste. The Bouls were another sub-sect of Vaishnavism.

The Boul sect was born out of the fusion of the Buddhist, Sahajiya, Sufis. A Boul did not abide by any social or moral injunction. The Hindu Bauls followed many of the Vaishnav practices. The Bauls philosophy was based on naturalism. Through their songs, they contributed much to bring about religious harmony among different religions. The Apapanthi sect came into existence during the 18th century and its founder was Munna Das, a goldsmith by caste. His gaddi existed at Madava, West of Awadh.

Dariya Saheb, who was a worshipper of Satyanama (true name) was another religious preacher who flourished in the 18th century. He was born in Sahbad district. His father was Piran Saha, a Sufi thinker. He was greatly influenced by Sufi thought and the teachings of Kabir. He did not recognize the external formalities of religion, such as, worship of idols or caste distinction.

SETUP OF CASTE

The most striking feature of the Indian society is represented by the caste system. This system is of very ancient origin and through the passage of time it has undergone profound changes, but it is still a very powerful institution in our present day socio economic organization. The Indian caste system is perhaps the most unique pattern of social organization in the world. The first literary traces of the caste system are to be found in the Rig Veda, and the Purusa-Sukta hymn. In the Bhagavad Gita, the caste system is sought to be justified on the basis of the ideas of Guna, Karma (deeds), and Dharma (Religion).

The features of caste prevailing through the past centuries may be described under nine heads hierarchy, endogamy and hypergamy, occupational association, restriction on food, drink, distinction in custom, dress, pollution, rituals and other privileges and disabilities, caste organization and caste mobility. Hutton mentions the following features as characteristic of the Hindu caste system: endogamy, hierarchical basis with the Brahman at the top, caste distance based on the notion of pollution, traditional caste occupations, and the fixity of caste status.

Ghurye put forth the following features segmental division of society, hierarchical arrangement of castes, restriction on social intercourse..., lack of unrestricted choice of occupation and restriction on marriage. Ketkar says, "A caste is a group having two characteristics, membership is confined to those who are born of members and includes all persons so born, and the members are forbidden by an unreliable social law to many outside the group.

According to Davis the hereditary basis of membership, fixity of status, caste endogamy and restrictions on social contact are certain common features of Indian caste. Nesfield writes, function and function alone is responsible for the origin of caste structure in India.

In theory the caste system is inter-linked with the varna model which divides the Hindu society into four orders — Brahmana, Kshatriya, Vaishya and Sudras. The first three caste are twice-born or dvija since the men from these caste are entitled to use the sacred thread at the vedic rite of upanayana, which the Sudras were not allowed to perform. The untouchable caste are outside the varna system. The term varna literally means colour and it was originally used to refer to the distinction between Arya and Dasa, in ancient India. According to the Rig Veda it was not applied to any classes, such as Brahmana, Kshatriya etc. The caste system is an all India [phenomenon] of which the Varna model provides an all India] macro-structural scheme.

Emile senert is of the opinion that the two terms (Varna and Caste) are confused in the literary tradition, which is less concerned with the faithful record of facts than with their arrangements in systems conforming to the tendencies of a strongly raised group. According to K. M. Panikkar, this four fold division is only ideological and is not in any social system. It is what Hindu sociologists wanted their society to be a theory of caste idealism unrelated to actual practise.

The people of each endogamous group follow certain characteristic patterns of behaviour and have certain assigned attitudes—among them a specialized occupation according to which a group is remarked in local hierarchy. The criteria for ranking have to do, village responds declare, with the ritual polluting and purity that are inherent in group practices. Every member of the endogamous group shares in the rank position of the group and his relations with members of other groups.

The term Jati is used here for this endogamous group. The word is common to a number of languages in Northern India being derived from the Sanskrit root meaning to be born. This word and equivalent terms in other Indian languages carry the connotation of social birth right as well as one's inherited group. The Varna model provides a framework within which the innumerable variations of castes throughout India are found. The Varna scheme is a hierarchy in the literal sense of the term because the criteria of ritual purity and pollution are at the basis of differentiation. According to Varna scheme there are only four castes, and it excludes the untouchables. But this is not true in reality since even during the Vedic period, occupational groups existed which, were not subsumed by Varna, although one cannot be sure whether these groups can be called caste or not. According to Srinivas:

> "Varna scheme has certainly distorted the picture of caste but it has also enabled ordinary men and women to understand and asses the general place of a caste within this framework throughout India. It has provided a common social language which holds good in all parts of India. This sense of familiarity, even when not based on real facts leads to a sense of unity amongst the people".

One of the common misconceptions about the Hindu social institutions is that they are unchanging. Hindu caste has been against the background frame of the Varna hierarchy. It is the Varna frame which remains more or less constant while caste vary from region to region. All modern scholars are agreed that caste (Jati) is not same thing as varna complex than the four fold division of the society. The Vedic varna divisions were not as rigid as caste divisions. The term caste or Jati refers to the occupational groups. As Srinivas writes, the varna scheme refers only to the particular categories of the society and not to its real and effective units.

PATTERN OF SOCIAL BEHAVIOUR

Caste structure is a pattern of social behaviour in which groups and individuals are guided by prescribed set of values and norms. Hierarchic gradation, social and other inequalities, endogamy, restrictions on dining, and the lack of freedom regarding the choice of vocation, were the principal features of the caste system. The caste structure of the society is hierarchy or system of subordination held together by the relations of superiority and inferiority at the apex of which are Brahmins and at the lowest rung are the Sudras. In the social hierarchy the lowest rung of the caste society is composed of the untouchables who are ritually the most impure. The concept of hierarchy forms the crux of the caste society.

The highest caste is that from whom a Brahmins will accept food. As a consequence of this hierarchy the Brahmins enjoy a number of social and religious privileges while they suffer a series of disabilities. Endogamy is the most important element of caste system. Marriage within one's own caste or sub-caste group is an essential feature of caste system. The system has become so rigid that inter-caste marriage have become too difficult. It is one of the main reasons for the persistence of caste system.

Caste is innate. A man dies in the same caste in which he is born and it is the caste that determines his station in life. Every caste regards some occupation as its own hereditary and exclusive calling and tries to debar the others from exercising it. Jajmani system, (the person receiving the services from a particular functionary is called Jajman), found in rural Indian enabled each caste to have a near monopoly over their hereditary occupation.

The original and exclusive occupation of Brahmins was to perform priestly duties. Each caste was also ranked higher or lower on the basis of the ritual purity. In course of time many adjustments and changes have been made in these rigid pursuits of occupation. Besides, each caste has its own caste council where the grievances of the caste members were heard. The caste panchayat usually exercises such authority and it is traditionally concerned with all matters belonging to the code and discipline of the caste.

It acts as a court of law and apply the penalty in the cases of the violation of the caste practices.

According to Ghurye:

> "In each linguistic area, there were about two hundred groups called castes with distinct names, usually birth on one of which determined the status in society of a given individual, which were divided into about two thousand smaller units generally known as sub-castes-fixing the limits of marriage and effective social life and making for specific cultural tradition. These major groups were held together by the possession with, few exceptions, of a common priesthood....complete acceptance of the system in its broadest outlines by the groups making up that system and their social and economic interdependence in the village not only prevented the exclusivist organization of the groups from splitting up the system into independent units, but created a harmony was not the harmony of parts that are equally valued, but of units which are rigorously subordinated to one another".

Caste structure is intimately related to the kinship system amongst the Hindus, this happens due to endogamous nature of caste system. An individual becomes a member of a caste in which he or she is born. Even if there is social mobility in the caste system through the process of sanskritization, it is only a positional change. Groups placed low in the social hierarchy seek to achieve such standards of conduct as bestow higher status within the system.

The objective scale of values behind caste stratification itself induces people to violate the main principle of caste. No doubt individual membersS of caste have not been able to change their caste and status, yet castes, or sub-castes as a whole have succeeded in rising their status. The process by which the objective has been achieved has been described by Srinivas, he call it Sanskritization. According to Srinivas:

> "Sanskritization is the process by which a low Hindu caste, or tribal or other groups, changes its customs, ritual, ideology and way of life in the direction of a high, and frequently twice-born caste. Generally such changes are followed by a claim to a higher position in the caste hierarchy than that traditionally conceded to the claimant caste by the local community. The claim is made over a period of time in fact, a generation or two, before the arrival is conceded".

However, the mobility associated with Sanskritization results only in positional changes in system and does not lead to any structural change. Sanskritization process promoted the sacred outlook, whereas westernization promoted the secular outlook. Lower caste peoples realized that mere sanskritization was not enough, which only helped them to improve their status within the immutable varna system. They realized that the adoption of the westernization process which helped them to move up in the social scale without the limitation of jati or varna.

In pre-British India, the self-sufficiency of the village community was one of the most important features of rural society. But after the British conquest of India village autarchy withered away. The establishment of private property in land brought about a change in property relations between castes. The growth of industry gave rise to new social conditions.

Kinship is a method by which individuals as members of society relate themselves with other individuals of that society. Kinship is an analysis of the internal structure of the sub-caste. Due to the practise of endogamy a person marries within the sub-caste group. In North India Hypergamy is practised according to which a man takes a wife from a clan which is lower in status to his own clan. In central India, there is general practice of caste endogamy. But the Southern region follow the patrilineal family.

The hereditary associations of caste with an occupation used to be a very striking feature of the caste system. A caste is considered to be high, if its characteristic way of life is high and pure. The term way of life mean whether its traditional occupation is ritually pure or polluting. There markable aspect of caste system is that the presumed hierarchy of way of life, which includes diet, occupation does not often correlate with the observed order of caste ranking found in several parts of India. The traditional association of a caste with an occupation determines its rank in the local caste hierarchy. In the association of caste structure with a hereditary occupation the Jajmani system forms the framework. The Jajmani system is a system of economic, social and ritual ties between different caste groups in the villages.

The person receiving the services from a particular functionary is called Jajman and the men rendering the services is called kameen of the Jajman. Though barter transactions have been a integral part of the Indian rural life, yet the traditional Jajmani relations are more conspicuous in the village life because they entail ritual matters and social support as well as economic success. Jajmani system is an integral part of the Indian rural life.

The advantages of Jajmani system for economic stability and security are still sufficiently great that many villages want to continue with at least some arrangements. The cultivators gain from them in that he gets better credit and a more certain labour supply than he usually can through caste transactions. Artisans and service families work for him through out the year without much pay and then are given a large payment at the time when the farmer can best afford to do so at harvest. The patron castes differ from one region to another depending on the socio-economic and political status of the castes.

The tendency of land ownership by the high castes serves to maintain and reimpose the caste hierarchy. At the top of occupational hierarchy stands a group of families which control and own most land rights in the village. However with the changing times, the general association of higher caste with higher class (in terms of wealth and power) has been disturbed. Land Ownership is a crucial factor in establishing dominance. The pattern of land ownership in India is such that the bulk of the arable land is concentrated in the hands of a relatively small number of big owners as a large number, who either own very little land or no land at all.

The big land owners are patron of the bulk of the poor villagers. Each household from serving and artisan castes provides goods and services to a certain number of land owning households, traditionally these ties have been stable, continuing from generation to generation. In Orissa, in Bisipara, an Oriya hill village, the warrior castes owned most of the land and combined soldiering with farm management. The out-castes, referred as Proja, were their servants.

The other castes, including the Brahmin were in a position of economic dependence and political subordination to them. In the district of Tanjore, there is a clear-cut hierarchy existing in the caste system with Brahmins as land owners.

In case of Punjab and Haryana, the dominance of a single agricultural caste referred to as Jats. According to Srinivas, a caste is said to be dominant when it is numerically the strongest in the village and economically and politically exercises a preponderating influence. But in regions where religious groups and tribals are inter-mixed and no single caste possess enough land, in such a condition, there is bound to be multiple domination in a region. The order of dominance among castes, parallels the order of caste rank.

The nature of high ranking castes is further reinforced by ritual notions of purity and pollution. High ranking Brahmin castes not only possess landed wealth, power, but also the traditional right to perform rituals and right to worship at temples. Other castes are obliged to worship as per their ritual prescriptions. Their economic and political subordination further enhances the dominant position of high ranking castes.

The mobility characteristic of caste in the traditional period resulted only in positional changes for particular castes or sections of castes and did not lead to a structural change. So, while individual castes moved up or down, the structure remained the same. A potent source of social mobility in pre-British India was the fluidly of the political power, however, a caste had to have a marital tradition, numerical strength, and preferably also ownership of a large quantity of arable land. Once it had captured political power it had to sanskritize ritual and style of life and lay claim to being kshatriya. Sanskritization has been a major process of cultural change in Indian history.

The consolidation of British rule involved, the abolition of feudalism. In the process territorial limitations on caste loyalties were lifted. Castes were able to organize themselves as political association on regional and country wide bases. The consequences of British rule on the economic aspect of caste have been even more pronounced. The growth of industry gave rise to new social conditions, occupational opportunities and social classes.

Many traditional occupations associated with inferior social status are being abandoned. New occupations have led to the formation of groups like trade union which cut across caste barriers. But the occupational aspect of caste is not at all an important factor. Caste as a ritual division of society is losing its importance. Caste continues to be preserved and protected in villages, towns by endogamy, caste has not as yet gone out, it has only changed its tactics.

5

CLASS CLASHES

MARX ON SOCIAL CLASS

For a proper appreciation of the several problems that the Indian society is presently facing, we must understand the nature of the underlying class conflict. This sounds very Marxian. I do not at all mind. Indeed, I shall feel proud if I am ever recognized as one belonging to that great school of social analysis. As I see it, it is not a single, inviolable, unchanging doctrine but a method of analyzing social change, founded on unsparing examination of social facts and merciless pursuit of logical analysis. As late Professor Kosambi said that Marxism is a method of thinking and not a substitute for thought.

Unfortunately, Marxism has been altogether too often taken as a substitute for thinking. Baran and Sweezy, the renowned American Marxists, rightly complain that "Marxists have too often been content to repeat familiar formulations, as though nothing really new had happened since the days of Marx and Engels—or of Lenin at the latest. As a result, Marxists have failed to explain important developments, or sometimes even to recognize their existence". This has led to stagnation of Marxian social science with lagging vitality and fruitfulness.

MARXIAN METHOD

The Marxian method emphasizes the importance of studying the society as a whole, how it works and where it is going. But I shall take into account new facts and developments that have occurred since Marx wrote and also the particular circumstances of the Indian society and, in the light of these, I shall be willing to modify Marx's conclusions wherever necessary.

It will be useful to begin by examining Marx's concept of social class and of class struggle. In his historical writings, Marx referred to several social classes. For instance, in his work *The Class Struggles in France,* 1848-1850, Marx distinguished six classes: financial bourgeoisie, industrial bourgeoisie, petty bourgeoisie, peasants, proletariat and Lumpen proletariat.

In this, Marx was merely adopting the concept of social class which was widely used by historians and social theorists of that time. But social classes meant much more to Marx. As Lenin said, anything which Marx wrote was in some way concerned with the question of class. Nevertheless, Marx never defined the basic concept of social class. Lenin gave the following definition:

"Social classes are large groups of people differing from each other by the place they occupy in a historically determined system of social production, by their relation (in most cases fixed and formulated in law) to the means of production, by their role in the social organization of labour, and, consequently, by the dimensions of the share of social wealth of which they dispose and the mode of acquiring it." This definition is commonly accepted as an adequate and faithful summary of Marx's views in the matter. But, it must be mentioned, it is nowhere found in Marx's writings.

It was only towards the end of his prodigious scholarship that, it seems, Marx decided to put down a systematic exposition of his concept of social class and his theory of social struggle. The evidence is in the last chapter of the third volume of *Capital*. Unfortunately, it remained unfinished and incomplete. He wrote barely a page in which he set out mainly the difficulties which he saw confronting his own concept of social class.

Marx wrote: "We have seen that this continual tendency and law of development of the capitalist mode of production is more and more to divorce the means of production from labour, and more and more to concentrate the scattered means of production into large groups, thereby transforming labour into wage-labour and the means of production into capital.

And to this tendency, on the other hand, corresponds the independent separation of landed property from capital and labour, or the transformation of all landed property into the form of landed property corresponding to the capitalist mode of production. The owners merely of labour-power, owners of capital, and landowners, whose respective sources of income are wages, profits, and ground-rent in other words, wage-labourers, capitalists, and landowners, constitute then three big classes of modern society based upon the capitalist mode of production."

Because of this, it is commonly supposed that, for Marx, the social classes are distinguished by the source of their income. But, this is precisely what, it seems, Marx wanted to refute. In the above, Marx continues: "The first question to be answered is this: What constitutes a class?—and the reply to this follows naturally from the reply to another question, what makes wage-labourers, capitalists and landlords constitute the three great social classes?"

"At first glance—the identity of revenues and sources of revenue. There are three great social groups whose members, the individuals forming them, live on wages, profit and ground-rent respectively, on the realization of their labour-power, their capital, and their landed property."

"However, from this standpoint, physicians and officials, for instance, would also constitute two classes, for they belong to two distinct social groups, the members of each of these groups receiving their revenue from one and the same source. The same would also be true of the infinite fragmentation of interest and rank into which the division of social labour splits labourers as well as capitalists and landlords—the latter, for instance, into owners of vineyards, farm owners, owners of forests, mine owners and owners of fisheries."

There Marx laid his pen aside for the last time and even the preliminary question he raised, "what constitutes a social class?"—remained unanswered.

We must therefore make do with what we can lay our hands on. I suggest that we should turn to the *Manifesto of the Communist Party*. It was published in 1848 and thus is one of the early writings of Marx. It is jointly authored by Marx and Engels. But, in the Preface to its English edition, Engels makes it clear that the fundamental proposition which forms its nucleus belongs to Marx.

The *Manifesto* is a little booklet of less than 50 pages and offers a concise statement, not so much of a theory but of Marx's vision of the development and future of the capitalist society which remained the basis for all his later theoretical work. Whatever your personal conviction or persuasion in the matter, you will not fail to be impressed by the grandeur and prophetic quality of his vision, particularly when you note that it was written in 1848 which is more than 125 years ago. To make my points, I may have to quote from it rather extensively. It will also give you a sample of the flavour, flair and power of Marx's writings.

The *Manifesto* opens with that historic statement: "The

history of all hitherto existing society is the history of class struggles" and proceeds thus: "In the earlier epochs of history, we find almost everywhere a complicated arrangement of society into various orders, a manifold gradation of social rank... The modern bourgeois society that has sprouted from the ruins of feudal society, has not done away with class antagonisms.

It has but established new classes, new conditions of oppression, new forms of struggle in place of the old ones... Our epoch, the epoch of the bourgeoisie, possesses, however, this distinctive feature: it has simplified the class antagonisms. Society as a whole is more and more splitting up into two great hostile camps, into two great classes directly facing each other—bourgeoisie and proletariat."

SOCIAL CLASSES

Marx did not define these two social classes. But, Engels in a footnote in the English edition, gives the following definitions: "By bourgeoisie is meant the class of modern capitalists, owners of the means of production and employers of wage-labour. By proletariat, the class of modern wage-labourers who, having no means of production of their own, are reduced to selling their labour power in order to live."

Let me first take the bourgeoisie. What distinguishes this class? Of course, the fact is that they are owners of the means of production and employers of wage-labour. How did the class emerge? Marx explains: "...the modern bourgeoisie is itself the product of a long course of development, or a series of revolutions in the modes of production and of exchange... the means of production and of exchange, on whose foundation the bourgeoisie built itself up, were generated in feudal society.

At a certain stage of development of these means of production and of exchange, the conditions under which the feudal society produced and exchanged, the feudal organization of agriculture and manufacturing industry, in one word, the feudal relations of property became no longer compatible with the already developed productive forces; they became so many fetters... Into their place stepped free competition, accompanied by a social and political constitution adapted to it, and by the economical and political sway of the bourgeoisie class."

DIFFERENT ERAS

Thus, what distinguishes bourgeoisie epoch from feudal epoch is *free competition* in place of feudal relations. Again it is worth quoting Marx: "The bourgeoisie, wherever it has got the upper hand, has put an end to all feudal, patriarchal, idyllic relations. It has pitilessly torn asunder the motley feudal ties that bound man to his 'natural superiors', and has left no other nexus between man and man than naked self-interest, than callous 'cash payment'.

It has drowned the most heavenly ecstasies of religious fervour, of chivalrous enthusiasm, of philistine sentimentalism, in the icy water of egotistical calculation. It has resolved personal worth into exchange value, and in place of the numberless indefeasible chartered freedoms, has set up that single, unconscionable freedom—Free Trade. In one word, for exploitation veiled by religious and political illusions, it has substituted naked, shameless, direct, brutal exploitation."

But mistake not. In two pages, Marx pays the most glowing tribute to what the bourgeoisie, by means of free competition and free trade, has achieved. I shall quote only a brief passage. Marx says: "The bourgeoisie, historically, has played a most revolutionary part...

It has been the first to show what man's activity can bring about. ...The bourgeoisie, during its rule of scarce one hundred years, has created more massive and more colossal productive forces than have all preceding generations together. Subjection of nature's forces to man, machinery, application of chemistry to industry and agriculture, steam-navigation, railways, electric telegraphs, clearing of whole continents for cultivation, canalization of rivers, whole populations conjured out of the ground—what earlier century had even a presentiment that such productive forces slumbered in the lap of social labour?"

What was then wrong? Nothing except that Marx believed that this could not go on for long. The reasons? Marx says: "Modern bourgeois society with its relations of production, of exchange and of property, a society that has conjured up such gigantic means of production and of exchange, is like the sorcerer who is no longer able to control the powers of the nether world whom he has called up by his spells.

For many a decade past, the history of industry and commerce is but the history of the revolt of modern productive forces against modern conditions of production, against the property relations that are the conditions for the existence of the bourgeois society on its trial, each time more threateningly. In these crises, a great part not only of the existing products, but also of the previously created productive forces, are periodically destroyed.... The conditions of bourgeois society are too narrow to comprise the wealth created by them. ...The weapons with which the bourgeoisie felled feudalism to the ground are now turned against the bourgeoisie itself." *Marx meant the weapons of free competition and free trade.*

In point of fact, the bourgeois capitalist society has survived many a crises since Marx wrote. It did this by modifying conditions of free competition. The last such crisis was the Great Depression of the 1930's. It accorded well with the Marxian theory and strengthened the belief that similar catastrophic economic breakdowns were inevitable under capitalism. Yet, in the three decades since the end of the Second World War, there has not been a single severe depression. Marxian theory is not able to explain this because it does not take into account the emergence of monopoly capitalism and the manner in which it modifies conditions of free competition.

Marx certainly recognized the tendency towards concentration and centralization inherent in the competitive system. He says: "The bourgeoisie keeps more and more doing away with the scattered state of the population, of the means of production, and of property. It has agglomerated population, centralized means of production, and has concentrated property in a few hands." But he concludes: "The necessary consequence of this was political centralization."

He did not at the same time investigate how the emergence of large-scale enterprise and monopoly would affect other conditions of bourgeois production, particularly the conditions of free competition. This is of course too much to expect from one who wrote more than a hundred years ago. But probably, as Baran and Sweezy suspect, "Marx anticipated the overthrow of capitalism long before the unfolding of all its potentialities, well within the system's competitive phase."

I need not dwell on this point further because that is not germane to my theme this evening. The important point to recognize, not often explicitly understood, particularly by Marxists, is that Marx's analysis of capitalism remained confined to the case of perfectly competitive economy and hence is inadequate to explain several phenomena of the present-day capitalism.

Let me now turn to the other class, namely, the proletariat. The proletariat is a product of bourgeois society. As Marx says: "The proletariat is its special and essential product." If bourgeoisie is defined as those who own the means of production and employ wage-labour, it is obvious that it must create a class which owns no means of production and hence, in order to live, must sell its labour. Thus, the bourgeoisie creates its own enemy. Marx says: "But not only has the bourgeoisie forged the weapons that bring death to itself; it has also called into existence the men who are to wield those weapons—the modern working class—the proletarians."

Let me outline, in his own words, Marx's concept of the class struggle between the bourgeoisie and the proletariat and the ultimate inevitable victory of the proletariat.

In proportion as the bourgeoisie, *i.e.*, capital, is developed, in the same proportion is the proletariat, the modern working class, developed—a class of labourers, who live only so long as they find work, and who find work only so long as their labour increases capital. These labourers, who must sell themselves piecemeal, are a commodity, like every other article of commerce, and are consequently exposed to all the vicissitudes of competition, to all the fluctuations of the market.

Owing to the extensive use of machinery and to division of labour, the work of the proletarians has lost all individual character, and consequently, all charm for the workman. He becomes an appendage of the machine, and it is only the most simple, most monotonous, and most easily acquired knack, that is required of him. Hence, the cost of production of a workman is restricted, almost entirely, to the means of subsistence that he requires for his maintenance, and for the propagation of his race. But the price of a commodity, and therefore also of labour, is equal to its cost of production. In proportion, therefore, as the repulsiveness of the work increases, the wage decreases.

EMERGENCE OF PROLETARIANS AS A CLASS

"But with the development of industry, the proletariat not only increases in number; it becomes concentrated in greater masses, its strength grows, and it feels that strength more. The various interests and conditions of life within the ranks of the proletariat are more and more equalized, in proportion as machinery obliterates all distinctions of labour and nearly everywhere reduces wages to the same low level. The growing competition among the bourgeois, and the resulting commercial crises, make the wages of the workers ever more fluctuating. The unceasing improvement of machinery, ever more rapidly developing, makes their livelihood more and more precarious; the collisions between individual workmen and individual bourgeois take more and more the character of collisions between two classes.

Thereupon the workers begin to form combinations (trades' unions) against the bourgeois; they club together in order to keep up the rate of wages; they found permanent associations in order to make provision before-hand for these occasional revolts.

This organization of the proletarians into a class, and consequently into a political party ... completes legislative recognition of particular interests of the workers, by taking advantage of the divisions among the bourgeoisie itself.

Finally, in times when the class struggle nears the decisive hour, a small section of the ruling class cuts itself adrift and joins the revolutionary class ...a portion of the bourgeoisie goes over to the proletariat, and in particular, a portion of the bourgeoisie ideologists, who have raised themselves to the level of comprehending theoretically, the historical movement as a whole.

Hitherto, every form of society has been based...on the antagonism of oppressing and oppressed classes. But, in order to oppress a class, certain conditions must be assured to it under which it can, at least, continue its slavish existence. The serf, in the period of serfdom, raised himself to the membership of the commune, just as the petty bourgeois, under the yoke of feudal absolutism, managed to develop into a bourgeois.

The modern labourer, on the contrary, instead of rising with the progress of industry, sinks deeper and deeper below the conditions of existence of his own class. He becomes a pauper and pauperism develops more rapidly than population and wealth. And here it becomes evident, that the bourgeoisie is unfit any longer to be the ruling class in society, and to impose its conditions of existence upon society as an overriding law. It is unfit to rule because it is incompetent to assure an existence to its slave within his slavery, because it cannot help letting him sink into such a state, that it has to feed him, instead of being fed by him. Society can no longer live under this bourgeoisie, in other words, its existence is no longer compatible with society.

"The essential condition for the existence and for the sway of the bourgeois class, is the formation and augmentation of capital, the condition for capital is wage-labour. Wage-labour rests exclusively on competition between the labourers. The advance of industry, whose involuntary promoter is the bourgeoisie, replaces the isolation of the labourers, due to competition, by their revolutionary combination, due to association.

This development of the modern industry, therefore, cuts from under its feet, the very foundation on which the bourgeoisie produces and appropriates product. What the bourgeoisie therefore produces above all, are its own grave-diggers. Its fall and the victory of the proletariat are equally inevitable." I have quoted Marx at length so that you may have faith in your mind his conception of the course that the struggle between the bourgeoisie and the proletariat would take leading ultimately and inevitably to the fall of the bourgeoisie and the victory of the proletariat.

In this, Marx quite rightly attaches great importance to the organization of the proletariat into trade unions, gaining political power, compelling legislative recognition of their rights and interests, and above all, keeping up the wages by collective bargaining. This is the exact counterpart of the development of large-scale industry and monopoly capitalism among the bourgeoisie. Indeed, it is only to the extent that large-scale industry and monopoly capitalism develop that trade unions of the proletariat can grow in strength. One modifies the conditions of free competition among the bourgeoisie; the other modifies the conditions of free competition among the proletariat. Marx failed to see the import of this because he continued to work and think within the confines of a perfectly competitive economy.

Hence, his assertion that "wage labour rests exclusively on competition between the labourers;" or that the modern working class of wage-labourers "sell themselves piecemeal and are consequently exposed to all the vicissitudes of competition, to all the fluctuations of the market" and that, like all commodities, they get their price which is equal to the "cost of production of the worker, namely, the subsistence that the worker requires for his maintenance and for the propagation of his race." He did not see that all this would change with the emergence of trade unions and the collective bargaining power of the workers, which he clearly foresaw.

Working as he was within the confines of a perfectly free competitive economy, it was necessary for Marx to postulate a perfectly homogeneous undifferentiated class of workers. Hence, he said: "Owing to the extensive use of machinery and the division of labour, (the worker) becomes an appendage of the machine, and it is only the most simple, most monotonous, and most easily acquired knack that is required of him"; or that "the various interests and conditicns of life within the ranks of the proletariat are more and more equalized, in proportion as machinery obliterates all distinctions of labour and nearly everywhere reduces wages to the same low level."

In this, Marx was clearly wrong. A worker working at a machine may appear, to an onlooker, as no more than an appendage of the machine. But, for that reason, it is not true that only the most easily acquired skills are required of him. As machines become more complex and demanding of higher precision of their output, not only specialized skills acquired through years of training but also a high degree of intelligence are required of the worker. In the range of skills which he acquires and exhibits, the modern industrial working class is at least as varied as the pre-machine class of artisans and handicraftsmen.

Large-scale industrial production also requires organizational and managerial skills of various order beginning with the shop-floor. In consequence, there emerges, even within the working class, a hierarchy of supervisors and chargemen. Men at the bottom aspire to move up in this hierarchy not only because wages there are higher, but also because the higher positions carry higher authority and because at the top there usually is a white-collar or near white-collar job accessible to the worker which carries not only higher pay and authority but also prestige and social status attaching to white-collar.

EMERGENCE OF WHITE-COLLAR CLASS

The white-collar represents the new middle class comprising office workers, supervisors, technicians and innumerable others who are essentially a product of the capitalist development. Marx did not anticipate the emergence and growth of this class.

He also did not anticipate the emergence of a welfare state within a capitalist society and consequent growth of an employee class providing the many welfare services such as education, public health, railways, road transport, post and telegraph and also the growth of bureaucracy overseeing them. Members of this class also do not have any means of production of their own except the skills acquired through often expensive education.

They are essentially wage-workers and may be classed with the proletariat as is commonly done. Nevertheless, we should note an important attribute of this class which distinguishes it from the proletariat narrowly defined as the industrial worker. That is the distinction between the white-collar and the blue-collar. A certain social prestige attaches to the white-collar occupations which, as Max Weber suggested, has its origins in the prestige which certain social groups such as the nobility, the officials of the state and the learned professions, enjoyed in the pre-capitalist society. The continuity is evident in the distinct life-style which the new white-collar middle class exhibits.

The social prestige attaching to the white-collar occupations and the life-style that goes with it have not left the blue-collar workers completely unaffected. Marx is not entirely correct in his assessment when he says: "The proletariat is without property; his relation to his wife and children has no longer anything in common with the bourgeois family relations. Law, morality, religion, are to him so many bourgeois prejudices, behind which lurk in ambush just as many bourgeois interests." Marx was probably right when he wrote. But, in the present-day society, even if it be true that the style and facts of proletariat life are far from those of the bourgeoisie, it is clear that aspirations everywhere are all very bourgeois.

It is for this reason that the blue-collar worker strives to move up in the hierarchy not simply because it gives him higher rewards but also because it brings him close to the white-collar class. Like the serf, in the period of serfdom, raised himself to the membership of the commune, so does the blue-collar worker raise himself into the white-collar society. The bourgeois capitalist society has created the aspirations and also the opportunities. Marx did not fully appreciate the vertical mobility that bourgeois society provides.

Developments, Marx couldn't Foretell : Marx also did not anticipate the emergence of the managerial class which forms so important an element in the modern capitalist development. In general, the managerial class do not own their own means of production and are essentially wage-earners though their purse is large. Marx is quite clear that the size of the purse does not distinguish a class of his concept.

In that case, the managerial class must be regarded as belonging to the proletariat. But, the size of the purse is not the only distinguishing characteristic of the managerial class. It stays close to the bourgeoisie, adopts the same style of life as the bourgeoisie, identifies its interests with those of the bourgeoisie and indeed aspires to join the bourgeoisie if opportunity presents. In its daily strife, the proletariat finds itself face to face, not with the bourgeoisie, but with the managerial class.

SEVERAL DEVELOPMENTS

These several developments, which Marx either did not anticipate or, when he did, did not fully appreciate their implications to his central proposition, have belied his expectation that the development of capitalism would progressively resolve the society into just two antagonistic classes: the bourgeoisie faced by a homogeneous, undifferentiated mass of proletariat. Instead, between the two classes of Marx's conception, is interposed a hierarchy of groups vested, not necessarily with property or means of production but, with social status and prestige.

This is not merely a matter of detail. It affects fundamentally Marx's theory of class conflict and final class struggle. The resolution of the society into just two antagonistic classes is a logical need of Marx's theory of class struggle. With too many classes or groups in-between, the conflict would not sharpen and the final struggle and the victory of the proletariat resulting in a classless society, would not materialize. Marx saw this clearly. The relations among a hierarchy of status groups are relations of competition and emulation, not of conflict.

Quite apart from the several status groups ranging between the bourgeoisie and the proletariat and merging one into another making a hierarchy, all creation of the capitalist system, one must examine what other groups or classes of the pre-capitalist society survive into the capitalist society. According to Marx, none. He says: "The other classes decay and finally disappear in the face of modern industry; the proletariat is its special and essential product." More specifically, Marx refers to what he calls the lower strata of the middle class and expects that it will gradually sink into the proletariat.

He says: "The lower strata of the middle class— the small tradespeople, shopkeepers, and retired tradesmen, generally the handicraftsmen and peasants—all these sink gradually into the proletariat, partly because their diminutive capital does not suffice for the scale on which modern industry is carried on, and is swamped in the competition with the large capitalists, partly because of their specialized skill is rendered worthless by new methods of production. Thus, the proletariat is recruited from all classes of the population."

Marx does not give a definition of the middle class and its lower or higher strata. But judging by whom he includes in the lower strata of the middle class, it is not difficult to see the implied scheme of classification. The basic division is of course between the bourgeoisie and the proletariat: those who own the means of production, do not themselves work but employ wage-labour; and those who do not own any means of production and must work as wage-labour.

In between the two, lies the middle class: those who own the means of production and also work by themselves. The middle class thus defined could be divided into higher and lower strata. In the higher strata are those with substantial means of production so that, though they are owner-operators they may also employ considerable wage-labour. In the process of capitalist development, they would accumulate more capital and move up into the bourgeoisie.

The lower strata have limited means of production and they are essentially owner-operator; if they employ any wage-labour at all, that would be only marginal. The small manufacturer, the shopkeeper, the artisan and the peasant belong to this class and Marx quite rightly put them together. His prediction that all these groups gradually sink into the proletariat and the reasons he gave for this process, namely, firstly their small capital and consequent inability to stand competition from the large capitalists and secondly their specialized skills becoming outdated by new methods of production, are well borne out by the capitalist development in the industrialized countries.

Nevertheless, we should note that the middle class, including a large lower strata, is yet very much a reality. The small shopkeeper has proved to be much more hardy than Marx imagined. The same is true of a number of professionals providing medical, legal and personal services such as tailors, launders, hair-dressers, taximen and automobile repair and service men. Besides, the development of large-scale modern industry itself has created several ancillary areas in which a new class of small manufacturer has emerged.

CAPITALIST DEVELOPMENT

The capitalist development has also created new classes of professionals such as chartered accountants, insurancemen, and industrial, financial and marketing consultants. These several groups constitute the middle class, a majority of them belonging to its lower strata of Marx's conception. It is not small or negligible by size and is far from disappearing. The lower strata of the middle class of the Marx's conception also includes the peasant. As such, in the present day Indian society, it constitutes the largest single group. Of course, this is partly because the capitalist development has not as yet gone far enough in this country.

Incidentally, I should mention, that having included the peasant in the lower strata and having pronounced that, along with its class, it will sink into the proletariat, Marx, in the Manifesto, does not pay any more specific attention to the fate of the peasant.

What is the role of this lower strata of the middle class, while it survives and subsists, in the class struggle between the bourgeoisie and the proletariat? Marx says the following:

> "Of all the classes that stand face to face with the bourgeoisie today, the proletariat alone is a really revolutionary class. The other classes decay and finally disappear in the face of modern industry; the proletariat is its special and essential product."
>
> "The lower middle class, the small manufacturer, the shopkeeper, the artisan, the peasant, all these fight against the bourgeoisie, to save from extinction their existence as fractions of the middle class. They are therefore not revolutionary, but conservative. Nay more, they are reactionary, for they try to roll back the wheel of history."

Thus, the lower middle class, comprising the small manufacturer, the small shopkeeper, the artisan and the peasant, has no role in the class struggle between the bourgeoisie and the proletariat. Its historical role is to decay and disappear as a class and sink into the proletariat. Bourgeoisie assists this process by pursuing relentlessly, by merciless competition, the advance of modern large-scale industry. To the extent the lower-middle class resists the bourgeoisie, it resists the historical process and tries to roll back the wheel of history. To that extent, and in this sense, the lower-middle class is a reactionary class. It follows that all policies aimed at protecting this class, the small manufacturer, the small shopkeeper, the artisan and the peasant, are reactionary policies. One must understand the sense in which Marx uses the term, 'reactionary'. I am surprised and puzzled when I find many, who call themselves Marxists, using the term 'reactionary' in quite the opposite sense and directly or indirectly supporting policies which Marx would have labelled 'reactionary'.

How important it is for Marx's theory of class struggle to have the society resolved into just two classes—the bourgeoisie and the proletariat is evident from Marx's reference in the *Manifesto* to yet another class. Marx says: "The dangerous class, the social scum, that passively rotting mass thrown off by the lowest layers of old society, may, here and there, be swept into the movement by a proletariat revolution; its conditions of life, however, prepare it far more for the part of a bribed tool of reactionary intrigue."

Which class is this? It owns no means of production. It also does not do wage-labour in the modern capitalist industry. In the Indian context, the description fits well the landless rural poor partly moved into the urban slums but without any wage employment. Marx's vivid description of the class as "the social scum, the passively rotting mass thrown off by the lowest layers of old society" also points to the scheduled castes of the traditional Hindu society and the bonded labour yoked to the feudal landlord-moneylender.

In the present-day Indian society, this class is not numerically negligible. Yet, in the two-class schemata of Marx, this class has no place except as a handy 'bribed tool of reactionary intrigue'. The meaning and implication are not clear, at any rate to me. But I should caution and emphasize once again that the term 'reactionary' has a very special connotation when Marx uses it and it is quite different from the one in which the term is often used by vulgar Marxists. Thus conceived, distribution of land to the landless or the houses to the bonded labour might be construed as a reactionary intrigue and the landless and the bonded labour being used as a bribed tool. May be. I do not know.

INDIAN LABOUR

Let me now turn to the present-day Indian society. I shall first describe its class composition and then put forward before you what in my opinion is the nature of the prevailing class conflict.

First, consider the class composition. I shall present some data from the 1971 census. This is now out of date by seven years. But it is unlikely that great changes in the class composition have occurred in the past seven years. The census classifies all persons into two classes: workers and non-workers. Workers are those who are gainfully occupied; they are not necessarily wage-earners. In 1971, out of the total population of 547.9 million, 180.4 million persons were classified as workers. I now propose to classify these workers in several classes according to the relations of production in which they stand in the system of social production.

In the first instance, I shall distinguish workers whose gainful activity is conducted within the framework of household; in other words, whose relations of production are pre-capitalist. They comprise mainly three groups: cultivators that is peasants, agricultural labourers mainly landless, and persons engaged in the household industry that is artisans and handicraftsmen. In 1971, their numbers were as follows: cultivators (78.2 million), agricultural labourers (47.5 million); and artisans and handicraftsmen (6.3 million). They add up to 132 million which is more than 70 per cent of the working population.

It is only the balance of 47.5 million workers who may be said to have entered into production relations of the capitalist economy. Even these cannot all be classified into the two Marxian classes: bourgeoisie and proletariat. There is a substantial middle class. They are neither employers of wage-labour nor are they wage-labour themselves. They own small means of production and employ themselves on them. Their number is 16 million which is one-third of the workers who may be said to be working in the capitalist system. It will be useful to note some of their major categories: 5.6 million of these are production workers such as tailors, bricklayers, transport vehicle operators and sundry labourers; 2.1 million are engaged in dairy, poultry and fishing; 1.9 million are engaged in providing various services such as restaurants, laundering and hair-dressing; and finally, 4.9 million are shopkeepers and salesmen of various description.

Almost all of these are pre-capitalist occupations which are drawn into the capitalist system under somewhat different relations of production. Besides, there are new occupations which are essentially a product of the capitalist system such as professional, technical, administrative and managerial services; a little under one million workers are engaged in these occupations as independent workers.

Let me repeat. Out of the 47.5 million workers who may be said to have entered into production relations of the capitalist system, 16 million, which is one-third, are independent workers; they are neither employers nor employees and hence neither the bourgeoisie nor the proletariat. It is only the remaining 31.7 million workers who are working strictly within the employer-employee relationship: 22 million of them are employers and 29.5 million are employees.

I am not sure that all of the 2.2 million employers could be called the bourgeoisie; many of them are small manufacturers and shopkeepers with small capital, themselves working and employing only a few wage-labourers. It is difficult to decide, on the basis of the data from the census, how many of them could be classified as the bourgeoisie; I presume that the number would be small. In the absence of data, I shall recognize the class of 2.2 million employers as such and equate them with the bourgeoisie.

In all, 29.5 million employees are wage-earners and constitute the proletariat in this country. However, they are by no means a homogeneous, undifferentiated mass. It will be useful to note the major categories: 11.8 million of them are wage-workers in production that is in the manufacturing industry, and transport; they also include pure labourers. We might add to these 1.9 million workers in dairy, poultry, etc., and 3.6 million workers in various service industries such as hotels and restaurant workers, housekeepers, cooks, waiters, maids, building caretakers, sweepers, launderers, hair-dressers, policemen, watchmen, etc.

The three groups add up to 17.3 million workers and constitute abut 60 per cent of the proletariat. We may call them the blue-collar proletariat though some of them, such as the policemen, would prefer themselves to be classified among the white-collar.

The remaining 12.2 million constitute the white-collar workers ranging from the clerical to the managerial. Among them, 5.6 million are clerks and 1.6 million are sales workers. They constitute the lower rung of the white-collar hierarchy. The balance of 4.7 million workers comprising professional, technical, administrative, executive and managerial personnel constitute the higher strata of the white-collar hierarchy some of them with their interests aligned with the interests of the bourgeoisie than those of the proletariat.

It is in the context of this class composition, that we should examine the nature of class conflict that is evident in the Indian society. The explicit evidence and the form of the conflict are to be seen in the numerous strikes which are now a common feature of the Indian polity. They cover the white-collar workers as well as the blue-collar workers. There is evident an admirable solidarity among the workers, whether white-collar or blue-collar, whether drawing less than Rs. 200 per month or more than Rs. 2,000 per month. We should therefore recognize all employees, that is all wage-earners, to constitute a class. This accords with the Marx's concept and hence we shall call them the proletariat.

Let me then summarize the principal classes in the present-day Indian society:

	Workers (in million)	
1. Pre-capitalist class:		
Cultivators	78.2	
Agricultural labourers	47.5	
Household industry	6.3	
	132.0	73.5%
2. Independent workers in capitalist society	16.0	8.9%
3. Employers	2.2	1.2%
4. White-collar employees	12.2	6.8%
5. Blue-collar workers	17.3	9.6%

Their number in the country is 29.5 million which is just about one-sixth of all workers. The proletariat in this country today is thus a small minority though a sizeable one. When, in the *Manifesto,* Marx called upon the proletariat to rise, he had a different perspective. Let me quote him: "All previous historical movements were movements of minorities, or in the interest of minorities.

The proletarian movement is the self-conscious, independent movement of the immense majority) in the interest of the immense majority." I submit that the proletarian movement in India today is not a movement of the immense majority; we should ask whether it is in the interests of the immense majority.

To answer that question we should ask another question: Against whom is it directed? Marx believed that the proletariat would stand face to face necessarily only with the bourgeoisie. The situation has become somewhat complicated since then partly because of Marx's own prescription. In the ten-point programme Marx outlined in the *Manifesto of the Communist Party,* the following three appear:

(1) centralization of credit in the hands of the state, by means of a national bank with state capital and exclusive monopoly;
(2) centralization of the means of communication and transport in the hands of the state; and
(3) extension of factories and instruments of production owned by the state. Under pressure from the proletariat, many capitalist states have made considerable progress along this path. India is one of the foremost among them. Besides, there has been a very great extension of welfare activities of the state which Marx did not anticipate. In consequence, the state is now a major employer in many capitalist countries. In India, the state is the largest employer.

LABOURERS IN DIFFERENT SECTORS

As I mentioned, there were 29.5 million employees, that is, wage-workers, in India, in 1971. Not all of them faced the bourgeoisie as their employer. Some faced the state as the employer. Some faced the bourgeoisie as the employer. Others faced a small manufacturer or a small shopkeeper as their employer. If we define bourgeoisie conveniently as employers of ten or more wage-workers, the *Employment Review* gives the following figures of employment as in March 1974: Public sector (12.5 million); and private sector in establishments employing ten or more workers (6.8 million). The two together add upto 19.3 million and is often referred to as the employment in the organized sector. The balance of employment is in the private unorganized sector that is in establishments employing fewer than ten employees each. The total number of employees in March 1971 was 29.5 million. In March 1974, it would be somewhat larger. But even taking the total employees in March 1974 to be the same as in March 1971, *i.e.*, 29.5 million, it is clear that a total of 10.2 million workers were employed in the unorganized sector.

To conclude, of about 30 million employees that were there in March 1974, more than 40 per cent were employees of the state; 35 per cent were employees of the small manufacturers and small shopkeepers; and only less than 25 per cent were the employees of the bourgeoisie even if we interpret that term liberally to include all owners of establishments employing more than ten employees each. (I recognize that one and the same owner might own more than one establishment). We should therefore examine the nature of the class struggle that the three categories of the employees are waging against their respective employers.

First, consider the employees of the state, that is, workers in the public sector. Their number is 12.5 million and they constitute over 40 per cent of the proletariat in the country. Out of these, 6.2 million, or half of the total are employed in administration and welfare services such as education and public health. Another quarter of the total, that is, 3.3 million, are engaged in various public utilities such as railways, post, telegraph, banking, insurance, electricity, gas, water and sanitary services.

In all these fields, the government has exclusive monopoly. The value it puts on these services is the value that it puts on the services rendered by the employees. No surplus value arises and hence no exploitation of the workers is possible in the sense of Marx. The remaining 3 million employees in the public sector are employed in the productive sectors to which the government has extended its activities; these are: manufacturing, construction, mining and quarrying and plantation and forestry. In many of these areas, again, the government has a monopoly, a virtual monopoly or an oligopolistic position. Hardly any profits are made.

What then is the justification of the public sector employees waging a struggle against the government? One can view the situation in one of the two ways. Either the government is regarded representing the whole society. In that case, the government employees can have a genuine grievance if, and only, if, their conditions of life and work are inferior to those of the large majority of the people they are called upon to serve. This is hardly the case.

The alternative is to go back to Marx and not make any distinction between the public sector and the private sector; in other words, not make any distinction between the government and the bourgeoisie. Did not Marx say? "The executive of the modern state is but a committee for managing the common affairs of the whole bourgeoisie." Leaders of the proletariat in the country apparently take this view. In that case, we should remember that Marx also said that in developing the modern industry, "what the bourgeoisie produces, above all, are its own grave-diggers".

The same would apply to the modern welfare state which undertakes planned economic development, expands its welfare services and extends its activities into production. All this requires expansion of employment in the public sector. If the employees and their leaders will not distinguish the public sector from the private sector, not distinguish the welfare state from the private capitalist, in so expanding wage-employment in the public sector, the modern welfare state would be producing, above all, its own gravediggers.

In recent years, labour governments in many capitalist

countries have increasingly come to realize this. Next consider the employees of the small employer. They are about 10 million in number. The small employer suffers from many disadvantages. His turnover is small; his costs are high. He can survive the price competition from the bigger capitalists only by paying somewhat lower wages and accepting lower profits which are often less than a manager's wage. As Marx said, if he is not able to withstand the price competition, he would go down and sink into the proletariat.

This is happening to many a small establishment and we find it taken under the wings of a bigger capitalist. By waging a struggle against the small employers, the workers only help them sink faster. Marx calls them reactionaries because in trying to survive in their small establishments, they are trying to roll back the wheel of history. On that consideration, the proletarian movement directed against the small employers must be considered progressive. As we shall presently see, there are independent and immediate reasons why it seems the workers would prefer the small employer to go down and be taken over by the big capitalist.

Finally, we arrive at the proletarian struggle against the bigger establishments, against the bourgeoisie. This is of course the form which Marx envisaged the proletarian struggle would universally develop into. In India, presently, it is confined to less than 25 per cent of the proletariat which itself constitutes only about a sixth of the working population. Hence, their struggle is essentially a movement of a small minority and not of the immense majority as Marx thought it would be. As I shall later explain, this circumstance gives the movement a character quite different from the one Marx postulated.

EMERGING PROLETARIAT

Presently, I invite attention to another noteworthy feature of this struggle, namely, that it seems to succeed better in bigger establishments. In other words, the collective bargaining power of the workers seems to increase in direct proportion to the monopoly power of the bourgeoisie. Marx saw this clearly and hence said that the bourgeoisie produced its own gravediggers. But because his thinking remained confined to the model of a perfectly competitive economy, he could not clearly see the underlying reason why the proletariat struggle succeeds better against a monopolist.

The reason is that the monopolist can pass his costs more easily to the consumer. In consequence, the workers are able to secure higher wages and better conditions of service in bigger establishments than in smaller ones. For instance, in the engineering industry in Poona, while many smaller units find it difficult to pay the statutory minimum wage, the workers in larger establishments are able to secure more than double the statutory minimum. No wonder that the workers in the smaller establishments prefer their employer to go down and be taken over by the bigger capitalist; at any rate, they do not seem to care if that happens. After all, that is the course of history as Marx saw it.

But this has serious implications. It means that the proletariat, as a class, is not homogeneous, not only because there are grades and status groups within its ranks, but also because the workers in the bigger establishments have inherently superior bargaining power than the workers in the smaller establishments.

I say inherently, because the superior bargaining power of the workers in the bigger establishments comes not necessarily because of better organization or greater political skill, but simply because they face an employer who is a monopolist or an oligopolist, who does not suffer price competition in his trade, he can therefore pay higher wages and pass on the higher costs more easily to the consumer. The workers do not mind. The fact of the matter is that, under the veil of class struggle, the workers in the bigger establishments join hands with the monopoly capital and share the gains of monopoly.

This strikes at the root of the Marxian dialectic of class struggle. Marx puts it as follows:

> "Proletariat and wealth are opposites; as such they form a single whole. The question is what place each occupies in the antithesis.
>
> "Private property, as private property, as wealth, is compelled to maintain itself, and thereby its opposite, the proletariat, in existence. That is the positive side of the contradiction."
>
> "The proletariat, on the other hand, is compelled as proletariat to abolish itself and thereby its opposite, the condition for its existence, what makes it the proletariat, *i.e.*, private property. That is the negative side of the contradiction."

With the character that the class conflict takes under conditions of monopoly capital and monopoly labour, I do not see why the proletariat, as proletariat, should feel compelled to abolish itself. Conflict is followed by combine and sharing of common gains. If this is true of the organized labour in the private sector, it is even more true of the labour in the public sector. There, the labour constitutes a monopoly and, in the form of the state, it faces an equally exclusive monopoly.

Whatever the cost can be easily passed on to the people. Marx said: "The executive of the modern state is but a committee for managing the common affairs of the whole bourgeoisie." With the emergence of monopoly capital, the bourgeoisie has found it possible and prudent to co-opt a few representatives of the monopoly labour on the executive of the state. It now manages the common affairs of the monopoly capital and the monopoly labour.

In explaining why the proletariat is compelled to abolish itself, Marx says: "All the preceding classes that got the upper hand, sought to fortify their already acquired status by subjecting society at large to their conditions of appropriation. The proletarians cannot become masters of the productive forces of society, except by abolishing their own previous mode of appropriation, and thereby also every other previous mode of appropriation. They have nothing of their own to secure and fortify: their mission is to destroy all previous securities for, and insurances of, individual property."

This is plainly not true under conditions of state and private monopoly capitalism. Under these conditions, the monopoly labour has seen that it can become, if not the master, at least the co-master of the productive forces of society. For this, it does not have to abolish its own or anybody else's mode of appropriation. It can do all this within the framework of state and private monopoly capitalism. It is also not true that monopoly labour has nothing of its own to secure and to fortify; it has a secure job with an assured minimum income on the first of every month without particular responsibility for production and performance.

Its mission is to improve the quantum and security of that income. Marx said: "All the preceding classes that got the upper hand, sought to fortify their already acquired status by subjecting society at large to their conditions of appropriation." Monopoly labour is no exception. Having got the upper hand, it is seeking to combine with monopoly capital and fortify its already acquired status by subjecting society at large to its conditions of appropriation. The monopoly capital is naturally willing to co-operate as it must in order to maintain itself. That indeed, as Marx says, is the positive side of the contradiction between capital and labour.

What happens to the negative side of the contradiction? It remains latent and dormant and does not surface so long as there remains a class at whose expense the monopoly capital and monopoly labour may combine and share common gains. Marx did not envisage this possibility because his thinking remained confined to the conditions of free competition and he believed that the society would soon split itself into two classes-bourgeoisie and proletariat-leaving no other class at whose expense the bourgeoisie and the proletariat may combine and share common gains. Marxian dialectic of class struggle follows there from.

The conditions in India are far from those postulated by Marx. Partly because the capitalist development has not gone far enough, there exists a large class, in fact as much as five-sixths of the working population, which is neither bourgeoisie nor proletariat and which is waiting to sink into the proletariat. The process is checked because of the rise of the state and private monopoly capital and monopoly of the organized labour; these monopolies restrict the admission into the organized proletariat. Hence, conditions exist, and will persist for a long time, in which the bourgeoisie and proletariat may combine and share common gains at the expense of the rest of the society.

As I have explained, it is only the monopoly capital, whether state or private, and monopoly labour, that is organized labour, which can combine and share common gains. This organized sector comprising about 20 million workers constitutes only one-ninth of the total working population. The apparent conflict between the state and private capital on the one hand and organized labour on the other, therefore leads to the exploitation of the unorganized majority constituting eight-ninths of the society. Because a small minority exploits a large majority, the process is imperceptible but it is certain and real nevertheless.

MODERN INDIAN SOCIETY

Thus, in the Indian society of today, the Marxian class conflict is subsumed within a larger conflict between the organized and unorganized sectors. The organized sector consists of the organized labour both in the public and private sector, and private monopoly capital, the state providing an executive committee to manage the common affairs of this sector. The unorganized sector consists of the cultivator, the agricultural labourer, the artisan, the handicraftsman, the new small manufacturer, the shopkeeper, several other working with small capital and finally the unorganized labour working with them.

Can we call these two sectors social classes in the Marxian sense? That takes us back to the questions which Marx asked and left unanswered: What constitutes a social class? Marx makes it clear that the existence of classes is bound up with particular historical phases in the development of production. The historical system from which Marx derived his theoretical model was the British economy of his day and he was led to believe that perfect competition and free trade were essential and permanent attributes of that system.

Within that system, quite appropriately, he discovered a criterion to define two fundamental social classes and postulated that, as the system developed, the society would split more and more into these two classes: owners of private property and of means of production and those without property and without means of production.

Circumstances have changed. Capitalism is now characterized not so much by competition but by state and private monopoly capital, and monopoly of the organized labour. Ownership of the means of production no longer provides the criterion to define basic social classes under this system. A new criterion based on the distinction between the monopolist and the rest must now define and distinguish social classes. That criterion is the distinction between the price-markers and the price-takers.

The monopoly capital, whether private or public, puts its own price on its product; the monopoly labour puts its own price on itself. All others take the price that the society places on their product and their labour. The society is now divided between two classes: the price-makers and the price-takers.

The Marxian dialectic of conflict between these two classes would appear as follows: Price-makers and price-takers are opposites; as such they form a single whole. The question is what place each occupies in the antithesis.

Price-makers, for their existence, need the price-takers to take the prices they make. Hence, to preserve themselves, the price-makers must also preserve the price-takers. This is the positive side of the contradiction. It explains several policies pursued by the ruling class aimed at protecting the price-takers, namely, the farmers, agricultural labourers, artisans, handicraftsmen, and small industrymen.

Such, for instance, are the policies to perpetuate small-scale farming by legislating ceilings on agricultural holdings; to protect artisans by make-believe support and assistance; and to promote small industry by supply of bank credit. What the ruling class will not do is to give these producers an assured price for their product or an assured wage for their labour.

In order to escape exploitation and privation, the price-takers must abolish themselves as a class. This they do, not by abolishing the price-makers, their opposite, but by invading the camp of price-makers and merging themselves into them. This is the negative side of the contradiction.

The process is already on. Farmers, agricultural labourers, artisans, handicraftsmen, small industry and businessmen, price-takers, all are trying to leave their trades behind and seek wage-employment in the organized sector; in other words, they are trying to join the camp of price-makers. They have nothing to lose except their petty property in land and means of production. And, they have a job to win, a job with an assured income on the first of every month, whether it rains or not, whether they produce or not, whether what they produce sells or not. With progressive exploitation of the price-takers by the price-makers, the gap between the two will widen, and the migration will accelerate until the class of price-makers reaches a critical level. The inherent contradiction in everybody trying to be a price-maker will then come to surface and the whole system will fall to the ground. I should be modest and not prophecy what will take its place.

A Recollection : I am grateful for the many comments my colleagues have offered on my analysis of the class conflict in the Indian society. It is customary to acknowledge such comments by means of a rejoinder. But, if I attempt to do it point by point, it will take far too much space. Moreover, it may take the argument away from the main focus of my analysis because, though a number of points raised in the comments deserve further discussion, in my opinion, they are not germane to the central theme of my Lecture. It is possible that, in spite of the length I have taken, I have failed to make clear my central theme. I shall therefore attempt a restatement.

I am attempting an analysis of the class conflict in the present-day Indian society within the framework of Marxian analysis modified in the light of the actual path and form in which development of capital has occurred since Marx wrote. Clearly, the development of capitalism has not proceeded quite along the lines Marx had expected. I have focused attention on a few major departures which I believe affect fundamentally certain crucial Marxian conclusions. Let me recapitulate them briefly.

DEVELOPMENT OF CAPITALISM

Firstly, the development of capitalism has not, in general, led to a division of the society into just two sharply distinguished and antagonistic classes. Certain middle classes of the pre-capitalist society, such as the new professions, have emerged.

Secondly, the development of capitalism has not reduced the proletariat to a homogeneous class of workers requiring no more than the simplest skills. On the contrary, it has created, within the ranks of the working class, a hierarchy based on skills and experience rewarded by higher wage and status. Besides, between the bourgeoisie and the proletariat, there is now interposed a class of professional managers, with its own hierarchy, the top of which merges with the bourgeoisie and its bottom with the top of the hierarchy within the working class.

Thirdly, capitalist development has not proceeded uniformly in all sectors of the economy. If we take monopoly capitalism as the highmark of capitalist development, it varies greatly between one sector and another, between one industry and another. In other words, the bourgeoisie again is not a homogeneous class.

Fourthly, within the capitalist system, the state has emerged as a major employer in nationalized or state-owned enterprises, public utilities, social welfare services, and general administration. This is a complicating circumstance for the working class movement. Not to see the difference between the bourgeoisie and the state as the employer is unrealistic; but to see the difference, divides the working class.

Finally, the working class is differentiated not only because of the private and the public sectors co-existing side by side but also because the bourgeoisie is itself differentiated. The workers, organized in trade unions, seem to succeed better when dealing with bigger employers with greater monopoly power, whether private or public.

Hence, the workers in each enterprise or establishment prefer to go it alone with only a general support from the entire working class in the name of its solidarity. Bourgeoisie has found this convenient. It has not only conceded legislative recognition to workers' rights but also accommodated the representation of their interests, in varying degree, in the government. In consequence, rather than organizing themselves into a single political party confronting the bourgeoisie in a single political party confronting the bourgeoisie in a revolutionary struggle, as Marx had expected, the workers have preferred to enter into agreement and arrangements with capitalism. In spite of protestations to the contrary, they have on the whole profited by this strategy.

In India, in terms of the working population, only about 10 per cent of the economy has witnessed capitalist development; 40 per cent of it is publicly owned and operated while 60 per cent is privately owned and operated. This is referred to as organized sector of the economy. Along with other features of capitalist development, the sector is characterized by the Marxian class conflict modified as described above.

I ask the question: How does this affect the remaining 90 per cent, unorganized, primarily pre-capitalist sector of the economy? My contention is that, whatever the intentions and the appearances, the class struggle in the organized sector results in the exploitation of the unorganized sector by the organized sector.

I should make it clear that when I say that the organized sector exploits the unorganized sector, I do not mean, even by implication, that there is no exploitation within the organized or within the unorganized sector. There can be exploitation within each sector and nevertheless one sector can exploit the other. This for instance is the case when an imperial power exploits a colony. There is exploitation within the imperial power as also within the colony. Nevertheless, the imperial power exploits the colony and, when it does, the conflicting classes within the imperial country combine in a common cause. This is the essence of the phenomenon.

One criticism is that the organized and the unorganized sectors, or what I have called the price-makers and price-takers, do not constitute social classes in the Marxian sense. I do not know. But I shall not quarrel about words if the phenomenon of the two interest groups, one exploiting the other, is recognized.

The division of the society into two classes, price-makers and price-takers, was mainly to draw the parallel with the Marxian classes and emphasize the different criterion I am suggesting to define classes. I request that, in the present phase of capitalist development, not the ownership of the means of production but the ability to dictate ones own price, should be the criterion distinguishing classes.

On that basis, I would recognize not just two classes but a hierarchy of classes, one more organized, that is with more highly developed capitalism, than another; with greater monopoly power than another; and hence with greater ability to dictate ones own price than another. My contention is that in a society so stratified, each class exploits another class less organized than itself and that, in this process of exploitation, capital and labour in each class combine in a common cause.

What is the evidence? In particular, what is the evidence that the working class in the more organized sector participates in the exploitation of the working class in a less organized sector? I take this opportunity to offer some illustrative evidence.

To simplify the argument, let me confine attention to the manufacturing industry. The manufacturing industry can be clearly divided into three sectors evincing different stages of capitalist development. They are: the registered factory sector; the urban unregistered sector; and the rural unregistered sector. In the following are a few relevant figures and ratios for the three sectors pertaining to 1974-75.

Manufacturing Industry

	Registered	Unregistered	
		Urban	Rural
Employees (million)	5.6	4.7	10.8
Wage workers (million)	4.4	1.0	0.8
Fixed capital per employee (Rs.)	12,100	1,449	601
Value added per employee (Rs.)	11,389	2,579	932
Annual wage per worker (Rs.)	3,831	1,551	822

Sources: Statistics of the Unorganized Sector. Central Statistical Organization.

Paper submitted to the Fifth Seminar on the Data Base of the Indian Economy.

First notice the difference in the stages of capitalist development in the three sectors on the basis of two characteristics: (a) fixed capital per employee, and (b) proportion of wage-workers among all employees. In the registered factory sector, which is capitalistically the most developed, nearly 80 per cent of all employees are wage-workers and the fixed capital per employee amounts to Rs. 12,100. In the urban unregistered sector, only a little over 20 per cent of the employees are wage-workers, and the fixed capital per employee amounts to Rs. 1,449. In the rural unregistered sector, which is almost pre-capitalist, only about 7,5 per cent of the employees are wage-workers and the fixed capital per employee amounts to a mere Rs. 601.

Now let us compare the average annual wage per worker in the three sectors. It varies from Rs. 3,831 in the registered factory sector to Rs. 1,551 in the urban unregistered sector to only Rs. 822 in the rural unregistered sector. Thus, the wage in the urban unregistered sector is almost double than that in the rural unregistered sector; and, further, the wage in the registered sector is almost two-and-half times compared to that in the urban unregistered sector. Clearly, in sectors with higher capitalist development, the wage workers get a better wage. This needs explanation.

It will be immediately pointed out that the value added per employee is also higher in the sectors with higher capitalist development. This is quite true. Indeed, if wage per wage-worker is related to the value added per employee, it is clear that the wage per wage-worker is a smaller proportion of the value added per employee in the sectors with higher capitalist development. The wage per wage-worker constitutes only 33.6 per cent of the value added per employee in the registered sector whereas it is 66.0 per cent in the urban unregistered sector and 88.2 per cent in the rural unregistered sector.

The three sectors represent successively higher stages of capitalist development and, in terms of the Marxian concept of exploitation, the exploitation of the wage-worker is clearly greater in the higher stages of capitalism. Nevertheless, the fact remains that with capitalist development, the wage-worker gets a better wage and that still needs an explanation.

It might be argued that the labour productivity as indicated by the value added per employee is higher in the sectors with higher capitalist development and that it explains the higher wage in these sectors. But the argument is patently un-Marxian. In terms of the Marx's analysis, to justify, a higher wage in the more highly developed capitalist sector, one must show that the 'cost of production' of labour employed in that sector is higher than that of labour employed in the less developed sectors. Marx does not accept this either. According to Marx, capitalist development reduces the worker to a mere appendage of the machine and his own cost of production is reduced to no more than his own means of subsistence. I have argued that in this Marx is wrong, that a modern industrial worker requires several specialized skills which can be acquired only through years of training, mainly on the shop floor.

The employer certainly recognizes this and is willing to pay a higher wage to an experienced worker than lose him and start all over again with a new worker. But two questions arise. One is that most of this training is at public cost and should we compensate the worker on that account? Secondly, even supposing that the training is done at the private cost of the worker, is this investment in himself essentially different from private property in the means of production? And if the reward to the ownership of the means of production is not justified, how does one justify the reward to education and training sunk in the worker?

This leads us to a harder question which also is the heart of the matter. As mentioned above, workers in the more highly developed sectors are better trained. Besides, they have the advantage of working with a larger quantity of fixed capital per worker. It is clear that the higher productivity of labour in these sectors, as indicated by the higher value added per employee, is largely due to the larger quantity of fixed capital, machinery and equipment, which is combined with labour in these sectors.

The focal point of Marxian analysis of capitalist development is that the bourgeoisie accumulates capital, combines it with labour, thereby improves the productivity of labour, but pays the wage-worker only his subsistence and appropriates the surplus-value for further accumulation This constitutes exploitation because, while the entire value created is the product of labour, the worker is paid only his subsistence and the surplus is expropriated by the bourgeoisie.

The bourgeoisie argue that what the worker produces over and above his own subsistence is due to the fixed capital associated with him and that therefore the surplus-value legitimately belongs to the owners of the fixed capital, that is the owners of the means of production, that is the bourgeoisie. Hence, the argument goes, the appropriation of the surplus-value by the bourgeoisie implies no exploitation of the worker. Marx does not deny that more fixed capital in better means of production improves the productivity of labour. He simply questions the legitimacy of the private ownership of the accumulated means of production which in their origin are all product of labour illegitimately appropriated by the bourgeoisie. Hence, the surplus-value being currently produced, which may quite rightly be attributed to the accumulated means of production, in the ultimate analysis, also belongs to labour. It is in this sense that all value created is the product of labour.

MARXIAN PROPOSITION

This Marxian proposition is often mistaken to mean that all value created in an enterprise is the product of labour currently employed in that enterprise and hence legitimately belongs to it. This is a mistake because it implies that the means of production employed in an enterprise are the product and hence the property of the workers currently employed in that enterprise. This is as un-Marxian as the proposition that the means of production are the private property of the bourgeoisie.

The correct Marxian proposition is that all value created over and above the subsistence of workers is due to past labour embodied in the means of production and hence belongs to labour in the aggregate. Hence, its appropriation either for capital accumulation or for consumption over and above subsistence must be a matter for social decision. It must not be left to the bargaining between the bourgeoisie and the workers in the several enterprises. If this is agreed to, it will be hard to justify the large wage-differentials obtaining in different sectors of the economy.

My contention is that the large wage-differentials presently obtaining in different sectors of the economy are the result of the fact that the appropriation of the surplus-value generated in each enterprise is left to the bargaining between the management, private or public, and the workers in each enterprise.

When this is 'done, the workers in the capitalistically more highly developed sectors are able to secure higher wages; firstly because, in these sectors, there is employed more fixed capital per employee and consequently is created larger surplus value per employee which, though it is due to past labour embodied in the means of production, is treated as available for splitting between the bourgeoisie and the workers; secondly because the workers in these sectors are better organized, and hence possess superior bargaining power, which power improves with every increase in wages they secure; and thirdly because the bourgeoisie in the private sector, or the state in the public sector, enjoy greater monopoly power and hence are able to pass at least part of the costs to the less developed sectors of the economy.

This is the central proposition of my analysis and, in my view, this constitutes exploitation of the less organized sector by the more organized sector in which process the capital and labour combine.

A point is made that, in spite of all its struggle to improve its wages and living conditions, the organized labour has been able barely to protect its real wage and that in some sectors, such as the public administration, the real wages have infect declined. I shall not dismiss this point. But, even if it sustains, I do not see that it refutes my contention regarding exploitation of the less organized by the more organized.

As I have argued, the evidence for the exploitation is the large wage differentials between different sectors; so long as they persist, the exploitation continues. If this is accepted, we can discuss independently whether the exploitation has progressively increased in the last one or two decades.

In evidence, we may enquire whether the real wages in the

organized sector have increased or, more appropriately, whether the wage differentials between organized and the unorganized sectors have widened. To examine this will require a much disaggregated analysis of wages. Such an examination, I suspect, will show that, in enterprises where capitalist development has proceeded faster, along with such development, the workers have improved their real wages.

In other words, in enterprises where, because of increased capital intensity and improved organization and management, the productivity of labour has increased, the workers have benefited by a share in the gains in productivity. But this is no more than a conjecture based on a general impression. It needs and deserves careful analysis.

If it shows that the wage differentials between different sectors have not widened, what are its implications? Does it mean that the gains of development are being shared by the organized and unorganized sectors equally or at least proportionately? This is hardly the case; nor is it the contention of my critics. Their contention, I presume, would be that all the gains of development are being appropriated by the bourgeoisie leaving the unorganized sector as also the wage and salary workers in the organized sector where they are. Subject to what I have said above and what I have to say in the following, I accept, this contention.

The bourgeoisie, supposing they do not dispute it, may say that only a small part of the surplus-value they appropriate goes into their luxury consumption but a large part goes into capital accumulation which provides the basis for expansion of wage and salary employment in the organized sector. I suppose this will be agreed to.

What does it mean? It only means that the surplus-value is used, if not for widening the wage-differentials between the organized and the unorganized sectors, for expanding the organized sector in which the wage and salary workers, by drawing much higher wages compared to those in the unorganized sector, combine with the bourgeoisie and the state in the exploitation of the unorganized sector. It is thus that, even if the wage differentials between the organized and the unorganized sectors might not widen, the process of exploitation of the unorganized by the organized progressively increases.

It might be said that the industrial employment has not increased in proportion to the increase in industrial production. This is true but is besides the point. For the process I am describing above, it is enough that industrial employment, with wages much above those obtaining in unorganized sector, is expanding at all.

That the employment is not expanding in proportion to the expansion of production only means that capitalist development is proceeding further and, with increased capital intensities, and improved organization and management, is strengthening the basis for continued exploitation. It does not affect my contention that the industrial workers, either by improving the real wages of their class or by numerically expanding their class, combines with the bourgeoisie or the state to keep all the direct and indirect benefits of surplus-value to that class and thus to exploit the unorganized class.

More than the expansion of industrial employment, or more generally what Marx would call productive employment, is of concern the expansion of what Marx would call the unproductive employment such as in general administration and welfare services.

The modern state appropriates a substantial part of the surplus-value and uses it for the purpose of general administration and welfare services. India is no exception. Indeed, in India, the expansion of such unproductive employment has been much faster than the productive employment in the organized sector.

The wages and salaries in this sector are as high as, if not higher, than those in the productive organized sector. Clearly, these workers are a party to the exploitation of the unorganized sector. Moreover, the general administration functions largely in the interest of the organized sector and the welfare services which the state provides are also used largely by this sector. Thus the general administration and welfare services of the state further strengthen the process of exploitation of the unorganized by the organized.

What does the unorganized sector do to escape this exploitation? It does not try to destroy the organized sector; being unorganized, it has no such power. Indeed, being unorganized, it does not even react as a class. Instead, its individual members try desperately to leave their class and join the other class. Their motivation, I said, is a job with an assured income on the first of every month, whether it rains or not, whether they produce or not, whether what they produce, sells or not. I should have made a distinction between a productive job and an unproductive job in the sense of Marx. Thus distinguished, the phrase, 'whether what they produce, sells or not' applies to the productive job; the phrase, 'whether they produce or not', applies to the unproductive job; 'a job with an assured income on the first every month, whether it rains or not' applies to both.

6

SCHEDULED CASTES

EDUCATIONAL PROBLEMS

Some time ago, a nation-wide study of the educational problems of the scheduled castes and the scheduled tribes was undertaken. A lot of data about students at various levels of education in regard to their enrolment, drop-out, hostel accommo-dation, scholarship, performance, attitudes, aspirations, etc. were gathered through the 'conventional' techniques of *schedule* and *interview.* However, data were also collected from secondary sources, namely, census reports, reports of Scheduled Castes and Scheduled Tribes Commission and governmental reports.

One of the serious limitations from which these studies suffer is that neither they have been rooted into the analysis of social structure nor they have any bearing on caste and class structure of Indian society. At the outset it may be stated that a proper study of social mobility among the scheduled castes must have its bearing upon social structure of 'caste society', that is, division of Indian society into caste and class groupings. Changes in the non-scheduled castes society would also have its repercussions on the structure of the scheduled castes. Therefore, a meaningful discussion would be possible if caste/class relations *vis-a-vis* scheduled castes are properly analyzed and all the 'ideological' points in the definitional and relational aspects of these two 'concepts', that is, caste and class, are discussed. What have been those conditions as a result of which several anti-Brahmin, anti-twice-born movements and other emulative movements by the scheduled castes have emerged?

Self-consciousness among these sections could be a result of the inhuman and exploitative conditions in which the scheduled castes were forced to live for centuries. It is quite possible that factors external to the caste system were strong enough to loosen its rigid strings tied to the scheduled castes and other lower sections. In such a situation, it was perhaps wise for the upper castes to grant certain concessions to the lower castes, and make search for new avenues of status, honour and power.

Social mobility among the scheduled castes should, therefore, be examined in view of their structural position in the caste system. Before we discuss the various viewpoints regarding caste and class, it is necessary to refer some points about social mobility. Regarding the social position of the scheduled castes in a village of Coimbatore district, Den Ouden points out the following questions:

> Do the scheduled castes comprise a recognizable category within the domain of regional norms and actual behaviour? To what extent do they constitute part of a more inclusive grouping in the eyes of the higher castes?
>
> Do the middle and high castes distinguish levels among the low castes?
>
> Do the low castes make similar distinctions?
>
> Is there a 'barrier of pollution' hindering or

preventing the vertical mobility of the low caste?

What sets the untouchable (and possibly sections within this category) apart from other castes?

Ouden rightly observes: "My principal concern was to identify and to interpret changes in the stratification system, to locate the causes of these changes and to evaluate their consequences for the low castes and their membership." Changes in caste rules struc-turing inter-caste relations may be of the following nature as observed by Ouden:

(a) Rules continue to exist but occur in the castes to which the rules refer.

(b) Rules continue to exist but situations formerly governed by these rules have declined in importance, some such situations are even disappearing.

(c) Rules lose stringency, weakened by new situations arising to which the rules hardly, if at all, apply.

(d) Rules become undermined by conflicting rules; more and more individuals conform to a new ideology and convert to new values and norms.

Ouden meticulously takes into account the role of caste hierarchy *vis-a-vis* 'caste relevant' and 'caste-irrelevant' roles. He also takes into account the role played by an individual in impro-ving his position within the caste system. However, the question regarding caste and class, both conceptually and operationally, remains unanalyzed in Ouden's work. Therefore, first we will deal with the viewpoints and approaches concerning caste and class, and then our emphasis will be on the nature of social mobility among the scheduled castes *vis-a-vis* caste and class as systems of social stratification affecting it.

THE DALITS

Despite various difficulties in defining the caste system, a large number of sociologists, anthropologists, social historians and indologists have engaged themselves in the study of caste system at the neglect of the studies of class, political power, etc. Studies of caste have been innumerable. The main features of the caste system, according to these studies, are: a common name, common decent, hereditary calling, and homogeneity of caste members.

Risely, Senart and Ketkar were among the early writers who studied caste exclusively as an Indian system. Later on, Furnivall, Hutton and Sherring in particular pleaded that caste system was 'functional' for the whole of the Hindu society. Even Marx's notion of the Asiatic mode of production and Maine's idea of caste as a case of non-contractual 'status-society' contributed to the stability and continuity of the caste system. Indologists such as Ghurye, Kapadia, Karve and recently Dumont have given caste system a renewed ideological strength rooted into India's specificity and cultural distinctiveness.

Singh observes that the abstracted and a historical detachment of caste from tribe, attribution of exaggerated autonomy to systems of religion and village community and the omission of the exploi-tative and alienative role of colonialism in India on its society and economy from most sociological analyses of its institutions, prove adequately the ideological foundation of such theorizing. Dube and Singh both realized that the demand for indigenization of social science paradigms now so widely voiced by social scientists in India is a product of such historical conditioning of concepts and theories.

However, such a demand for indigenization of social science paradigms and schema is not a recent one only. Marxist scholars like Thorner pleaded for it in 1950s for a better under-standing of agrarian relations. Even some non-Marxist scholars and indologists such as Karve and Saran made similar demands.

However, reasons for them were different from that of Thorner. Mukerji made a vehement plea for making Indian tradition as the sole basis of analyzing social change. Desai realized the role of colonialism in Indian society, polity and economy, and felt that the Marxist concepts and paradigms could provide a fuller under-standing of the Indian society.

One of the criticisms against the lack of proper paradigms is the western education and academic socialization of Indian sociologists and social anthropologists. Srinivas has been accused of a wrong application of the British functionalism by Mencher, Leach and Saberwal.

Ideological contents have been predominant in the various approaches to the study of caste system. These elements were reflected even in the methodology and data which were used for substantiating the numerous explanations about the origin and functioning of the caste system. However, caste was never treated as a 'social formation', which also included components other than traditionally known as 'caste' components of Indian society.

Some scholars for certain ideological reasons again equated caste with entirety of Indian social system. Whatever may be the reasons for stability and continuity of the caste system, the following formulation seems appropriate:

"My basic assumption is that the continuity of the caste system is a solid proof of its adaptive capacities. It has adapted to innume-rable varied situations, forces, and constraints. Because of its adaptability, caste has evolved simultaneously in several directions and adjusted with ideologically antagonistic systems, adjusting its principles whenever necessary.

It has never paved the way to the emergence of an alternate system of stratification and social rela-tions, though the contents of its functions and other paraphernalia changed from time to time".

Sinha observes certain trends in regard to the studies of caste in India. These trends which refer to stability and change of the caste system could be taken for studying caste system as a part of a 'social formation' which certainly comprised of class, ethnicity, power, religion and economy along with caste. However all these aspects were webbed into each other should provide a proper understanding of the historicity of social formation of Indian society.

Caste and class were parts of this formation in various ways. Such a perspective has not been formulated, nor a realization about indigenization of concepts and theories could provide the necessary understanding of Indian social structure as a social formation. As Singh has rightly hinted that historical and fragmented nature of understanding has been at the core of the studies of social stratification.

One of the serious limitations of the studies of social stratification is that caste has been considered as a logical opposite of the 'class'system. The class system has been thought of a basic feature of the western world. Beteille has outlined the basic features of the 'caste' model of Indian society while examining its usefulness as a scheme of analysis. Beteille's trio of 'caste, class and power' is an imitation of Weber's theory of social stratification, namely, 'class, statute and party.'

The other Weberian adaptations are 'caste, class and polities' and 'caste, religion and power'. These adaptations have undermined the role of historicity of Indian society while accepting Weber's notions of rationality and historical specificity. Secondly, Weber's macro-analysis implied a certain method of study and research which has been neglected by Beteille, Bhatt and Aggarwal in their empirical studies of social stratification.

Caste and class are not polar opposites. Changes in caste and class have not occurred as 'replacements.' The view that "caste is changing into class", or change is "from hierarchy to stratification" or "from closed to open system" (the first implying caste and the latter referring to class) are not, therefore, true. At no point of time caste system was a 'closed'system, and class was not so 'open' system even in the western world. Therefore, the notions that class inheres mobility, openness and freedom to individuals are implanted in the minds of Indian intellectuals through western text-books and funding of researches.

Caste was named by the western academics as a feature of an archaic society and charac-terized it by all those features which were just opposite to that of the 'class'system. Class has existed along with caste as an inseparable phenomenon. It is a different thing that caste has been a more 'elaborate'system of ranking in some regions than others, and similarly class-like relations have been more pronounced and visible among certain groups and in certain contexts than others.

It is admitted by several scholars that caste incorporates the elements of class, and class has a cultural style of functioning in Indian society. Historians of both Marxist and non-Marxist dispositions have poin-ted out the co-existence of class relations with caste stratification. Therefore, the ideas that 'caste alone' could explain Indian social reality or that 'class alone' could explain Indian problems or both 'caste and class'should be taken as the basis of understanding of Indian society are not very relevant.

Alternative to all these views should be the notion of 'social formation' which explains the totality of social relations from various viewpoints and at various levels in terms of historicity of the Indian society.

SOCIAL FORMATION

Borrowed approaches such as functional, dialectical, psychological and structuralism are inadequate to explain the totality of social formation and its dynamics. As we have pointed out earlier that the impact of western scholarship has been immense on Indian sociology. The two most popular views about caste are:

(i) it is a cultural phenomenon; and

(ii) it is a structural form of social stratification. Caste as a cultural phenomenon is mainly upheld by Dumont and Leach, and as a structural form it is upheld by Barth and Berreman. Caste as a cultural phenomenon is particu-laristic and Indian in substance, and according to the 'structural' view it is a form of general theory of social stratification.

It is true that systems analogous to caste are found elsewhere also, and it is also true that caste system is one of several stratifi-cations found in other societies. Singh taking a clue from these two views formulates a paradigm of social stratification in view of cultural versus structural, and particular versus universal characteristics of social system. He suggests four types:

(1) cultural-universalistic;

(2) cultural-particularistic;

(3) structural-universalistic; and

(4) structural-particularistic. Singh does not indicate his preference for one of these types that resembles with the Indian situation; however, it seems that his view is nearer to the structural-particularistic category.

In a recent study, Singh categorizes the theoretic concerns in the seventies in the studies of social stratification as:

(1) structural-functional,

(2) structuralist,

(3) structural-historical, and

(4) histori-cal-materialist or Marxist. These approaches are not discussed here in detail. However, some of the basic points in regard to caste-class debate could be

mentioned. Class relations are subsumed by caste and any departure from caste in terms of incongruence between caste, status, wealth and power is considered as emer-gence of class relationships by the structural-functionalists. Struc-tural-functional studies are characterized by mobility within the caste (sanskritisation), and norms relating to mobility are of a con-sensual sort. These studies lack historicity. However, in some studies, structural mobility (downward social mobility, namely, proletarianization and bourgeoisification, namely, upward social mobility) have been reported. Resilience is the main feature of caste, according to the structural-functionalists. Future of caste is seen quite safe as it is a localized system of social relations. Kolenda and others do not agree with the view that 'organic solidarity' existed in a congruent fashion at any time in the caste system. Bailey and Beteille assumed 'organic solidarity' in the traditional caste system. Not only Kolenda does refer to a point which goes 'beyond organic solidarity', several historians such as Panikkar, Stein and Thapar have pleaded that there was never perfect congruence between caste, class and power; and mobility and migration were quite normal activities in ancient and medieval India.

Another serious limitation of structural-functional approach is its reliance on analytical abstraction in the form of statistical-mathematical indicators or analytical typologies. D' Souza treats class as a category conceptually abstracted, hence class does not exist as a community unlike caste. Class is defined operationally in terms of certain indices. Marxists would accept this as a non-humanistic view of a system of social relations. It is considered as a 'Brahminicar or 'hierarchical' model of caste society. Leach has labelled Srinivas as the father of 'Brahminocentric'sociology. The 'dalitcentric'sociology or 'upside down' view has been advocated by Mencher, Parvathamma and several others in some recent writings.

Dumont's *Homo Hierarchicus* is the most significant represen-tative of the structuralist approach to the study of caste system in India. Singh points out that pivotal notions of structuralism such as ideology, dialectics, transformational relationship and comparison have been brought in the analysis of caste stratification in India by Dumont.

For Dumont, 'hierarchy' is 'ideology' and hierarchy implies 'pure' and 'impure' in regard to all sorts of social relations, hence binary tension or dialectics. 'Pure' and 'impure' are separate in all aspects as well together as parts of the theory of caste hierarchy. 'Hierarchy' also implies the relationship of 'encompassing' and the 'encompassed'. The 'pure' encompasses the 'less pure' or 'impure'. This applies to all the sections and aspects of society. Thus, according to Dumont, change is *in the society* and not *of the society*.

Dumont's view falls in the category of 'cultural-universalistic' type of social stratification. According to Singh, Dumont's structuralism suffers both theoretically and substantively. Pure and impure are fused together instead of being disjunct. The notion of 'contra-priest' by Gould also negates such a separation between the two at a substantive level. Dumont wrongly understands that tradition displies representation of structural relations irrespective of time, place and situation, and which might have changed disproportionately to the changes in the tradition.

It is not at all a new idea that caste and class have been treated as binary notions by Dumont. All along the western scholars have done it for the reasons best known to them. Singh observes: 'The structuralist's treatment of dialectics is dissociated from history. History, indeed, links essence to existence, form to content, superstructure and theory to practice. Devoid of such a sense of historical conjecture structuralism amounts to a set of conceptual schema, devoid of a basis in evolutionary changes in society. Its transformational relationships being a historical abound in tautologies." Dumont's structuralism is no exception to these criticisms.

Structural-historical approach has been applied by both Marxists and non-Marxists scholars. The main emphasis is on structural orientation, historical evolutionary typologies and proce-ssual analysis of structures as social movements. The question of origin of caste has recently been resurfaced by Klass.

Marxists such as Namboodaripad and Ranadive have made propositions about the nature of caste. The scholars of both the dispositions have not been able to prove their common thesis that social stratifi-cation in India has emerged from its ancient egalitarian character. Secondly, the view that from clan-like organization caste has emerged, is not factually tenable. On the contrary, class has emer-ged from inequalitarian system like caste due to recent change in it.

To us, structural-historical approach does not refer to origin of caste or clan or class. It offers a new theoretic interest implying Indian society as a social formation with its different aspects having inter-linkages and inter-relationships which have evolved over the years due to their constraints and contradictions. This approach has not been applied earnestly by historians, sociologists and anthropologists. Singh is inclined to have a preference for this approach, but he has not analyzed the phenomenon of social stratification with such clear theoretic and methodological prepa-redness.

Some studies of the social origin of equality/inequality have been undertaken but mainly as parts of the studies of social movements without having a direct bearing upon the structural-historical approach.

Marxist categories and concepts have been used in the understanding of national movement in India. The basic tenets of the Marxist approach refer to locating the historical forces in the mode of production and the contradictions of classes. It is essentially evolutionary and developmental and has a dialectical quality of self-transformation. Gough combines Marxist approach with the anthropological tradition of field-work. She considers mode of production as a social formation in which she finds inter-connec-tions of caste, kinship, family, marriage and even rituals with forces of production and production relations.

Her study of colonial rule in Thanjavur explains the emergence of new bourgeoisie, polariza-tion of peasantry, and the pauperization of the working class due to historical transformations in the modes of production. Totality of contradictions in social stratification could be seen through the contradictions in the mode of production. Thus, Marxists like Gough and even ideologies like Namboodaripad and Ranadive consider class relationships as the domain assumption in the under-standing of caste and kinship in India.

Even *varna and jajmani* systems could be explained in terms of class relations as embeded in the mode of production. The mode of production framework has been put to test at the village level by Djurfeldt Goran and Lindberg, Heera Singh, Thorner, Saith and Tanakha, Bhardwaj and Das.

Caste-class congruence and/or incongruence has been exa-mined in several studies of social movements. 'Caste feudalism' refers to class relations, or caste relations encapsulate class relations, or that caste relations are another name for class relations—are some of the recent expressions based on several studies conducted by social scientists in India.

There are four basic features for understanding caste and class relations and their transformations in regard to Indian society. These are:

(1) dialectics,

(2) history,

(3) culture, and

(4) structure. Dialectics does not simply refer to binary fission in the cognitive structure of the society. It refers to the effective notions which bring about contradictions and highlights relations between unequal segments and men and women. History is not again a conjectural construction based on mythology, scriptures and idealistic formulation, but it provides a substantial account of existent conditions of work and relationship; culture does not include just cultural practices, rituals, *rites de passage*, etc., it defines the rules of the game, the nature of relations between the haves and the have-nots and so on. Structure is no doubt a product of dialectical contradictions, historical forces, and certain rules of the game, but it becomes a 'formation' once it has emerged, and in return, becomes a sort of 'force' to determine in some way the course of history, nature of contradictions and the evaluational standards. Thus, structure refers to relations between social segments at a given point of time, but as a historical product and reality. Having these elements as the kernel of structural-historical approach, changes in caste and class structures could be considered as 'transformational' rather than replacements. All the debates regarding caste and class such as caste is closed and class is open, caste is 'organic' in its structure rather than 'segmentary', there is either caste or class, both caste and class are there, class is replacing caste, caste is weakening, class is emerging, etc. may be taken up with this perspective for a better understanding of social stratification.

Jajmani was never an 'organic'system in reality, though apparently it provided such an impression. The idea of 'contra-priest' even cannot undermine the hierarchy which is built into the *jajmani* system. It is necessary to understand the following patterns of change with a historical perspective:

(1) Downward mobility and proletarianization.
(2) Upward mobility and embourgeoisiement.
(3) Urban income for rural people and mobility in the village.
(4) Rural non-agricultural income and mobility.

COMMON NORMS

Bougie writes: "To sum up on these points: hereditary specialization, hierarchical organization, reciprocal repulsion, as far as any social form can realize itself in its purity, the caste system is realized in India. At the very least it penetrates Hindu society to a level unknown elsewhere. It plays some part in other civilizations but in India it has invaded the whole. It is in this sense that we may speak of the caste system as a phenomenon peculiar to India."

Srinivas, following Bougie, observes pre-eminence of religious values in the caste system, and these values centre around the ideas of pollution and purity. However, Hocart finds that religion encompasses power, hence priesthood is not 'absolute' in nature. Relations between Brahmin and Kshatriya are defined in terms of certain reciprocity, namely, the former represents the 'religious' authority, and the latter enjoys 'political' power.

Srinivas refers to various types of purity and impurity in regard to the Coorgs of South India. He writes: "Normal ritual status is the status which a person enjoys most of the times." Further, he observes: "Ritual impurity, normal ritual status, and ritual purity form a hierarchy. If a person in an impure condition touches another in a condition of either purity or normal ritual status, the latter becomes impure. If a person in a condition of normal ritual status touches another in a pure condition, the latter losses his purity and is reduced to normal ritual status. That is, normal ritual status is a mild form of impurity." Dumont and Pocock, however, observe: "We must discard the reassuring but unjustified expression of 'normal' ritual status." Normal ritual status, which is mildly impure is really outside the realm of the hierarchy of pure and impure in the context of the caste system in India. Ritual bath could eliminate such impurity and after the occasion is over, it could recur. Relations between castes in the caste system are not based on this sort of ephemeral purity or re-impurity after the purification.

Srinivas adds to the confusion that is also realized by Dumont and Pocock when he writes: "The concept of pollution governs relations between different castes. This concept is absolutely fundamental to the caste system." Srinivas further writes: "Some occupations are considered defiling because of the contact with some defiling object or other necessary to their practice. Swine-herding is defiling because swine defiles. Leather defiles, and consequently the making and repairing of shoes is an occupation of the untouchables.

Finally, any occupation, however, remotely implying the destruction of sentient life in any form would be prohibited to the high castes." According to Srinivas, sanskritisation is the only way to remove impurity or minimize it. We may quote two points made by Dumont and Pocock about Srinivas' notion of pollution and purity among the Coorgs. One is that an object or a person is purer, or less pure (or of course more or less impure) than another. Secondly, a person or an object is impure in relation to one another, for example, when there is avoidable relationship between the two.

Srinivasian sociology is commented upon by Parvathamma: "In all the writings of Srinivas, the Brahmin-non-Brahmin values are juxtaposed." Hierarchy remains basic to Srinivas' thinking in regard to all aspects of human life even if it is not so pronounced or less existent. Srinivas does not try to analyze the tensions and contradictions which could be caused by what he calls 'sanskriti-sation'. His main emphasis still remains on concepts of dominance and solidarity.

It is not only Srinivas, Dumont, Marriott, Mandelbaum, etc. also have overworked on the themes of caste hierarchy, pollution-purity, religion, rituals and other allied aspects. Their impact on the younger scholars relating to the study of caste has resulted into the neglect of the study of social structure in totality as a social formation.

The notions of pollution-purity, hierarchy and domi-nance have made a strong impact on the minds of scholars, refor-mers and political leaders as they do not see the social structure beyond these parameters. It is, therefore, necessary first to look into the measures taken for the welfare of the scheduled castes, and then to relate them to the reality of relations between the scheduled castes and caste-Hindus.

We are not comparing India's Dalits with Muslims or Blacks for the simple reason that they are a part and parcel of India's social formation at all the levels of its evolution and development. The Blacks have had never been part of the Whites and the same is true about India's Muslims and the tribes.

We do not have to go into the genesis of the names 'untouchables', 'ex-untouchables', 'Harijans' or 'scheduled castes, '*dalits* which have been used for the lowest sections of Hindu society. Issacs makes a detailed reference to the beginnings and uses of these names for the scheduled castes of today.

To us, there are two patterns of social mobility among the scheduled castes: 57

(i) the welfare measures have brought about mobility among some selected sections of the scheduled castes, adversely affecting hegemony of the dominant castes in the fields of education and employment; and

(ii) social mobility among the scheduled castes is also directly a result of certain socio- cultural movements which in turn has created anti-upper caste attitudes and awareness about their own low position. It is not that these two patterns are quite independent of each other. Since the sche-duled castes were also a highly differentiated lot before Indepen-dence, that differentiation could be reflected in these broad patterns of social mobility among them. Certain sections of the scheduled castes have taken more advantages of the constitutional safeguards and welfare measures, hence they have more migration to urban centres, education and white-collar employment. The others who perhaps due to their earlier weak position among the scheduled castes had to choose the path of 'sanskritisation' for social mobility, and this created tensions without much benefits in concrete terms. Though latently 'sanskritisation' might have brought some benefits to the scheduled castes.

We have observed in an earlier article that the scheduled castes suffer today not only because of the imposed social and cultural disabilities but perhaps much more because of the imbalan-ces created by the emergence of structural differentiation within them due to the policies and plans undertaken ostensibly for their uplift and welfare. The differential benefits received by the sche-duled castes is a major reason for these continuing inequalities. The two patterns of social mobility on the one hand accentuate class-like distinctions among the scheduled castes, and on the other the demands of equality in relation to the mobile sections of the caste Hindus are not met. Data about Rajasthan in regard to enrolment, hostels and scholarships relating to SCs have amply revealed inter-district, intra-district, inter-caste and disparities.

The atrocities on Harijans and their exploitation by the dominant Hindu castes may be analyzed in view of the distinctions which we find among the scheduled castes *vis-a-vis* their relations with caste Hindus. All types of Harijans have not been equally victims of atrocities of the landlords, rich peasants and upper castes. To say that it is a situation of total class war between caste Hindus and Harijans is not a correct observation. The relations between caste landlords and Harijan labourers are quite intriguing.

The institution of untouchability is not functioning in a wholesome way. Its pollutional aspect has receded, but its reflections are seen quite effectively in economic and social relations. Untouchables have changed along with the changes in structural and cultural aspects of Indian society. The areas of untouchability and non-untouchability have become crystal clear in recent years. Like caste resilience, untouchability has more or less disappeared.

It is not that caste has withered away with all its class-like character, and untouchability has been continuing and *vice-versa.* Since caste in the garb of class remains a pivotal force to a large extent, untouchability refers to a situation of exploitation, suppression and powerlessness of the wretched of the earth. Naturally, the exploiters are the well-off caste Hindu landlords and big peasants. Hari-jans or untouchables may not be doing today what they were forced to do a couple of decades ago, but the Harijans remain under the economic and social hegemony of the landed interests.

PROVISIONS IN THE CONSTITUTION

Article 46 of the Constitution of India provides: "The state shall promote with special care the educational and economic interests of the weaker sections of the people and, in particular, of the scheduled castes and scheduled tribes, and shall protect them from social injustice and all forms of exploitation." In view of this clause several provisions have been made for the reservation of seats for the scheduled castes in the states of union and in the parliament and reservation for jobs and services at various levels.

Further, Article 17 declares: "Untouchability is abolished and its practice in any form is forbidden. The enforcement of any dis-ability arising out of untouchability shall be an offence punishable in accordance with law." In pursuance of these constitutional provisions, several programmes have been undertaken for the uplift of the scheduled castes.

The question is: "How close to equality are scheduled castes?" Chandi Das reviews the achievements of social welfare programmes for scheduled castes for two decades and finds that their position compared to that of the non-scheduled castes is still very inferior as regards titles to land as well as size of landholdings.

He further writes: "Their depressed position is reflected again in their economic and social mobility. Their rates of urbanization and education, compared to those of non-scheduled castes, are low. And their economic poverty is poignantly underscored in the fact that, as between districts which are at the same level of development, the average per capita income of those with a higher proportion of scheduled castes is much lower."

A similar observation is made by Ramaswamy. The policy of preferential treatment of scheduled castes has been in practice for over two decades, but has barely scraped the surface of the problem. Even in the urban areas only a fraction of the posts in the administration which are reserved for them is actually filled. The same is the case in regard to completion of formal education even upto secondary level.

In regard to educational opportunities for the scheduled castes, Premi observes that new inequalities are creeping up among the scheduled castes themselves. She writes: "Mere existence of facilities does not ensure their optimum use. Awareness and acceptance are essential for utilization. To maximize the use it is necessary to generate better awareness. More publicity is needed to ensure the wider use of the facilities and to find out the reasons for the poor use". Premi arrives at the following conclusion:

(i) Education among the scheduled castes may not filter down as expected.

(ii) Equal access for unequal groups is not true equality.

Chauhan observes that the spread of education among the scheduled castes has created social classes among them on lines parallel to those existing in higher society. Chitnis concludes that the scheme of post-matric scholarship is neither equitably distributed not optimally used. Caste patterns within the scheduled castes determine differential distribution and utilization of scholarship and other amenities. Ramaswamy, in another article, reconfirms unevenness among the scheduled castes independent of the imbalances created by education and other measures for their welfare. She writes:

> 'In terms of social and economic status, there are clear differences among the scheduled castes. There is a well recognized hierarchy among them. Not all of them are untouchables, even among those that are, there are degrees of pollution. There are also religious cleavages among the scheduled castes." Each one of the scheduled castes is aware about its identity among themselves, and at the same time is conscious of their shared status as scheduled caste.

The realization that unevenness exists among the scheduled castes has led to the exploration of what is popularly known as 'scheduled caste elites'. Harold's *India's Ex-untouchables,* Saber-wal's *Scheduled Caste Elites of Punjab,* Sachchidananda's *The Harijan Elite* and Deshpande's *Scheduled Caste Elites and Social Change* are some of the most well known titles on this theme. Issacs interviewed 50 educated persons from the scheduled castes; Saberwal added eight more, that is, he interviewed 58; Sachchidananda interviewed 200; and Deshpande slided down much below Issacs, and interviewed only 29 Harijan elites.

Two points of methodological and substantive nature emerge from these studies of scheduled castes and their elites:

(i) The reliance is on the information which the researchers could gather from their respondents (elites in this case); and

(ii) it is by and large realized that 'unevenness' among the scheduled castes inherently prevalent as well as created by the implementation of policies and programmes for their welfare is mainly responsible for their backwardness. Awareness about this unevenness could have a levelling effect on the weaker sections. However, it would not be correct that nature of elites could be understood by inter-viewing them. The number of respondents studied is not signi-ficant. The nature of investigation is important. Secondly, that diffusion of ideas about the welfare programmes and awareness about their status in the post-independence period could minimize the gap between the caste Hindus and the scheduled castes is also based on erroneous premises. It is quite likely that we get neither proper understanding of the structure of the scheduled castes *vis-a-vis* caste Hindus nor of the substantial reduction of the hiatus between the scheduled castes and caste Hindus as the problems of the scheduled castes are dealt at the surface level only.

SCHOLARS' VIEWS

Patwardhan observes: "The overall perspective is that there is an increasing possibility for upward mobility for all the

Harijans." She further states that there are two processes of mobility:—

(i) through corporate efforts; and

(ii) by competing between castes and within a caste. Patwardhan also notices inter-caste variability in regard to social mobility, and "sacred and secular models in different contexts." Migration, education and white-collar jobs, particularly outside the village, have been the main source of social mobility among the scheduled castes. The gist of Partwardhan's analysis is that social mobility among the scheduled castes has been immense and a multiplicity of factors have contributed to this particularly since independence. However, Patwardhan's view that 'ascription' does not play such a role in social mobility looks only superficial. Ascription- achievement dichotomy is not viable for understanding mobility at the empirical level. Ascription promotes achievement, and in turn such an achievement adds to ascription, and in this way, in real life, it is found as a complicating process, and if it continues for decades and centuries no significant change may be brought by Constitution or Untouchability Offences Act of 1955 or other measures. In a recent study, Malik observes that as a consequence of social mobility among scheduled castes, their social status, pattern of interaction, levels of aspirations, family pattern, employment of wives and awareness of government policies have also changed. However, these aspects have been studied without knowing the basic structural questions and the complexity of ascription and achievement. Duskin and Lynch refer to unity among the scheduled castes beyond the village particularly for political action in towns and cities. Menchar and Mahar also find the similar political mobilization among the scheduled castes. Mobilization

> of such a sort may be counterproductive, and consequently the non-scheduled castes also mobilize themselves perhaps with greater resources and vigour than the scheduled castes.

All Dalits are not equally victims of atrocities committed by the landlords, the rich peasants and the upper castes. Why is it so? Is it perhaps due to the fact that the Harijans who are not victims belong to a higher 'class' than other Harijans who fall a prey to the rich landlords? The following questions are quite revelant:

> Why some of the families of Harijans are tortured and exploited?
>
> Why the Harijans of a particular village who have generally a low and poor status among the Harijans are victimized?
>
> Why only certain sections of Harijans have extracted most of the benefits extended to them by the central and state governments and voluntary agencies?
>
> Why some castes and groups have advanced in the field of education, and others have migrated to towns from their native places just for bare survival?
>
> Why atrocities are committed only on Harijans and not on their non-untouchable counterparts (in the sense of class) from among the caste Hindus?

Massacre, loot and rape of the scheduled castes in Belchi, Agra, Pant Nagar, Marathwada, Bajitpur and other places are known to all of us. In an attempt to understand the role of caste system *vis-a-vis* class struggle and class organization, the Atyachar Virodhi Samiti in Maharashtra was constituted. It observes: "The caste system functions both as a relation of production and as an ideology." The Samiti further observes: "The caste system functions as an extremely effective method of economic exploitation. The class which has economic power also acquires political power and social prestige which helps it to perpetuate, consolidate and justify its position in the hierarchy. Caste hierarchies also effect ownership of land. Economic hierarchy is closely linked with social hierarchy. The caste system is not merely division of labour. It is also a division of labourers. Capitalist relations make agricultural and industrial labourers into a distinct *class in itself,* but the caste system prevents them from being a *class for itself."* Caste and religion are used to perpetuate a particular class structure. Caste persists as a part of feudal ideology.

The Samiti observes that caste system has preven-ted formation of consciousness and struggle on class lines with any commonalty of interest or unity of function. This function is one of the main resources for its persistence. The Samiti agrees with Mencher's observation that "conflicts between social classes stem ultimately from the social relations of production." The new functions of the caste resemble with the old class-like functions of the caste system, hence discouragement to the emergence of class consciousness.

Such a situation is not peculiar to Maharashtra only. Singh has reported about a similar situation in Punjab. One could find 'class character' in the 'spectre of caste war' in Gujarat in regard to reservation of seats for scheduled castes in state's medical colleges.

The above point is very well brought out by Bose in a study of the riots in Gujarat. He observes that literacy, education and employment are the most important indicators of social mobility among the scheduled castes, and geographical spread of the violence is closely related to social mobility of the scheduled castes affected by violence.

Those sections of the scheduled castes who are relatively better educated, more mobile and have some access to jobs have been most seriously affected by the present caste riots. The areas, thus affected, have also a relative concentration of the scheduled castes. Bose also admits that there may be deep-rooted caste prejudices among the upper castes against the Harijans, but at the same time it is also a fact that the rivalry is now between the well-off scheduled castes and the caste Hindus who are entrenched into lucrative jobs, positions of power and high status. In effect, it is a 'class war' between the apparent caste riots, between the scheduled castes and *savamas.*

I.P. Desai, who has earlier written a book on *Untouchability in Rural Gujarat,* also looks at the relations between the scheduled castes and the caste Hindus from a class point of view. Ingle finds that Untouchability Offences Act, 1955 has been flouted by caste Hindus in Maharashtra quite frequently, and without much corresponding corrective steps. Desai observes: 'The system of reservations, even though introduced by the state, has now become a weapon in the hands of the various deprived groups in their struggle against socially entrenched upper caste and upper class interests."

The upper castes and classes want to maintain the social and economic status quo under the cover of seemingly progressive ideology and demand that 'merit' and not 'caste'should be the determining factor in higher education, jobs, promotions, etc. The scheduled castes and the scheduled tribes and other socially disadvantaged groups through their agitation have tried to attack on this status quo by insisting upon reservations which apparently might appear as a particularistic ideology.

Some empirical studies at the village level reveal a high con-centration of socially backward castes among the tenant cultivators. Reddy and Murthy find that as many as 73 per cent of the pure tenant cultivators belong to the backward castes, and of the owner-cum-tenant cultivators 70 per cent belong to these backward castes. The backward caste tenant cultivators are predominant in the small and medium size groups. The socially backward castes in Andhra consists of Settibaliji and

Harijan, and the socially advanced castes consist of Brahmin, Kapu, Devanga and others. Thus, most of the tenants of small and medium size belong to economically and socially depressed castes and pure rent receivers except 12 percent who belong to the dominant castes. The latter are getting more benefits from technological changes than the small size cultivators.

While discussing realities of agrarian relations in India, Mukher-jee discusses caste/class dichotomy and observes that at the root of different forms of social organization, namely, caste and class are the common causal factors which have brought caste, religion and class on the same political and economic dimensions. He cites the example of caste riots and observes: "Caste riots are frequent in those areas where the castewise 'social' deprivations are manifestly correlated with the classwise economic deprivations, such as in Bihar, Maharashtra, Tamil nadu, etc." According to Mukherjee, these caste contradictions are due to inherent class contradictions in the caste system.

Vagiswari compares the income and occupation of Harijans and non-Harijans. He finds that the position of the Harijans has worsened over the past ten to twenty years. He estimated that the per capita annual income of the Harijans in 1970 was Rs. 227 as against Rs. 406 for the non-Harijans. He finds that in terms of all economic indicators—size of landholding, employment, occupa-tion, savings—the position of Harijans had progressively worsened between 1950 and 1970; also it had deteriorated compared to the non-Harijans during the same period.

Consequently, the *dalits* or Harijans are attacked, murdered, their womenfolk raped, and other cruel and inhuman treatment is meted out to them. The accounts of such atrocities are innume-rable. In case the scheduled castes react even mildly against the atrocities, they are forced to pay a very high price including social boycott, denial of public facilities and employment on farms by the landlords. Such incidents have taken place quite frequently in Bihar, Uttar Pradesh, Gujarat, Maharashtra, Tamil Nadu, Rajasthan, etc. In the Belchi killings on May 27, 1977, nine Harijans and two others—all agricultural labourers were tortured and then burnt alive by dominant caste Hindus. Singh provides a vivid account of atrocities and oppression of the scheduled castes in Madhya Pradesh.

In a forthright despatch, Sinha comments on Bihar situation and observes that it is class war against Harijans, and not atrocities. In 1977, Bihar, among all states, accounted for the largest number of cases of atrocities against Harijans. The outrages occurred in Kargdhar, Belchi, Pathadda, Chhaundano, Gopalpur and Dha-rampur. People were killed or persecuted not because they were Harijans, but also because they were agricultural labourers and sharecroppers working with the rich and dominant landlords, hence cruelties against them were of the nature of a class war as the interests of the two did not coincide and class contradictions had become more than manifest.

The issues behind these happenings were struggles for minimum wages, the occupancy rights of the sharecroppers, and a challenge to the absolute feudal power of the landlords. Therefore, such atrocities (class war) could be against the non-Harijan proletariat, the backward castes, and even against the poor intermediate and upper castes proletariat. Logically this view could be accepted on the basis of class war thesis. But it is only partially true. There is an element of Harijanness in the atrocities committed by the caste Hindus on the Harijans. There is a difference between a situation of atrocity and that of oppression and exploitation.

There is a difference between a Brahmin prole-tariat and a Harijan proletariat, hence the differential treatment meted to the two by a Brahmin or Rajput landlord for the same reason. What is known as "the rise of the Kulak power at the centre and in the states", can be held responsible for the oppression of the scheduled castes. The attitude of patronhood or patronage has slowly been disappearing away particularly since independence.

Mukherjee, while writing about the peasant revolt in Bhojpur district of Bihar, observes that *izzat* (dignity) and *unche-neeche jaat ka sangharsh* (upper-lower caste conflict) are the two main causes of bitterness between the upper and lower castes and class people. He writes: "The dehumanization of the lower castes is violent and physical: rampant sexual tyranny perpetuated by the upper castes on lower caste women; the pride of Bhumihars, whose unwritten law prohibits lower classes to remain seated in their presence even at their doorstep; its viewing even the wearing of a clean *dhoti* or receiving education as intolerable ignorance; the 'hakim' suffix after every sentence; at places, the taking of *dole*, i.e., the Bhumihar or Rajput landlord's privilege to sleep with the new bride of a lower caste labourer on the wedding night."

Movement for creation of Jharkhand State for the *adivasis* and slogans like "Harijanisthan lar ke leinge" (we will fight for a state for Harijans) are expressions of the oppression and sufferings of the Harijans and tribals at the hands of the dominant castes/classes in Bihar.

In Marathwada, the riots began due to renaming of Marath-wada University as Dr. Babasaheb Ambedkar University in July 1978. The Students Action Committee, which naturally consisted of *non-dalit* student activists, launched an agitation against the *dalits* which continued for 67 days. The Protection of Civil Rights Act did not help the victims in getting out of the inhuman situation prevailing in the region.

The movement provoked violence inclu-ding killing of people, molestation and rape of Harijan women, burning of Harijan houses and huts, pillaging their *basties*, evicting them from their houses and villages, killing of their cattle, denying them drinking water and refusing them work, etc. This act of the caste Hindu capitalists, landlords with the help of the state power was planned to give a serious setback to the *dalit* movement and its vocal leadership. Thus, an explanation for understanding the pitiable position of Harijans should be searched in the character of social structure of Indian society. The causes of their exploitation, oppression and intimidation are not casual, shortlived, and contingent in nature. Dignity and upper-lower caste/class have been the two focal points of discord and contradictions throughout the history of the Hindu society.

A study was conducted by the Harijan Sevak Sangh in 1976 in 179 villages of nine districts of Madhya Pradesh. It is reported that important programmes like land distribution, irrigation, distribution of homestead plots, debt redemption, freeing of bonded labour and financial help schemes were only marginally implemented. Most of the 54 lakh Harijans in the state are agricultural labourers or landless peasants and their future is in the hands of a few big farmers.

They were paid as low as Rs. 1.50 for a day's labour. They were put to all sorts of inhuman treatment and indignity. Uttar Pradesh tops the list of atrocities, and Madhya Pradesh comes next to Uttar Pradesh. In the first half of 1973-74, 254 cases were reported, and 18 of these were murder, 37 rape, 38 arson, 81 grievously hurt cases, and 80 offences under Untouchability Offences Act. During 1974-75, 11812 cases were registered.

In 1977, there were 8,905 cases of alleged atrocities on the scheduled castes, and that highest number of atrocities were reported from Uttar Pradesh (4, 974), but according to another source the number was 5,739, and in 1976 it was 3,428 and in 1975 it was 6,760—higher than those of both 1976 and 1977. As many as 2,133 incidents of atrocities were reported from Madhya Pradesh. Other states had: Andhra Pradesh (70), Bihar (421), Gujarat (331), Kerala (136), Maharashtra (367),

Rajasthan (179), and Punjab (81). The report refers to land disputes, payment of wages at lower rates, indebtedness and forced labour, forcing the Harijans to perform manual jobs and creating obstruc-tion in the use of public places, particularly drinking water wells.

In 1975-76 and 1976-77, the Scheduled Castes and Scheduled Tribes Commission received, 2, 295 and 1, 761 complaints, respectively, regarding harassment and untouchability, land and agriculture, housing and education from the scheduled castes and the scheduled tribes. The Commission reports that all the cases are not reported, and out of the reported cases, only some are found punishable because of legalities and other factors such as lack of evidence, etc.

There was a time when studies on caste by ethnographers, anthropologists, sociologists and lately by political scientists, econo-mists and historians became quite popular. Every aspect of the society was viewed in the idiom of caste. To the students who studied caste, class remained almost invisible as a social reality. But others who studied class quite consciously thought that 'caste divisions' persisted along with 'real class divisions' in Indian society. Scholars of either hue and orientation did not see the existence of the social formation of Indian society which absorbed caste, class, race, ethnicity, minorities, religions and regions.

The change in the emphasis on the studies from caste to class, or from hierarchy to stratification, or from closed to open stratification or change in the application of the methods of study from 'indological' to 'empirical' and now 'experimental' are no doubt indicators of the realization of the need for studying what is more relevant than what was in the past. However, even these shifts in the foci of studies and research are not properly perceived. To think of Indian society simply in terms of 'caste' as the social formation implying harmony, hegemony, reciprocity, hierarchy, division of labour and stability of the society and vice versa from a class point of view would create confusions and misconceptions.

A scholar of the eminence of Srinivas does not take cognizance, perhaps inadvertently, of the continuity of 'social formation' of Indian society, and prefers to adhere to "caste model" of Indian society. He refers to 'rural caste' and 'urban caste' like some American scholars such as Rosen and Marriott. Caste and class, theoretically speaking, are principles of status determination, hence not concerned with 'rural' or 'urban' people as such. Rural and urban are patterns of living and not principles of ranking.

Srinivas observes that "even today agricultural production requires the co-operation of several castes, and even traditionally competition between different castes did occur though it was not very common." He further notes that "caste idiom is widespread", but does not realize that it could also be called as 'class idiom', or idiom of Indian society itself. Srinivas states that there are caste continuities, discontinuities, and fuzzy/areas without clear-cut boundaries with multiple and contrary forces at work. Thus, Srinivas refuses to admit existence of 'class relations'.

We have pointed out that mode of production and differentiation of peasantry are dynamic in nature. Transformation in these could be understood by a framework which includes dialectics, history, culture, and structure. Structural-historical perspective is found quite useful. The rules and regulations to bring about social mobility among the scheduled castes have become quite ineffective.

The frame of pure and impure and sanskritisation has been unable to account for structural changes among the scheduled castes. Differentiation among the scheduled castes has accentuated unevenness of a new sort among them. Atrocities and violence against the scheduled castes are a clear indicator of a 'class war' between the well-off caste Hindus and the well-off scheduled castes. Oppression and exploitation are not new to the scheduled castes. The only difference is that now there is more possibility of making a hue and cry than before whenever violence takes place. A class view of the status of the scheduled castes in the caste system could reveal the dynamics of social mobility. Srinivas is perhaps not prepared to accept clearly that caste has also been a system of class relations as well.

He says: 'there is fuzziness," this is just to avoid the issue and clinch to his well known position of 'caste sociologist'. Leach feels that the tradition of British empiricism has been used the way it suits for the purposes of analyses—it has become a matter of convenience rather than a matter of scientific investigation. Leach's fear is that such an attitude in use of empiricism brings in the subjectivity and cultural idiosyncracies of the researcher. We are very often accused of doing Brahmin or Rajput or Raiyot sociology. We have to guard ourselves from such accusations by bringing refinement in our methodology and understanding.

BASE OF THE CUSTOM

The untouchability is an age-old phenomenon. It has been said that the untouchables of India occupied the lowest position in the *varna* or caste system, hence untouchables and stratification were correlated. But this statement does not stand valid today in India to a large extent, and it was not completely true in the past as well. The untouchables were a highly differentiated category of people, and they had a hierarchy of their own, and therefore their relations with caste Hindus were not of a similar nature.

In other words, different castes and subcastes of untouchables had differential relations with different caste Hindus depending upon the ranks of both the untouchables and the *swarnas*. Some of the families of the untouchables found positions of respect in the courts of the feudals while others did 'forced labour' during their life-time. Some untouchables were close to the upper caste families, while others were not so. Some castes and sub-castes were less impure than others, and therefore, they had different relations with the caste Hindus.

Such a situation was not just due to the notions of pollution and purity of birth ascription. Distinctions among various castes and sub-castes of untouchables were of a wholesome nature as they were reflected in their styles of life, traditional callings, relations with 'clean' and the upper castes and opportunities for mobility and migration etc. The situation of untouchables today cannot be understood without viewing the stratificational relations which they had in the past.

Today, all types of Harijans are not equally victims of atrocities of the landlords, rich peasants and the upper castes. Why some of the families of Harijans are tortured and exploited? Why the Harijans of a particular village, who have generally a low and poor status among the Harijans, are victimized? Why only certain sections of Harijans have extracted most of the benefits extended to them by the central and the state governments and voluntary agencies? Why some castes and groups have advanced in the field of education and others have migrated to towns from their native places just for bare survival? These are some of the very relevant questions for understanding of the problems of the Harijans of India today.

The institution of untouchability is functioning selectively, but quiet effectively, in certain arenas of our social relations. It has eroded in regard to its pollutional aspect to a large extent, but it does not show encouraging trend of decline in regard to its social and economic dimensions. This shows that the institution of untouchability has been a dynamic institution of Indian society. Changes in the institution of untouchability have occurred from time to time corresponding with the changes in other institutions such as caste, property, land tenure, hereditary occupations etc. Some of the ex-untouchables are not strictly 'untouchables' today, and some others continue to sail in the same boat. Such a situation demands an analysis of structural factors which have brought about mobility, migration and awareness among the Harijans of today. Secondly, untouchability is a contextual and relational phenomenon. The untouchables are treated as 'untouchables' in a given context, and they are treated like 'non-untouchables' in some other contexts. We could call these as 'sacred' and 'mundane' contexts, respectively.

Thus, the view that an untouchable must not be 'touched' physically, has no meaning in a secular context. For example, when the upper caste Hindus work with the untou-chables on their farms, or when they wish to extract work from them, or when they visit Harijan houses during elections, we could refer these as secular contexts. However, the untouchables are treated as 'polluting creatures', when they are invited to eat at the patron's houses on certain occasions. The discriminatory treatment meted to them is an ample testimony of the 'sacred' context. It could be said, therefore, that all untouchables are not equally 'untouchables' among themselves, and also in relation to the caste Hindus.

Further, it could be said that untouchability is not the sole criterion of untouchable's status in our society. Since untouchability and caste stratification are closely inter-related and caste has been a dynamic and adaptive system, untouchability should be studied through a processual perspective.

DIFFERENT ASPECTS

There are different views regarding untouchability. First, the functions performed by the untouchables are considered necessary, useful and important for the entire society. In other words, untou-chability would continue so long as the untouchables performed these functions. Contrary to this is the view according to which untouchability refers to a situation of exploitation, suppression and powerlessness. The untouchables are pauperized and the wretched of the earth. They are the lowliest of the lowest. Their exploiters are the well-off caste Hindu landlords and big peasants. However, both the views do not explain singularly or together the position of Harijans in relation to other castes.

The positions of Harijans as well as caste Hindus have changed to a large extent, hence no traditional web of relations between the two. For example, the upper castes do not continue to be landowners, and the Harijans do not work on the traditional basis. The inter-mediate castes have gained the status of landowners, and the Harijans work on their fields as agricultural labourers on a daily wage basis.

When the poor Harijans refuse to work due to some genuine reasons including less wages, they become a target of the fury of the landlords. Bihar, Uttar Pradesh, Haryana and Rajasthan have this sort of conflict between the Harijans and the rich peasants, and the latter are generally from among the intermediate peasant castes.

According to a third view, violence and insecurity are an off-shoot of the elite sponsored developmental system. In such a situa-tion, which we have, violence by elites on Harijans, and 'violence of protest' by Harijans are found simultaneously. However, the elites always get an upper hand even after the violence is deciding the affairs of the society and fate of the downtrodden. It is quite foolish to expect justice from the vested interests.

The institution of untouchability has changed in recent years, not due to the Untouchability Offences Act of 1955, but due to the pragmatism of the upper and upper middle castes and classes. They have realized lately that observance of untouchability might be quite disadvantageous for them economically and politically in the changed circumstances after independence. It is felt that without working with the Harijans on farms, in factories or in elections, the upper castes cannot continue to dominate or reconsolidate their position. This has been acquired due to some of the structural changes initiated since independence to bring down the age-old ascriptively determined monolithic dominance of the upper castes. However, partly due to legal loopholes and other lacunae, and partly due to pragmatic stratagems, the upper and the upper middle castes and classes have remained in positions of power, both politically and economically.

Today, therefore, one finds dissonance between the formal and the real status of the Harijans, and there is also a hiatus between the form and the content of their position and standing in Indian society. One cannot understand the position of Harijans in terms of the existing legislation, constitution and other governmental measures.

The untouchables suffer a number of disabilities ranging from their most personal relations to the utterly formal and latent actions. These disabilities have been noted in regard to recruitment to army and police, admission to schools and colleges, bondage to the land, denial of services by Brahmins and other upper castes, use of sacred places and temples, and entry into shops and tea-stalls etc.

The disabilities are not the same for all the untouchables as differential treatment given to the Harijans by the caste Hindus is found on the basis of their economic condition, education, occu-pation etc. Mahar observes that the nature of untouchability is too variegated in social and cultural phenomena and diversity of groups subsumed under such labels. Thus, there is no single measure or uniform criteria for identifying an 'untouchable'.

Appa-rently, untouchability is a stigma, but in reality, it is a contextual phenomenon and a behavioural norm. It is not, therefore, just a cultural entity. The untouchables have complained against the upper castes on account of discrimination meted out to them, and the upper castes have complained against the Harijans as they have interfered in their exclusiveness of practices etc. The law does not provide a satisfactory solution to this antithetical, but apparently legitimate situation of self-righteousness.

Why there are atrocities only on Harijans and not on their other non-untouchable counterparts from among the caste Hindus? An answer to this question could explain the role of 'untouchability' as a factor responsible for the exploitation of the 'untouchables' by the *svarnas*. A number of studies have shown that the policy of preferential treatment has not given its desired fruits. The Harijans have not changed their traditional callings, nor they have acquired formal education to the extent caste Hindus have acquired.

Moreover, these developments have created cleavages also among various scheduled castes. The Mahars, the Malas, the Balais, etc., are ahead of other scheduled castes of their respective regions. Thus, certain new forms of inequalities have emerged among the scheduled castes themselves. The caste Hindus and the Harijan elites have combined, may be unwittingly, to prevent the flow of facilities and new opportunities to the rank and file of the Harijans just to safeguard their vested interests or to promote further their own interests by directly or indirectly diverting the resources for sabotaging the welfare plans meant for the scheduled castes.

The crux of the problem is that an equalitarian structure cannot be built without removing the structural bottlenecks of the already existing unequal groups.

We know that the Harijans earn their livelihood by working on land, and they are deprived of control over the land on which they have been working. The incidence of landlessness is more among them compared to other groups. The size of their land-holdings is also smaller than that of caste Hindus. As many as 33 per cent of the total agricultural labourers are from among the scheduled castes. Most of them have uneconomic landholdings. The Harijans have barren and fallow lands. The fertile and strategically important lands have been allotted to the caste Hindus with the connivance of the local leaders and district administration. Therefore, it is necessary to ask: What is the meaning of develop-ment for the scheduled castes? There is a need for a basic change among the planners, leaders, scheduled caste elites and adminis-trators to ensure the filtering down of the benefits to the rank and file of the Harijans.

Eminent economists such as K.N. Raj, V.K.R.V. Rao, B. S. Minhas, Dandekar and Rath have shown that the planning has hit the poor badly, and they have become, indeed, poorer. The way modern education, technology and legislation have been initiated, has led to the breeding of inequality. The rich can escape, and the poor can be trapped. Consequently, the Dalits, the Chamars and Harijans are beaten, their houses are burnt and their womenfolk are molested and raped by the landlords and other caste Hindus.

These victims are not the well-off Harijans, Harijan leaders and the Harijan white-collar workers. In fact, they are the people who could not have proper education, could not migrate to urban centres for better prospects, and who could not escape the fury of the landed interests. We have ample evidence to show that the poorest of the Harijans are dehumanized and oppressed by the caste Hindus.

In 1975-76, Uttar Pradesh had highest number of atrocities as reported by the state government. About 50 per cent of the total number of such inhuman incidents occurred in the most populous state of India. In 1976-77 also, Uttar Pradesh topped the list of atrocities followed by Delhi, Bihar and Madhya Pradesh. About 80 per cent cases were of beating, and only 10 per cent were of untouchability.

An overwhelming number of these clashes with Harijans are over land and agriculture. Atrocities by police have also been on the increase. However, the cases reported to the government are only a small fragment of the total atrocities which have been committed on the Harijans.

On June 22, 1974 two scheduled caste persons were killed by Kanbi Patels in Surendranagar district of Gujarat because they wanted to fetch water from a village well. The scheduled castes had a well, exclusively for themselves, but it had dried up. The Patels had to come to a compromise due to police intervention and allow the scheduled castes to draw water from the well during fixed hours of the day. However, the Patels did not tolerate the decision and considered this as their direct insult, and hence planned murder of two scheduled caste men who had raised voice for fetching water from the village well.

In 1976, a study was conducted by the Harijan Sevak Sangh in 179 villages of nine districts of Madhya Pradesh. It is mentioned that "important programmes, like land distribution, irrigation, distribution of homestead plots, debt redemption, freeing of bonded labour and financial help schemes were only marginally implemented." Most of the 54 lakh Harijans in the state are agricultural labourers or landless peasants, and their future is in the hands of a few big farmers. They were paid as low as Rs. 1.50 for a day's labour.

The Harijans were terrorized by anti-social elements belonging to the upper castes. Their crops were destroyed or looted, houses were burnt and womenfolk were raped. All the Harijans suffered from one or another disability. Uttar Pradesh tops the list of atrocities on the Harijans, and Madhya Pradesh comes next to Uttar Pradesh. During 1972-73, 200 cases of atrocities were reported in Madhya Pradesh. In the first half of 1973-74, 254 cases were reported, and 18 of these were murder, 37 rape, 38 arson, and 81 grievous hurt cases, and 80 offences under the Untouchability Act. During 1974-76, 11, 812 cases were registered.

Arun Sinha, while commenting on Bihar situation, observes that it is 'class war' against Harijans, and not atrocities. In 1977, Bihar, among all states, accounted for the largest number of cases of atrocities against Harijans. The outrages occurred in Kargdhar, Belchhi, Pathadda, Chhaundadano, Gopalpur and Dharampur. The people were killed or persecuted not because they were Hari-jans and the actions of the landlords were not just atrocities.

The issues behind these happenings were struggles for minimum wages, the occupancy rights of the sharecroppers, and a challenge to the absolute feudal power of the landlords. Therefore, such atrocities could be against non-Harijan proletariat as well belonging to the non-scheduled castes, the backward castes, the intermediate castes and even the upper caste proletariat. However, this view is only partially true. There is an element of Harijanness in the atrocities committed by the caste Hindus on Harijans. We could explain this point by making a distinction between a situation of atrocity and that of exploitation.

It is true that all proletariat, irrespective of their caste background, are subjected to inhuman treatment by the caste Hindus. But there is a difference between a Harijan prole-tariat and a caste Hindu or a Brahmin proletariat. The differences between the two are found in regard to their occupational back-ground, prestige of occupation, numerical strength in their respec-tive castes, patronage from caste dominants and cultural milieu. The fact is that a Harijan becomes a target of landlord's fury, but a proletariat belonging to his own class does not get the similar treatment even if he works on his farm as an agricultural daily wage labourer. This is, what we would like to call as 'Harijanness' in the phenomenon of atrocities on Harijans.

We find somewhat different explanation of the atrocities on the Dalits. On May 27, 1977, in Belchhi, a village in Bihar, one villager was shot and 13 others were burnt alive. This was assessed as 'systematic harassment' of the Harijans by the upper caste Hindus according to one political party. However, the Janta Party maintained that the murders were the culmination of a feud bet-ween two groups of criminals, each including Harijans and upper caste Hindus.

We do not have to enter into the controversy regarding the veracity of the incident, but it was said that the Bharatiya Lok Dal-Jana Sangh combine in eight of the Janta ruled states in 1977 encouraged the upper caste Hindus to persecute the Harijans. In other words, it was rumoured that the Harijans would remain defenseless so long as the Janta Party remained in power.

A section of the Harijans made a demand for arms to protect themselves against the toughs and anti-social elements of the upper and upper middle caste Hindus. Thus, the emergence of Janta Party with BLD and Jana Sangh as its two important constituents was characterized as "the rise of the Kulak power at the centre and in the states." Oppression of the Harijans was considered a logical consequence of this change of power in the country.

The Atyachar Virodh Samiti recently made an analysis of riots in the Marathwada region of Maharashtra. The massacre, loot and rape of Harijans in this region have been quite frequent like Uttar Pradesh, Bihar and Madhya Pradesh. The Samiti observes that caste represents a specific form of oppression at the level of relations of production. There are both class and caste issues, because caste divisions persist beyond purely economic classes. A link should be established between fights against caste oppression and class exploitation, that is, caste discrimination and caste oppression are, in effect, representative of class hegemony of the upper castes.

It is reported that during 1966-76, 40, 000 cases of atrocities were recorded. During the 19-month rule of Janta, the cases of atrocities were more than 17, 000. Regarding the cases of atrocities (only murder and rape), Uttar Pradesh (183) tops among the states, followed by Madhya Pradesh (100), Bihar (100) and Rajasthan (78).

In Marathwada, the riots began due to renaming of Marathwada University as Dr. Babasaheb Ambedkar University in July 1978. The Students Action Committee launched an agitation against the change of the name of the university. The violence against the *dalits* took many forms which continued for more than two months. The Protection of Civil Rights Act did not help the victims in getting out of the inhuman situation prevailing in the region.

The violence was of a wholesome nature. It included killing of people, molestation and rape of Harijan women, burning of their houses and huts, pillaging their *basties,* evicting them from their houses and villages, killing of their cattle, denying them drinking water and refusing them work, etc. It is reported by the Atyachar Virodh Samiti that 1,200 out of 9,000 villages of Marathwada were affected by the attacks of the caste Hindus, 5,000 people became 'homeless and stateless, and 2,500 became totally demoralized and helpless. This was an offensive launched by caste Hindu capitalist landlords with the help of police, patels, sarpanches and anti-social elements. Breasts of one woman were cut off after raping her. Those who had left their homes were not ready to go back in spite of starvation.

SAMITI OBSERVERS

The Samiti observes that renaming of the Marathwada Univer-sity was only a pretext; the real issues were different. These included preferential treatment given to the *dalits,* namely reservations in educational institutions and jobs, the policies and character of *dalit* movement itself and its leaders, the increasing unity among the *dalits* themselves and between *dalit* and *swarna* agricultural labourers, and the linkages between the rural and the urban *dalits*. Thus, the issues such as language, separate statehood, caste exclu-siveness, communal freedom, establishment of steel plants, and opening or renaming of a university, etc. are only apparent causes of the atrocities on Harijans.

The real cause of all this is the desire of the upper castes and the landlords to maintain their monolithic control over the resources of the society, and to keep the Harijans and other proletariat as their servants and slaves. As such, caste becomes a mechanism of exploitation of the poor people, particu-larly the Harijans. It is, in effect, a system of relations of production; it promotes conservatism and helps the rich and the entren-ched few in Indian society.

Charan Singh when he was Home Minister of India said that the caste system was the root cause of the problems of the Harijans. Atrocities on Harijans would continue so long as the caste system continued. He made the suggestion that the preferential treatment should be given to those marrying outside their own caste.

Attitude of the persons towards caste should also be considered while giving them jobs. Jagjivan Ram, an acknowledged Harijan leader, observed regarding molestation and rape of Harijan girls: "Why did such things happen? Harijan girls were not known for their beauty and there were far more beautiful girls in other commu-nities. The reason was economic weakness of the victims. They would not put up a fight against the 'ruffians', whether they belonged to the police force or other communities."

The backward class movement particularly in Bihar and Uttar Pradesh has further sharpened caste divides in the countryside. Brahmins, Rajputs, Kayasthas and Bhumihars who comprise about 7 per cent of total population, hold 75 per cent of government jobs. In Karnataka, the backward classes constitute 38 per cent of the population, but hold only 12 per cent of the jobs. Besides this discrimination, the backward class people like Harijans are kept at a distance in social and cultural arenas by the upper castes. Parvathama observes:

> The Indian social structure itself is based on graded hierarchy of status where religious, economic, educational, political and judicial powers increase in the ascending order thus directly limiting the status of lower castes. While the instances of disabilities and backwardness are in the descending order, they are thinly spread over a whole range of Sudra castes, but greatest concentration obtains with reference to the untouchables who fall traditionally outside the *chaturvarna* scheme and thus constitute a class of *avarnas* called as *panchvnas.*

Thus, we must search for an explanation of the position of today's Harijans in the social structure of Indian society. The causes of their exploitation, oppression and intimidation are not casual, shortlived and contingent in nature.

Our study of educational inequalities among Rajasthan's scheduled castes shows that their alarmingly backward condition is connected to the deprivation they suffer in relation to the higher status groups and to the differential treatment they receive from the power elites from among themselves. We have found that the distributive disparities affecting the scheduled castes are at three levels: between the scheduled castes and the general population; between the various scheduled castes; and among scheduled castes in a particular district or area. Emergence of inequalities among scheduled castes has become a new stratificational problem, and this has accentuated class distinctions within the scheduled castes. Such a phenomenon would give a setback to unity, mobili-zation and movement among the scheduled caste people.

Available data reveal that the lowest castes, namely, Harijans, become the targets of violence. Such violence has very frequently occurred in Uttar Pradesh, Bihar, Maharashtra, Gujarat, Tamil Nadu, and Andhra Pradesh. Atrocities on Harijans are inflicted both by upper and upper middle castes in these and other states. Our view is that caste divisions in Indian society are not outside the purview of class divisions. Since caste and class co-exist, class consciousness and class unity are hampered by norms of caste divisions. It is, therefore, necessary to give a proper attention to the factor of 'caste' in the analysis of class relations, and also to see caste divisions from the class point of view.

In fact, caste is a double-edged weapon being used against the Harijans by the caste Hindus, and to oppress them in the name of their exclusive-ness and freedom. Resilience of the caste system has promoted the interests of the upper castes and suppressed the Harijans and other lower castes to a great extent. In other words, the processes of social change initiated after independence have helped the upper castes in the fields of education, politics and jobs. Violence against the Harijans is an expression of the hostile attitudes of the upper castes towards the Harijans, as this results into suppression of class consciousness among them and promotion of the vested interests of the caste Hindus.

[illegible] "Tiger" [illegible] "Mithuna" [illegible] cultural [illegible] positions are [illegible] are [illegible] and upper middle classes [illegible] and other castes [illegible] that [illegible] Indian society are not [illegible] pathway to class [illegible] since caste and class [illegible] hampered by [illegible]

[illegible] relations [illegible]

[illegible] caste systems [illegible] of the [illegible] [illegible] social change [illegible] of education, politics and [illegible]

7

THE TRIBES

TRIBAL PEOPLE

The tribal people have been seen as an undifferentiated lot. However, they have/had gradations based on age-sets, sex and kinship which did not form the basis of social stratification as found among the non-tribal people like property, wealth, power and authority. Several studies of social stratification, ranking systems and class formation among the tribes all over the world have reported absence of social differentiation in tribal societies.

Social stratification, as an existential phenomenon among the tribes, is, however, different from that of the advanced agricultural and industrial societies. It is not unique as it is generally considered. The principles of social stratification such as ethnicity, class and power are the same everywhere. The difference lies in the opera-tionalization and actual functioning of these principles due to structural differences in various tribal societies in regard to their history, level of economic development, nature of colonial impact and exposure to modern forces of social transformation. Thus to the extent the tribal people are different in terms of these criteria social stratification and class formation are also different among them in comparison to the non-tribal societies.

POLICY MAKERS

For a long time it has been debated by the academia and policy-makers whether tribals should be allowed to retain their cultural identity intact or they should be assimilated with the rest of Indian people. This culrurological perspective is not specifically articulated for the study of social stratification as such among the tribal people, but rich data have been generated regarding intra-tribal and inter-tribal status distinctions (Vidyarthi, 1974).

More specifically, the ethnic and class perspectives have been in currency for the study of tribal social stratification (see, for example, Sachchidananda, 1990; Badgaiyan, 1986; Doshi, 1990; Singh, 1985). Emphasis in the ethnic perspective is laid on inter-tribal distinctions in terms of historicity, land relations, colonial impact, contact with non-tribal people, economic development and socio-political awakening, etc. However, the class perspective emphasizes upon formation of class relations among tribes keeping in view their economy, patterns of exploitation, alienation, and backward-ness. In a couple of studies convergence between the ethnic and the class perspectives has been greatly emphasized (see Badgaiyan, 1986; Doshi, 1990).

Finally, we may identify the major tribal ethnic structures in terms of their internal differentiations and interethnic differences and ties to ascertain ramifications of social stratification and class formation. Class formation, as a structural process, is based on increasing differentiation among the tribal people in terms of property, wealth, landownership, exploitation, pauperization, education, political power, social movements, migration and social mobility. We may relate these aspects of class formation with the ethnic structures to find out the nature of correspondence/non-congruence between ethnicity and class.

THE ADIVASIS

'Tribe' may be distinguished from 'caste', but it is not that 'tribe' is a homogeneous entity and 'caste' is characterized by complexity and heterogeneity. There are distinctions within a given tribe and between different tribes. Certainly, tribes are considerably distinct from the non-tribes. But then the question is: What is so distinctive about 'tribe' that makes it distinct from other entities such as caste, class, race, etc. Some tribes are quite large in size and are also spread over several states of India. Surely, tribes are not 'organically' related to each other as castes are under a common principle.

But tribes are also not exclusive systems as they are not small in size and bear a great deal of heterogeneity. Historically, a 'tribal society' has not been static, and yet it has retained its exclusivity from a 'caste society'. There are 427 tribes in India, and these can be classified on the basis of language, religion, degree of their isolation, and pattern of livelihood (Beteille, 1974). Some of these attributes of tribes often resemble with the non-tribal people in a given region than the tribal people of another region. The tribals are hunters, fishers, shifting cultivators, settled agriculturists, plantation workers and industrial wage earners, hence some of them resemble with the non-tribal people.

The large tribes such the Bhils, Gonds, Santhals, Oraons and Mundas are not only settled agriculturists, some of them are found in modern occupations in like members of caste Hindus. Tribal economy is also largely like the peasant economy. Division of labour based on gender, work specialization, tenurial differentiation and class distinctions are found among the tribal people like any non-tribal peasant community. Despite these similarities, tribes remain distinct from castes because of their geographical isolation, language or dialect and religion (Beteille, 1974). Even these criteria are not a rigid basis of distinguishing tribes from castes. For example, Meenas in Rajasthan are listed as a scheduled tribe, but they have always lived in multicaste villages as a part of the village system. Meenas were also one of the functionary castes under the *jajmani* system and, in fact, they are/were always referred as a caste.

Certainly, tribes have been large and small both, but never without internal social differentiation. Beteille argues that a substantial number of tribal people are peasants today, hence tribes are in transition (Majumdar, 1937; Sinha, 1965; Oraon, 1969). There is class and social stratification (implying stratified peasantry) among tribes in India. In no way, tribes can today be treated as 'primitive'. Besides differentiation of peasantry, there is also a middle class among the tribal people.

Migration, education, mobility, social and political awakening have contributed to the emergence of a small middle class. State-sponsored measures including the constitutional provisions and special programmes for their development have set in a new process of differentiation and stratification which would mean consideration of more or less same criteria of status determination which are normally applied to the non-tribal people.

There is more or less unanimity among the students of tribal social life in India regarding the presence of social stratification. However, Roy Burman (1984) cautions that social stratification by itself is not enough to mobilize the people to actively resist alienation of their land. More important is the nature of social stratification. Roy Burman cites a few examples in support of this observation. The Gonds were a highly stratified community, but no significant revolt took place amongst them till the forties of the present century. The presence of a state structure and the shifting nature of political contacts with the outside world led to both stratification and segmentation of Gond society. Like the non-tribal people, "the upper strata emerged as a multi-focal aristo-cracy." A new elite emerged among the Gonds, and the British rulers transformed them into new Zamindars.

Thus, the Gonds synthesized the old and the new, the tribal and the peasant cultures. A tribal movement gets a start generally when it has support of a combination of factors including iniquitous relations, middle class interests, philanthropism and ethnic/community identity. But the point is that tribal people are like other people engaged in similar pursuits in the same area(s), and they are also different from them, and it is this difference/dissimilarity that makes social stratification in tribal society somewhat different from the non-tribal people.

Let us describe a 'functional' formulation of 'tribes' here. Tribes are not castes or caste-like entities though some of them have followed the path of sanskritisation and conversion to Christianity and Islam. Tribes are a highly differentiated lof ethnically and culturally. Some adhere to 'tribalism', others have converted to Christianity by rejecting tribal pantheon, and some have taken up Hinduism by adopting vegetarianism, teetotalism and other Brahminic ideals and practices.

Tribes are also differentiated based on landholdings, rural-urban background, education, occupation, income and political power. Tribes have been granted special treatment under the Constitution of India. They have also many attributes, practices and styles of life that distinguish them from the non-tribal people. It may be seen how their 'distinct' and 'general' characteristics get reconciled in their social life. What keeps them partly different from others, and what impinges upon their life to bring them closer to the non- tribal people? The tribal situa-tion is complex in the sense that the tribals depend upon forest-based sources of livelihood, they are also engaged in settled agriculture, they are working in factories and industries, some of them are educated and are employed as professionals, civil servants and white-collar workers, and some are active politicians and social workers. Ethnic and cultural differentiation can be seen in terms of tribal identities and religious pursuits.

Thus, the nature of social stratification is also quite complex corresponding with the hetero-geneity of their socio-cultural and economic structure. Therefore, it would be unwise to consider tribes as the people dependent mainly upon forest produces, simple agriculture, living far off from modern civilization. They are a people who have a lot of attributes in common with the non-tribal population, and at the same time, have their own 'tribal identity'.

Social stratification among the tribal people is, therefore, neither simply based on criteria like age and kinship nor it can be characterized by property, education, occupa-tion, income and power. A semblance of the two sets of criteria may distinguish the tribal people from the non-tribal population.

THE HISTORY

Sachchidananda (1990) reports that social stratification in the states of West Bengal, Bihar, Madhya Pradesh and Orissa in the pre-colonial period could be observed through the ranks such as the *khuikattidars,* the village headmen and the masses. Later on some artisan castes such as blacksmiths, potters and weavers further differentiated the tribal society. From class point of view, the village society was divided into the *khutkattidars* and the *paria lioroko* (masses). The later depended on the goodwill of the *khut-kattidars* and were rated as second class citizens. The *khutkattidars* were the real owners of the village land. Sachchidananda writes: "The *khutkattidar* system was thus an arrangement for the management of land resources on a communal basis. The headman managed the affairs of the village with the help of some influential village leaders. He dispensed justice, fixed the dates of village deities and collected dues from landholders for payment as *chanda* (contribution) to the tribal chief.

Under such a situation lineage or clan was the basis of socio-economic differentiation. The *khutkatti* system was mainly confined to the Munda tribe. Thapar and Siddiqui (1991) also find the *khutkatti* system as the basis of the Munda society. The *mundas, pahans* and *mahtos* were heads of their clans. Besides these heads of the clans/lineages, the *khut-kattidars* were powerful as they collected a tribute from the villages. Thapar and Siddiqui after tracing the history of social structure and its differentiation in ancient period write:

"Thus, the tendency towards social stratification which had already begun with the *khutkatti* system was not only intensified and accelerated under the state, but was also made more complex with the interpolation of various levels of intermediaries". The tribal mode of production broke down and gave a way to the emergence of a new correlation of social status with landholding and power. The lineage rights over land became weak, and a feudal state on tribal society was superimposed. Tribal identity was also weakened by commodity production.

Individual ownership of land was found among other tribes. The headmanship was not confined to a member of a clan or lineage as it was in the case of the Munda tribe having the *khutkatti* system. But all the tribes had the institution of *headman* who acted as a patriarch. The *khutkattidars* were not completely autonomous as the king was the supreme authority in his state. Sachchidananda observes that such a system did not persist for long as feudal superstructure was set in place not only in Chhota-nagpur but also among the Gonds in

Madhya Pradesh. He writes: "Scions of the Raja's family carved out feudatory estates and principalities, the most famous of which was the kingdom of Chanda. The emergence of the feudal system marked the beginning of the breakdown of the tribal polity characterized by communal ownership of land" (Sachchidananda, 1990). At this stage, a clearly visible system of social stratification could be seen among the tribal people. A sort of economic explanation of this is provided by Sachchidananda though without using clearly relevant concepts and categories. He writes:

"Social stratification based on differential command over economic resources began to emerge. The development of trade and commerce facilitated the growth of small urban centres. A variety of castes, ranging from *brahmans* and *rautias* to many artisan communities, flocked to these centres".

Sachchidananda mentions about the grant of *jagirs* by the Raja of Chhotanagpur in early seventeenth century. As a result of this a new class of merchants, money-lenders and Brahmin priests emerged. The emergence of this new class proved antithetical to the principle of communal and equalitarian character of the tribal society. Since the new grantees of lands in the tribal areas enjoyed more or less permanent and usufructuary rights, they soon began to exploit the tribal people uninhibitedly with the help of village officers such as the *munda* and the *pahan*. The *khutkatti* system also began to crumble down along with the *parha* system.

Thus, a new basis of power and social status emerged and replaced the traditional arrangement. Land did not remain any more a commu-nally owned and controlled phenomenon. However, the village officers like the *munda*, the *manki* and the *majhi* were given police powers by the British in their interests to establish their rule over the masses by granting a small minority such benefits which made them to fight for the *raj* and to suppress their own people.

It can safely be deduced from the available literature that isolation of the tribal people has been decreasing, and this has benefited some sections of the tribal society and, at the same time, new forms of social stratification among tribes in India has been variously characterized in terms of peasantization, detribalization, Hinduization, conversion to Christianity, etc.

Some caste-Hindus because of pre-eminence of tribal society in a given region have adopted some tribal attributes, and such a process has been called as 'tribalization'. Despite these changes, tribal society can be distinguished from the Hindu, Muslim, Christian and other non-tribal communities. However, this does not imply that tribes in India have remained or continue to remain isolated, homoge-neous, small in size and unique compared to the non-tribal people.

The British affected the tribal people in several ways. The intrusion of the British in the management of forests dipossessed the tribals from their age-old control and use of forests. Besides the British officers, a lot of other sections like suppliers, traders, clerks and workers started living in the tribal areas. In course of time, some tribals were also benefited by the British encroachment, and they became a distinct class of the privileged few. Education was one way by which a select group of tribals became superior to the masses. Conversion to Christianity also helped the converts in education, employment, and in fact, in acclaiming a higher status for them.

Singh (1978) highlights some dysfunctional consequences of the British colonialism. The agency system established by the British was used for ruthless suppression of the tribal uprisings. The colonial system also strengthened the feudal elements in tribal society as it encouraged the chiefs and landlords to extract surplus from the tribals as much as possible for the well-being of the *raj* in India. The moneylenders had their heyday as no one was there to check the usurious activities perpetrated by them.

From various accounts, it is evident that during the British period class-based distinctions were replacing the traditional status system among the tribes of India. It could be seen in the alienation of land, control of forest economy by the state, emergence of moneylenders and traders, close but exploitative contacts by the non-tribals with the tribal people, etc. All these sections of society, including the British officers, Zamindars, moneylenders and traders and non-tribal agriculturists were superior in skills and resources even before they landed on the tribal soil.

This implanted a hiatus between them and the tribals, and the policy of the government created status cleavages among the tribals. This is why some non-tribals are regarded as *diku* (exploiters). The tribals, in general, faced acute pauperization and were forced to migrate in search of employment to far off places in Bengal, Assam, Maharashtra, etc. The tribals are found divided even today due to the processes of acculturation started by the Christian missions and Hindu organizations. Conversion to Christianity and Hinduization brought about at least three orders, namely, Christian convert tribals, Hinduized tribals, and non-converts. All these tribals were also stratified internally based on their economic standing and ethnic status.

Inter-ethnic relations between different groups with varying degrees of structural distance have been highlighted by Badgaiyan (1986). Ethnicity and class as the two main principles of social differentiation have provided multiple ways to the people for organizing their social relations. Within the same ethnic group there are wide-ranging class differences, and the hostile ethnic groups may be found in the same class. The searching questions posed by Badgaiyan are:

(1) How people resolve the contradictory claims on their sentiments and impulses to act?

(2) Do they allow their ethnic sentiments to ride over class interests or do they let class interests prevail over their ethnic obligations?

(3) Is it the context that decides as to which affiliation will prevail over the other?

(4) Do all ethnic groups behave the same way?

(5) Are ethnic groups swayed more by primordial sentiments than by contextual logic? These questions are explicated in the context of the historical development of Munda society. The four phases noted by Badgaiyan are:

   (i) the traditional Munda society before the emergence of kingship among them;

   (ii) Munda society under kingship but before the imposition of British colonialism;

   (iii) Munda society under British colonialism; and

   (iv) Munda society in independent India. The account provided by Badgaiyan about the pre-British period resembles with those given by Sachchida-nanda and Thapar and Siddiqui. The rent collectors in Chhota-nagpur were recognized as Jagirdars (owners of land) after the British had taken over the Diwani of Bengal in 1765.

The Jagirdars accelerated the process of expropriation of native owners of land. Ejection became an easy affair, and some proprietary cultivators were forced to become tenants and agricultural labourers. By the middle of the last century the number of Jagirdars had gone upto 600. In addition to rent, they imposed new taxes and levies.

Badgaiyan writes: 'Praetorian obligations of service, gifts and presentation now became necessary for holding the land. Forced labour came to be extracted more and more. The Jagirdars introduced the *thekedars* to collect revenue. These *thekedars* used all their means and power to extract as much as they could from the tenants". Thus, three new classes, namely, Jagirdars, *thekedars* and tenants emerged replacing the rent collectors and cultivators. With the intervention of the

British, the moneylenders and the merchants also entered into socio-economic fabric of tribal life. Another dimension to social stratification among the tribes of middle India was added by the coming of Christianity as it brought about differentiation initially on religious basis and later on the basis of education, occupation and income. By the end of nineteenth century, the divide between the non-tribal elite and the tribal masses had become so wide that the Birsa movement emerged as a strong wave against the Hindus, Christians, Jagirdars, *thekedars* and colonialism.

TRIBAL SITUATION

Badgaiyan observes that by the end of the nineteenth century the tribal situation had become quite complex. For example, the Mundas had to deal with a number of other tribal groups like the Oraons, Hos and Cheros; they had also to deal with the non-tribal groups like the Hindus, Muslims, Sikhs and Christians and Birsaite sections from among themselves. These ethnic distinctions reflected to some extent status distinctions.

The tribals who conver-ted to Christianity were able to improve their socio-economic status by having modern education and white-collar employment, hence were generally considered superior than those who adhered to their traditional pattern of social life. All these developments accentuated the role of class in patterning of social relations. What Badgaiyan observes is that "the objective reality was thus characterized by a multiplicity of social groupings based on ethnicity and class, religion and language. But the Munda consciousness visualized this diversity falling into a trichotomy: tribals, *diku* and non-tribals but *non-dikus*".

Around this time, the word *'diku'* became quite expressive signifying non-tribal exploiters such as Jagirdars, merchants and moneylenders. The character of the *dikus* has changed considera-bly after independence as the north Biharis employed in govern-ment departments are treated as *dikus* because they deprived the tribal people aspiring for white-collar jobs. In any case the word *diku* is used for the non-tribal exploiter of the tribal people. Thus, from the point of view of class, there are the classes of the exploiters and the exploited. However, both the classes are internally differentiated, hence no uniform pattern of exploitation. These outsiders also became local administrators and this too helped them in the oppression of the tribal people.

But Singh (1978) takes a different view as he observes that the most of the tribal population in India was integrated within the administration of the provinces of British India or within that of the Indian states. He calls it the mode of protective administration. The administration established *chatties* along highways to supply the army which brought in merchants, traders and peddlers and set up canton-ments and centres of administration and trade.

The colonial system ended the relative isolation of the tribal society; brought it into the mainstream of the new administrative set-up, policies and progra-mmes; but put an end to the political dominance of the tribes in the region; and roped the tribal communities which had been spared from the strain of the surplus generation by their states into a new system of production relations. Singh's observations thus do not synchronize with that of Sachchidananda and Badgaiyan.

However, Singh makes a reference, though a passing one, about the dual policy followed by the *raj* as it strengthened the feudal crust on the one hand and the forces of market cutting the very roots of tribal economy and polity on the other. All these changes were reflected in social stratification. Let us now discuss the situation in the post-independence period.

CHANGE IN SOCIETY

K.S. Singh observes that the economic and political

processes of tribal transformation get reflected in social stratification. Social stratification among tribes has always existed in various forms such as social and physical distance, notion of purity and pollution, prestige and status, habits and customs, and the like. The system of social stratification in the form of the feudatory chief Zamindars at the top, the well-to-do headmen in the middle and the general mass at the bottom has changed since independence.

A class of insider *diku* and professional tribal moneylender as a result of the anti-land alienation laws has emerged in the post-independence period. A small section of the tribes has gone up in socio-economic hierarchy, and they are engaged in land transactions and moneylending. In another context, Singh provides a four-fold classification of social movements with special reference to middle India. These movements are:

(1) movements for political auto-nomy;

(2) agrarian and forest-based movements;

(3) sanskritisation processes; and

(4) cultural movements based on script and language. All these movements could be understood as efforts on the part of tribal society to find for itself a place of honour and status at least equal to other sections of Indian society. In other words, the tribal people expressed their anger against their political and economic suppression and also desired to move up in socio-cultural hierarchy as reflected in their efforts to convert and or adopt Christianity and Hindu way of life.

There are not many studies available on social stratification among the tribes in India. The Indian State has provisions in its constitution with regard to uplift of the tribal people living in diffe-rent parts of India by reducing age-old socio-economic inequality. In the field of education, socio-economic and political awakening and employment part-successes have been achieved as a result of the policy of reservation of jobs, seats in educational institutions and earmarking of scheduled tribes' and scheduled castes' constituencies. The anticipated consequence of these provisions could be seen in new forms of socio-economic and political inequality between different tribal communities.

Sachchidananda seems to be (apparently though unintentionally) inclined towards an economic analysis of social stratification among the tribals of middle India. He writes: "Since the advent of colonial rule and the unrestricted movement of plainsmen into the tribal areas, the tribal population has been subjected to unemi-ting economic exploitation. Massive alienation of tribal lands to moneylenders and superior cultivating castes left the majority of agriculturists steeped in poverty and debt" (1990).

Such a situation, characterized by isolation, economic backwardness, lack of educa-tion, social fragmentation, and distinctive ethnic, religious and linguistic affiliations, forced upon the state to declare the tribal people as a 'scheduled' category, providing them protective discri-minatory treatment leading to their integration with the wider society in India. Sachchidananda's description of the tribal situation lacks requisite rigour as it neither makes use of the categories like class, class consciousness, class antagonism, change, relations of production and role of state, etc. nor it examines the role of ethnicity, isolation, assimilation, kinship, etc. as the main tools of his analysis.

However, studies by Rose (1981), Pathy (1984) and Shah (1979, 1986) examine the tribal situation from the class perspective about which we would make a brief reference later on.

Sachchidananda (1990) reports that the weak impact of the measures taken by the Indian State for the welfare of the scheduled tribes has resulted into the continued dominance of the new outsiders as the colonial rulers have been replaced by the indige-nous elites. The illegal transfer of land from tribals to non-tribals has become an established fact of life. Surplus land has not been distributed to the poor and deserving tribals. Even the land distributed is in fact so meagre and qualitatively so poor that it has not proved to be a viable source of livelihood. Industrialization has displaced the tribals as their lands have been taken over by the state.

A large number of outsiders have again come to the tribal areas due to industrialization further widening the gap between the tribals and the non-tribals *(dikus).* Contractors, petty businessmen and government officials have taken strong roots in tribal society though still they look to be anachronisms and unwelcome elements. Even infrastructural facilities like roads, electricity and means of communication have been made available in the tribal areas keeping in view the needs of the outsiders rather than the tribal inhabitants.

Education, employment and represen-tation in legislative bodies from village panchayat to parliament through the policy of protective discrimination have created an elite section among the tribals rather than bringing about social mobility among the tribal masses.

Sachchidananda observes that "a significant impact of politico-economic change in independent India is the accentuation of social inequalities in tribal society." Sachchidananda's argument is that most tribal societies in middle India were egalitarian. Social stratification emerged among them in the pre-colonial and colonial periods in the form of semi-feudalism and exploitation by dividing the tribal society into the upper class and the commoners.

The outside moneylenders were a third notable class which has been replaced by the inside *dikus* after independence. Social stratification is a relational and relative phenomenon, and therefore, it can be observed only in terms of relations between individuals, between individuals and groups and between groups over a period of time based on a certain value-frame.

It has been reported earlier that social stratification has always existed among the tribes of India though its value-frame has changed from time to time. Social stratification existed not only between tribals and non-tribals, but it was also found among tribes, clans and lineages based on kinship—status, age, sex, hereditary—office, possessions, etc. After independence, education, employment and political power, though these are in a certain way inter-related phenomena, have become the main bases of social stratification among the tribal people.

Since these did not exist earlier, their emergence after indepen-dence in a particular way cannot be taken as an accentuation of inequality. A small section of tribals has come directly close to the non-tribals through these new bases of social status, and some of the tribals have even gone higher than the non-tribal people based on these criteria. Other tribals have been beneficiaries at the secondary and tertiary levels.

A large number of tribals still remain unbenefited from these scarce resources like education, white-collar jobs and positions and offices of power. Class distinctions have crystallized among the tribals like the non-tribal people in terms of upper, middle and lower classes because all the people have not been benefited in equal measure, and it is hard to believe that a majority of the tribals have been harmed by the develop-ment process in the post-independence period.

The high level of socio-political awakening among the Mundas, Oraons, Santhals, Hos, Bhils, Raj Gonds, Chaudharis, etc. is self-explanatory of their betterment compared to their own past during the British period.

The most important bases of social stratification among the tribes of middle India are ethnicity and class. Despite being inter-related aspects these are not found in the same proportions of interconnections and efficacy in all tribal societies. Tribal people who have been exposed more to the influences like

Christianity, modern education, developmental programmes and industriali-zation would have more of *class* and power as the bases of status determination rather than ethnicity in the form of stratified lineages or clans. Let us have a look at these criteria in the context of the present day tribal society.

TRIBAL GROUPS

Ethnicity becomes distinctly observable if a community is viewed in terms of its independent existence rather than as an interdependent entity. The creation of scheduled areas, provisions for special measures for the development of tribal blocks, reserva-tion for representation in parliament, state legislatures and local bodies and for admissions in schools and colleges/universities and jobs have further strengthened the ethnic identities of the tribes of India.

Thus, in any given region, we may find ethnic differentiation within a given tribe in terms of the non-converts and the converts. The benefits accruing from adhering to one's own religion or from conversion to Hinduism, Christianity and Islam would determine to a large extent social status of the tribal people.

Fuchs (1977) is, however, right in his observation that most tribes are divided in two sections—a Hinduized upper section and a lower tribal section. He cites examples of the Gond (Raj Gond and Jungli Gond), Kokru (Muasi and Paharia), Bhilala (Bara Bhilala and Barela), Raj Banshi and others. Hinduized tribes have been relegated to the status of outcastes and untouchables.

Only some tribes living in Chhotanagpur have developed some degree of consciousness and they also assert themselves almost equal to the non-tribal people. Fuchs shows his serious concern about adoption of the Hindu way of life by the tribes in central India, but his silence regarding conversion to Christianity speaks volumes of his approval. Fuchs also deplores the absence of a strong tribal soli-darity among the aboriginals of central India. They do not have organizational support-base nor they are economically and socially well-placed.

Thapar and Siddiqui (1991) ask the question as to how tribal identity survived. Though they do not provide a complete answer but observe that the preservation of tribal identity was in part due to the nature of land relations. The expansion of tribal identity was to some extent watered down by the cultural legitimation of the tribal elite in terms of a wider Indian context (sanskritic courtly culture). With the emergence of a well established agricultural base and a network of trade connections not only further elaborated the system of social stratification but also weakened the exclusivity of tribal/ethnic identity. Thus, going by Thapar and Siddiqui's view, we may infer that the tribal identity was always coloured by economic differentiation and power hierarchy.

Class and ethnicity were inextricably intermixed in Chhotanagpur in the nineteenth century (Badgaiyan, 1986). In the context of the Mundas of Chhotanagpur, Badgaiyan mentions about *khutkatti* clan Mundas, *non-khutkatti* clan Mundas, non-Munda tribals and Hindu caste functionaries in the period before the emergence of kingship among them. The Munda and the Manki were not only heads of their clans and villages, respectively, but were also *khutkattidars.* Later on the *khutkatti* system was destroyed and replaced by Bhuinhari, Rajhas and Manjhihas tenures.

There were non-tribal jagirdars in large number when the Munda society was under the system of kingship. Hinduism made inroads into the tribal heartland, and it was strengthened by the recruitment of Hindu militia and administrative staff. Brahmin priests and other functionaries found a convenient place for themselves with the patronage of the king as lower level feudatories, Hindu and Muslim merchants also found opportunities for trade and barter in the region.

In the first phase, new ethnic groups entered into the Munda society as a subordinate class, the producers of surplus; but in the second phase the class that entered was the subordinate class, the appropriators of surplus. Badgaiyan observes: "Entry of this new class radically changed the production relations. In order to justify and support the new production relations new concepts of owner-ship and authority as well as new ideology came to be imposed on the Munda society and polity". "The Munda themselves became greatly differentiated on class lines". Thus a new complexity arose between class and ethnicity.

In fact, Badgaiyan also analyzes the patterns of dominance along with ethnicity and class. He refers to the subordination of all non-Munda ethnic groups in the early period followed by the subordination of the Mundas by a dominant section of the immigrant ethnic groups. The ethnic divide gets further blurred by sharing of class positions by the Mundas with the non-Mundas. There were Munda Zamindars and non-Munda Zamindars, and there were similarly Munda tenants and non-Munda tenants. Perhaps ethnicity has an edge over class because "relations between non-Munda Jagirdars and Munda tenants were reported to be far more strained and antagonistic than those obtaining between Munda jagirdars and Munda tenants". However, Badgaiyan infers a somewhat different conclusion from such a situation. He writes:

"This leads one to hypothesize that agrarian relations are more strained when class stratification is compounded with ethnic differentiation." We may make two observations here:

(i) the Munda Jagirdars had a legitimacy of their rule much before the non-Mundas encroached upon the tribal areas as jagirdars, hence they were not acceptable to the Mundas as their masters; and

(ii) the strained relations between the Munda tenants and

the non-Munda Jagirdars symbolized the non-acceptance of the alien rulers on the Munda land.

ETHNIC STRUCTURE

The ethnic structure of the Mundas became further weak due to two factors:

(i) the British takeover of Bengal in 1765 (Bihar was part of Bengal); and

(ii) Christianity. Rack-renting and ejection from Rajhas and Manjhihas land became frequent reducing the Mundas to the status of tenants and agricultural labourers. Forced labour was almost a routine activity. *Thekedars* as collectors of revenue were a new institution in the system of exploitation. Thus, with Jagirdars, *thekedars,* British administrators, money-lenders and merchants, the authority of Mundas and Mankis deteriorated further. Earlier Hinduism and later on Christianity proved to be an attack on the ethnically monolithic character of the Mundas as a community. The Birsa movement was a direct reaction to the onslaught committed on the Mundas by the British administration and Christianity.

Ethnic situation had become quite complex as the tribal groups came closer to each other and they also dealt with the non-tribal groups like the Hindus, Muslims, Sikhs, and Christians. Besides this, the Mundas had Hindu, Christian and Birsaite sections among themselves.

Badgaiyan observed that it was not that every-thing was seen in terms of ethnicity alone. Social relations were defined by both ethnicity and class. Mundas and Hindus both had Jagirdars and tenants. Ethnicity was thus not coterminous with class. Objectively, there were several groupings based on ethnicity and class, religion and language. The Mundas perceived, according to Badgaiyan, three main groups, namely, tribals, *dikus* and non-tribals but *non-dikus.* Ethnicity and class co-exist among the Mundas. Badgaiyan writes: 'In the light of the behaviour of the Munda tenants and agricultural proletariats with regard to Munda and Hindu Jagirdars, it can be said that the ethnic solidarity is diluted by class differentiation and class hostility is heightened by ethnic differentiation." Class solidarity is eroded by ethnic differentiation. Identity of both class and ethnicity has resulted in greater solidarity among the Mundas. Today the question is: Whether ethnicity represents a bundle of primordial sentiments and ties or is it an identity which is contextually manipulated?

Many a times ethnicity is articulated and twisted according to the compulsions of given situations. Badgaiyan writes: "Ethnicity is not just having a set of external attributes. It is essentially a question of subjective perception. It is this subjective perception that gives people a sense of belonging to an ethnic group." Members of one ethnic group could belong to more than one class, and members of one class could belong to more than one identity at a given point of time, and they may not be in mutual harmony.

Ethnicity in the context of wider socio-political and economic development has acquired a great deal of instrumental significance. Measures like the constitutional provisions and reservations and special schemes for development have strengthened rather than weakened the ethnic and primordial solidarities among the scheduled tribes.

It is felt by the articulate section of the tribal people that they could persist with the existing benefits and also demand more and better amenities for their development by asserting their ethnic unity and solidarity as expressly as possible. In this way 'ethnicity' among tribes and 'caste' among Hindus have become a convenient means of political mobilization. Sachchidananda (1990) does not find any real contradiction between elaboration of stratification and hardening of ethnicity. Though apparently the two seem to be antithetical to each other, but in real life they are found in specific contexts without being anta-gonistic. Diversification and development impinge upon the monolithic character of the tribal society, hence weakening of ethnic solidarity becomes a logical and natural consequence, but 'ethnici-zation' is brought in by making best possible efforts to ensure availability of maximum benefits from the processes of deve-lopment.

Expression of ethnic identity depends upon the contexts and the issues at a particular point of time. Lack of inter-tribal solidarity has always been one of the serious obstacles in achieving the most urgent common ends. Different tribes have not come together to share the same platform mainly because of the perception of exclusivity of one tribe and a sense of pride of being superior or at least not inferior compared to any other tribe. Mobilization even against the non-tribal people has suffered from such perceptions regarding inter-tribal and intra-tribal relations and notions of superiority and inferiority. However, ethnic identity has found its place in different spheres of life such as language, education, politics and culture. Students have formed from time to time associations and unions comprising *adivasis* alone.

A detailed treatment of the 'tribal question' in Chhotanagpur is provided by Weiner (1978) as a part of his study of *Sons of the Soil: Migration and Ethnic Conflict in India.* One gets the impression from Weiner's study that the main cause of the backwardness among the *adivasis* is economic as he emphasizes on the problems of land alienation, exploitation by *dikus* (earlier moneylenders and Zamindars and now white-collar workers, politicians and traders and businessmen), unemployment, etc.

This explanation is based on the perceptions of the tribals themselves about their own problems. Their perceptions about the outsiders and their impact on politics in the region have been considered by Weiner as the basis of his argument in regard to what he calls 'tribal encounters' for analyzing relationship between tribals and migrants. The economic problem forced the tribals to emigrate in large numbers to work as plantation labourers in Assam and Bengal. Ethnicity is reflected in some of the statements made by the respondents. All *dikus* were Bihari Hindus and that they (tribals) were exploited by the Bihari landlords.

The tribals lost their lands to non-tribals. Weiner observes that some well-to-do tribals who have acquired land, and some of them are themselves substantial money-lenders are not hated by the tribal folk. In fact, some tribals feel proud of their wealthy tribals, whereas they express antagonism against the wealthy non-tribals. Thus, Weiner clearly advocates an ethnicist perspective rather than a structural view for analyzing relations between tribals and non-tribals.

He writes: "given a choice, people prefer to hate others because of their religion, race, caste, or tribe, rather than because of their wealth. The wealthy in one's own community is a source of vicarious pride. The status (and accomplishment) of members of one's own community pro-vides self-esteem to all members of the community.

For this reason, it is not easy to create class cleavages and class parties in a multi-ethnic society except where class and ethnic cleavages coincide. Class antagonisms then become veiled expressions of ethnic hostility. This is probably why ideological parties of the left based upon class appeal have not done very well in India, and why peasant revolts against landlords are more likely to occur when the peasants and landlords belong to different religions or castes, or one is tribal and the other is not".

MIGRATION OF THE TRIBALS

Migration of the tribals from their native places has certainly weakened ethnic bondage because class differentiation forces to treat themselves also as unskilled workers, mechanics, clerks, teachers, rural, semi-rural and urban inhabitants etc. Some tribals have become professionals like university teachers, doctors, engineers, lawyers, social workers and politicians. Professionals from among the tribals identify themselves more with the non-tribal middle class people rather than with the rest of the tribal people. Weiner over-emphasizes the ethnic perspective undermining the role of class and power in weakening the ethnic character of the tribals on one hand and socio-political differentiation among the tribes on the other. All the queries made by Weiner refer to the ethnic question. Some of the questions are as follows:

(1) Why have the tribals remained 'backward?'
(2) Why are they looked down upon by non-tribals?
(3) Why have they not moved into skilled positions in industry, or into managerial posts?
(4) Why have they not successfully competed against the migrants who have moved into Chhotanagpur?
(5) What can be done to change the situation?

Certainly, ethnicity holds its strong ground among the tribes of India, but it is also a fact that as a result of some reforms, administrative measures and implementation of given policies, ethnicity has become visibly weak and class differentiation has surfaced significantly. Therefore, a simple formulation referring to tribals versus non-tribals or local people versus outsiders in the context of jobs and opportunities forecloses the analysis of the role of class and power in the context of social changes since independence. Without any conscious effort, class differentiation itself brings about de-tribalization among the tribes of India.

Conversions to Christianity and Islam and impact of Hinduism and other cultural forces have already shown a great deal of de-tribalization. The Christian tribals are superior to the non-converts in socio-structural terms. The Hinduized tribes consider themselves culturally superior to the non-converts as they have adopted vegetarianism and have discarded drinking of alcohol.

Despite conversion to Christianity, the ethnic dimension remains intact though in a somewhat new and changed form. Conversion to Christianity has brought about 'double allegiance' among the tribals as they are unable to forget their past and simultaneously they are made to be a part of a new world-view, namely, Christianity. This double identity, though broadens economic and socio-cultural base of the converts, but they are not able to get out of ethnic bondage in larger sense of the term. Most of the educated tribals converted to Christianity have/had their training in theology and have remained attached to one or other church. Missionary schools, colleges and other organizations have invited strong reactions in which some of these convert educated tribals are employed.

PRESTIGE IN SOCIETY

Economic and political processes, accompanied by urbanization, industrialization and political awakening, have brought about visible differentiation among tribal people on class lines. Singh (1985) observes: "The major thrust of change has been from tribes into peasants. By the end of the eighteenth century communities of peasantized tribals had emerged in Assam, Rajasthan, middle India, fete." A hierarchy of land tenures in the form of tribal chiefs and occupancy tenants emerged with the coming of the British administration. Taking over of the forests from the control of the tribals made them to work as manual workers. With the emergence of industrialization in post-indepen-dence period tribal people have also become unskilled, semi-skilled and skilled workers in industries. A class of well-off non-tribal people co-existed with the tribals in the form of moneylenders, shopkeepers and white-collar workers. These non-tribals are now expressly considered as 'outside exploiters'. Class differentiation is a double-edged phenomenon because there has been a differential impact of the factors and forces of social change due to the uneven nature of intra-tribal and inter-tribal situations. As a result of this, we can find today hunting and food-gathering tribal people on the one end of the continuum and highly educated people engaged in government jobs and other lucrative persuits on the other.

Thus, there is no uniform principle of hierarchization among the tribes of middle India. The differentiation between various tribes and between the families of a tribe in a given context indicate clearly that different segments of tribes and specific families have carved out particular 'social spaces' or placements for themselves. In many ways, they resemble with each other and also with the non-tribals though in varying degrees. Neither all tribal people have been equally involved in class and power struggles against their oppre-ssors nor have they been benefited uniformly from the positive consequences of those collective or semi-collective mobilizations. But all tribals were not oppressed or deprived of in the same manner, hence their involvement in the emancipatory efforts has also varied. Some of these points have remained unattended in most of the studies of class and power among the tribes of middle India.

Observations made by Thapar and Siddiqui (1991) seem to be quite convincing about connection between socio-cultural and politico-economic dimensions among the Mundas in ancient period. They write: "The more fundamental changes however related to rights over land. The axis shifted from clan to territory: tenurial rights based on kinship were encroached upon by those based on professional services. The Raja granted lands and villages on perpetual tenures of military, administrative and personal services— the services required by the infrastructure of a state.

The grantees were appointed to appropriate the maximum rights". Certainly, a distinction existed between the lineage lands or *bhuinhari* and the *rajhus* lands. Thapar and Siddiqui report presence of *manjhas* (grantee), *rajhus* (crown) and Kanwars, Thakurs and Lallas (who were given maintenance grants), and retainers. Thus, along with ethnic (clan, lineage) stratification, a quite elaborate class stratification existed. They write: 'Thus, the tendency towards social stratification which had already begun with the *khutkatti* system was not only intensified and accelerated under the state, but was also made more complex with the interpolation of various levels of intermediaries". Now, from lineage, economic and political functions passed into the hands of professionals outside the lineage. A new nexus emerged between social status, landholding and power, though lineage still did not become defunct. It is evident from this account that feudalism had taken over the tribal society and the classes mentioned above also existed in the princely states till India achieved her independence.

The hypothesis put forward by Thapar and Siddiqui regarding decline of ethnicity and emergence of class relations also finds substantiation in Badgaiyan's systematic historical analysis of 'class and ethnicity' among the Mundas of Chhotanagpur. Badgaiyan provides a detailed account of the simultaneous emergence of feudalism and complex class structure among the Mundas, and observes that "social relations were defined not entirely by ethnic membership. They were influenced also by the class structure.

" However, the two were not coterminous nor were they reducible to each other. Another important point in Badgaiyan's analysis is regarding what he calls "objective reality and subjective disposi-tions" particularly in the context *of dikus* (exploiters) in Chhota-nagpur. The Mundas consider all the non-tribal exploiters despite their ethnic and class differences as *dikus*. "The definition of an objective situation is subjective" (1986). The tribal exploiters today and carrier the tribal jagirdars have/had not been perceived as *dikus*. Thus, the objective reality and its subjective perception do not necessarily coincide, and therefore class and ethnicity co-exist in certain respects and cut across each other in some contexts. When class and ethnicity are perceived in consonance, there is greater solidarity among the tribal people. Leaders of various tribal movements generally strive to emphasize on such an accord between ethnicity and class.

A large number of researchers observe that in the pre-British period with the encroachment of feudalism on tribal life, the process of emergence of a new class structure set in replacing the tribal patriarchal clannish system rooted into the *khutkatti* system of land tenure. Thus, feudal classes such as Raja, Jagirdars, grantees, *bhuinhars,* retainers, tenants on the one hand, and priests, mer-chants, moneylenders and masses emerged on the other. Such a change affected significantly the tribal polity too. Sachchidananda (1990) observes that the political authority of the head of the *parha* (confederation of villages) disappeared, and many Mundas migrated to other parts of tribal Bihar where they could retain their traditional institutions.

In Madhya Pradesh and Orissa too, individual ownership of land had become a fact of life. The British used some traditional/hereditary village officers for collecting revenue by granting them powers of a police force. In Bihar, *munda, manki* and *majhi* thus became once again powerful under the British patronage. But the market forces further more rapidly accentuated in the British period along with new administrative system. Land alienation, moneylenders' usurious practices, hetero-geneity brought in by the influx of non-tribal communities and new categories of people like traders, contractors and petite administrative officials not only proved a serious blow to the pre-colonial tribal system, but also accentuated two-pronged class-based stratification between the tribals and the non-tribals and among the tribals. Now one could easily find among the tribals proprietary tenants, tenants-at-will, share-croppers and landless agricultural and manual workers. The classes other than these were formed by the non-tribals to a large extent. These included government employees and officers, professionals like doctors, lawyers and professors and merchants and traders. The post-independence period has witnessed strengthening of this class structure, and side by side some new communities and social categories too have acquired an access to some scarce and much desired positions and offices. The new political system has certainly created a class of tribal power elite. This new class is largely a transformation of the class of educated tribals of pre-independence period who were engaged in various reform and other movements and also employed as professionals and administrative workers.

Socially and culturally, the tribals have not assimilated to a considerable extent with the non-tribals. Conversions and adop-tions of other religions and practices have created somewhat limited cleavages among the tribals rather than restructuring the tribal society. But this is not true in the same way about economic and political relations among the tribals and of the tribals with the non-tribals. Class structure and relations among the tribals resemble with the non-tribals, and so are power relations. The hiatus between the socio-cultural and politico-economic structures and relations could be attributed to the differential impact of macro-structural forces and factors which was perhaps intended by the colonial rulers and it is persisting even today because of the policies pursued by the Indian State since independence. Ethnicity has thus remained a force to reckon with for mobilizing the *adivasis* against the atrocious class structure which was superimposed upon them by the pre-colonial and the colonial rulers and continues to be there to a great extent even after independence.

STUDIES IN SOCIAL STRATIFICATION

Some recent studies of social stratification among tribal people highlight on class hierarchy and its socio-cultural consequences. A study of the Chaudhari tribe in Surat district of Gujarat by Shah (1979) shows the presence of four economic strata on the basis of occupation and ownership of land. These strata are:

(i) agri-cultural labourers and poor cultivators;

(ii) middle cultivators;

(iii) rich cultivators; and

(iv) white-collar employees. The first three constitute more than 92 per cent of the total working population of the Chaudharis, while in the fourth category there are less than 3 per cent people. Shah (1991) writes: "Labourers and poor cultivators are at the bottom of the occupational hierarchy. It is the single largest stratum, constituting 61 per cent of cultivators, of which 24 per cent are almost landless and 37 per cent have land between one and five acres. Their main source of livelihood is manual labour." Shah provides other details about economic life of this largest segment of the Chaudharis of Gujarat. Of the middle cultivators 33 per cent own land between five and 15 acres. These are a better off section as 20 per cent of them have wells for irrigation and half of them have diesel or electric pumps. They use chemical fertilizers, and about 70 per cent of them have a pair of bullocks. Rich cultivators are about 5 per cent and own more than 16 acres of land. They are better off than the middle and poor cultivators. They have electric or diesel pumpsets, use chemical fertilizers, hire wage labourers, produce for market, and their women-folk and children are educated and do not do manual work even on their own farms. All these three classes are related to agriculture though unevenly and enjoy different social statuses. The white-collar workers who are about 3 per cent of the popu-lation are engaged in non-agricultural

> white-collar jobs, particularly in lower level school teaching. Besides teachers, there are also clerks, postmen, *talatis, gram sevaks,* extension officers, etc. Some are employed in co-operative societies in various capacities. "Middle and rich cultivators dominate the stratum of educated white-collar employees."

In another study of stratification among the scheduled tribes in the Bharuch and Panch Mahals districts of Gujarat, Shah (1986) observes that status distinction based on achievement in such respects as wealth, property, income, occupation, education and power is emerging, and it is similar considerably with the pattern in the wider Indian society. Status determination based on ethnicity is being slowly replaced by the new criteria such as wealth, income, occupation, education and power. Economic and educational aspects and style of life are today the bases of newly emerging stratification. Differences in these aspects between the tribals and the non-tribals and within the tribals would provide an objective assessment of social stratification.

The categories and groups in these two districts are more or less the same as Shah has found in Surat district. Different tribes are divided on the basis of interests. Besides land as the principal basis, there are differences of status based on education and life-style. Stratification is reflected in almost all aspects of social life of the tribal people. Contradictory changes have also been noted. Some have become quite rich and better-off, and others have slided down in class hierarchy. However, change in social stratification has not been uniform in Bharuch and Panch Mahals districts. Shah observes as follows: "There is sharper stratification in Bharuch than in Panch Mahals. The number of landless labourers is larger in the former area than in the latter district. The rich and the middle peasants of Bharuch purchased more land than their counterparts in Panch Mahals. So is the case with government benefits. The differences in life-style between the rich and the middle peasants on the one hand, and the poor peasants and the labourers on the other, are more widespread and sharper in Bharuch. These differences are perhaps because of uneven development in the two districts. Because the one which is more developed grows faster and develops sharper stratification, inequality increases and becomes sharp with development."

From both these studies of three districts of Gujarat, namely, Surat, Bharuch and Panch Mahals, Shah concludes that there is nothing like an all-India tribal culture and world-view. Tribals are also not isolated from the non-tribal people. It is a fact that they have become highly differentiated, socially and economically, and in certain respects the persisting socio-economic distinctions between them and the non-tribals have also accentuated mainly due to uneven consequences of lopsided development policies and their faulty execution. Despite this the tribal people are being 'integrated' with the wider society though not in a uniform manner.

The better off tribals, namely, the middle class Chaudharis of Surat, have developed a certain commonness, cutting across tribal boundaries, with their counterparts of other tribes, in social and cultural matters and in life-styles. In fact, middle and rich cultivators as well as the middle class (white-collar workers) do not have a clash of interests, hence commonalty of attitudes and aspirations for further betterment of their status.

Bose (1981) also identifies four main classes among tribes in Gujarat, though mainly based on landholdings. These are: rich peasants, middle peasants, poor peasants, and agricultural labou-rers, and these have also been found by several researchers among the non-tribals as well. A given tribe is generally distributed among all the four classes. However, all the tribes are not the same as some are better off than others, and accordingly the proportions of different classes would also be different. Bose reports that the tribes in Gujarat today are equally affected by the processes of planned and unplanned change and by the continuous structural and institutional shifts in rural India. He writes: "They are stratified in terms of control over resources," hence the above mentioned four classes. This class hierarchy is reflected in all aspects of tribal life including education and political power. But Bose does not highlight the emerging patterns of social mobility among tribals brought about by developmental programmes and education as we find it in the two studies of three districts of Gujarat by Shah. Pathy's study (1984) of five tribal villages in Gujarat is similar in terms of its framework and methodology.

The five economic categories in Pathy's study are: landlords, rich peasants, middle peasants, small peasants and farm workers. The distribution and characteristic features of these classes are the same as we find in the study conducted by Shah and Bose. It seems that in a broad sense, the studies of class stratification among the tribes of Gujarat reinforce each other. While referring to an earlier study by Pathy, *Political Economy of Kandhaland in Orissa,* Shah (1986) observes that "there is a case for closer examination in the tribal commu-nities." Further, Shah finds that the rich have become richer, and the poor poorer, because of 'free competition' among the unequal competitors.

Roy Burman (1989) emphasizes on both class and ethnicity perspectives, but he does not spell out the nexus between class and ethnicity and status and class. The notion of status is inherently present in the ethnic identity and kinship system of the tribal society. In a recently published (edited) volume, Bhadra and Mondal (1991) also emphasize the role of class and ethnicity as the main bases of social stratification in North-east India. There are tribes like Meenas of Rajasthan which have hardly any tribal features in terms of ethnicity and class, and yet they are scheduled as tribes. The Tharus of Bihar have all the prerequisites for being scheduled as a tribe, but they are not scheduled as such.

Singh though admits the emergence of social stratification as a historical reality created by the colonial administration and the processes of sanskritisation and conversion to Christianity, but observes that "there are also contrary pulls in the opposition direction. The bonds of ethnicity and the appreciation of the political advantages of the tribe as an ethnic minority are still strong" (1985). This view is also shared by Sachchidananda. He writes while commenting on the class approach of Pathy:

"These economic categories may be considered classes only in a limited sense; ethnic consciousness dominates over class consciousness. Similarly, production relations cannot be clearly characterized as feudal or capitalist. Primordial forms of slavery, revolving indebtedness of small peasants and agricultural labourers for consumption loans, the lack of a free labour market, forced labour, labour exchange, institutional credit and some commodity production confuse the total picture" (1990).

But the question is: Do these four or five classes not exist among the tribes of Gujarat, Bihar or Rajasthan? Are they simply 'constructions' and not identifiable groups of people? Kulkarni (1979) observes that the question of class in the tribal society is more pervasive than the caste- tribal approach. Class interests do not obey caste or tribal boundaries (Sengupta, 1980). Land alienation is a class question. The demand for the formation of Jharkhand State is a class question. The 'tribal question', the 'forest-question' are all questions of 'class interests'. The forest policy in India in its present form serves the capitalists rather than the poor (Guha, 1983). 'Tribal unrest' is a class question. Both positive and negative consequences of the role performed by law and the state refer to the question of class in terms of gainers and loosers, more gainers and less gainers, more loosers and less loosers and so on. Thus, there are three viewpoints regarding ethnicity and class as the bases of social stratification:

(i) mainly ethnicity,
(ii) mainly class, and
(iii) both class and ethnicity.

Social stratification among the tribes of India is different com-pared to the non-tribes to the extent the tribal people are dissimilar in terms of their history, level of economic development and impact of modern forces of social change. Several studies of social stratifi-cation bring out the convergence of ethnicity and class as the main basis of status distinctions within and between different tribes. However, emphasis on ethnicity and class as exclusive bases of social stratification remains central to some scholars who look at the tribal social stratification either in terms of ethnic reality or as an economic phenomenon—*a* part of global class formation.

The *raj* created new structures and institutions and thereby provided a new system of social stratification. Landlords, contractors and money-lenders were alien to the tribal society before the advent of the British. Differentiation of the peasantry in terms of tenure-holders, tenants-at-will and jagirdars was also created by the British. A class of outside exploiters in terms of Zamindars and moneylenders was not known to the tribals till the British took over the forests.

Since Independence ethnicity is being viewed in a changed form as a means of mobilizing the tribal people with a view to have access to economic and political opportunities. Inter-tribal and tribal-non-tribal distinctions on the one hand and processes of conversion and initiation on the other are being highlighted by the tribals as the basis for demanding special treatment by the government.

However, the tribals are not an exclusive component in India's fast changing social situation. A new middle class is emerging among them like the one we find among the non-tribals. Ethnicity is on decline on the one hand, and it is being revived in myraid ways on the other. De-tribalization and ethnicization co-exist today both as a reality and as a strategy for change. Unifor-mity is not found in regard to convergence between ethnicity and class. Processes of socio-cultural and structural transformation are also not uniform in different parts of India.

At the same time, now the 'forest question' and the 'tribal question' are being considered more as class questions. The phenomenon of power and domi-nance is increasingly dependent upon the questions of ethnicity and class.

8

MINORITY COMMUNITIES

TERMS OF MINORITIES

The term "minority" has not been defined in the Constitution or in any other enactment or in the Government Resolution under which the Minorities Commission was established. However, the Commission has been treating Muslims, Christians, Sikhs, Buddhists and Zoroastrians as religious minorities at the national level because -their numerical strengths as compared with rests of Indian citizens-is smaller and as such they are entitled to any protections that may be designed for religious minorities. According to the 1981 census, the religious (minority) communities constitute about 16.46% of the population of India (excluding Assam) comprising 11.35% Muslims, 2.43% Christians, 1.96% Sikhs, 0.71 Buddhists and 0.01% Zoroastrians (Parsees).

The picture of the population by religions at the national level is different from-that at the State levels. At the national level Hindus are the dominant majority but at the State level they are hot in a few States and Union Territories. The Muslims are in majority in Jammu & Kashmir State and Lakshadweep, whereas Christians are in majority in the States of Meghalaya; Nagaland and Mizoram, Sikhs in the State of Punjab and the followers of other than Hinduism, Islam, Christianity, Sikhism, Buddhists, Jainism and Zoroastrianism are in majority in the state of Arunachal Pradesh.

The linguistic minorities are those who have separate spoken language without necessarily having a distinct script and which constitute numerically smaller sections of the people in a State. In other words, linguistic minorities are determined on a State wise basis. Majority of the population speak 15 major languages mentioned in the Eighth Schedule of the constitution *viz.* Assamees (speaks 0.7%), Bengali (3%), Gujarati (4.7%), Hindi (38.4%), Kannada (3.9%), Kashmiri (0.4%), Malayalam (4%), Marathi (7.6%), Oriya (3.6%), Punjabi (2.5%). Sanskrit (.00004%), Sindhi (0.3%), Tamil (6.9%), Telugu (8.1%), Urdu (5.2%), and other languages (4.60%).

Ours is a multi-religious, multilingual and multi-cultural society. Secularism is the bedrock of our nationhood. Uniquely among world civilisations, ours has combined antiquity and continuity with a heterogeneity. Our diversity is not a weakness but the basic source of our strength as a nation. We have built our nationhood on the values of tolerance and self-confident synthesis, of openness to the best in all cultures without losing our distinctive identity, of coexistence among different ways of life and the cross-fertilisation of ideas, Ours is a tradition of "sarva dharma sambhaava," equal respect for all religions, and full freedom for all religions to be practised and propagated. `Safeguards for the protection of the minorities and provision for their welfare were provided in the constitution, and necessary measures initiated in pursuance thereof.

National Integration Council was constituted by Pt. Jawaharlal Nehru in 1961; Prime Minister's 15-Point Programme for the upliftment of the minorities was devised by Mrs. Indira

Gandhi and the Minorities Commission was constituted by her in 1978. All these institutions and various programmes and schemes being implemented for the welfare of minorities are discussed in detail below:

PROVISION IN THE CONSTITUTION

The Constitution is replete with provisions for the welfare of the minorities. Specific articles in this respect are the following:

Prohibition of Discrimination on Grounds of Religion Race, Caste, Sex or Place of Birth:

(i) The state shall not discriminate against any citizen on grounds only of religion, race, caste, sex, place of birth or any of them;

(ii) No citizen shall, on grounds only of religion, race, caste, sex, place of birth or any of them, be subject to any disability, liability, restriction or condition with regard to

(a) access to shops, public restaurants, hotels and place of public entertainment; or

(b) the use of wells, tanks, bathing ghats, roads and places of public resort maintained wholly or partly out of State funds or dedicated to the use of the general public;

(iii) Nothing in this article shall prevent the State from making any special provision for women and children;

(iv) Nothing in this article or in clause (2) of Article 29 shall prevent the State from making any-special provision for the advancement of any socially and educationally backward classes of citizens or for the Scheduled castes and Scheduled tribes.

Equality of Opportunity in Matters of Public Employment:

(i) There shall be equality of opportunity for all citizens

in matters relating to employment or appointment to any office under the state;

(ii) No citizen shall, on grounds only of religion, race, caste, sex, descent, place of birth, residence or any of them, be ineligible for, or discriminated against in respect of any employment or office under the State;

(iii) Nothing in this Article shall prevent Parliament from making any law prescribing in regard to a class or classes of employment or appointment to an office under the Government of or any local or other authority within a State or Union territory, any requirement as to residence within the State or Union territory prior to such employment or appointment;

(iv) Nothing in this Article shall prevent the State from making any provision for the reservation of appointments or posts in favour of any backward class of citizens which in the opinion of the State is not adequately represented in the services under the State;

(v) Nothing in this Article shall affect the operation of any law which provides that the incumbent of an office in connection with the affairs of any religious or denominational institution or any member of the governing body thereof shall be a person professing a particular religion or belonging to a particular denomination.

Freedom of Conscience and Free Profession, Practice and Propagation of Religion:

(i) Subject to public order, morality and health, all persons are equally entitled to freedom of conscience and the right freely to profess, practise and propagate religion:

(ii) Nothing in this article shall affect the operation of any existing law or prevent the State from making any law;

(a) regulating or restricting any economic, financial,

political or other secular activity which may be associated with religious practice;

(b) providing for social welfare and reform or the throwing open of Hindu religious institutions of a public character to all classes and sections of Hindus.

Explanation —The wearing and carrying of kirpans shall be deemed to be included in the profession of the Sikh religion.

Explanation ii—In sub-clause (b) of Clause (2) the reference to Hindus shall be construed as including a reference to persons professing the Sikh, Jain, or Buddhist religion, and the reference to Hindu religious institutions shall be construed accordingly.

Freedom to Manage Religious Affairs: Subject to public order, morality and health, every religious denomination or any section thereof shall have the right:

(a) to establish and maintain institutions for religious and charitable purposes;

(b) to manage its own affairs in matters of religion;

(c) to own and acquire movable and immovable property; and

(d) to administer such property in accordance with law.

Freedom as to Payment of Taxes for Promotion of any Particular Religion: No person shall be compelled to pay any taxes, the proceeds of which are specifically appropriated in payment of expenses for the promotion or maintenance of any particular religion or religious denomination.

Freedom as to Attendance at Religious Instruction or Religious Worship in Certain Educational Institutions:

(i) No religious instructions shall be provided in any educational institutions wholly maintained out of State funds;

(ii) Nothing in clause (1) shall apply to an educational

institution which is administered by the State but has been established under any endowment or trust which requires that religious instruction shall be imparted in such institutions;

(iii) No person attending any educational institution recognised by the State or receiving aid out of State funds shall be required to take part in any religious instruction that may be imparted in such institutions or to attend any religious worship that may be conducted in such institution or any premises attached thereto unless such person or, if such person is a minor, his guardian has given his consent thereto.

Protection of Interests of Minorities:

(i) Any section of the citizens residing in the territory of India or any part thereof having a distinct language, script or culture of its own shall have the right to conserve the same;

(ii) No citizen shall be denied admission into any educational institution maintained by the state or receiving aid out of state funds on grounds only of religion, race, caste, language or any of them.

Right of Minorities to Establish and Administer Educational Institutions:

(i) All minorities, whether based on religion or language, shall have the right to establish and administer educational institutions of their choice;

(ii) In making any law providing for the compulsory acquisition of any property of an educational institution established and administered by a minority, referred to in clause (i), the State shall ensure that the amount fixed by or determined under such law for the acquisition of such as would not restrict or abrogate the right guaranteed under that clause;

(iii) The State shall not, in granting aid to educational

institutions, discriminate against any educational institution on the ground that it is under the management of a minority, whether based on religion or language.

Special Provision Relating to Language Spoken by a Section of the Population of a State: On a demand being made in that behalf the President may, if he is satisfied that a substantial proportion of the population of State desire the use of any language spoken by them to be recognised by that State, direct that such language shall also be officially recognised throughout that State or any part there of for such purpose as he may specify.

Language to be used in Representations for Redress of Grievances : Every person shall be entitled to submit a representation for the redress of any grievance to any officer or authority of the Union or a State in any of the language used in the Union or in the State, as the case may be.

Facilities for Instruction in Mother-tongue at Primary Stage: It shall be the endeavour of every State and of every local authority within the State to provide adequate facilities for instruction in the mother-tongue at the primary stage of education to children belonging to linguistic minority groups; and the President may issue such directions to any State as he considers necessary or proper for securing the provision of such facilities.

Special Officer for Linguistic Minorities:

(i), There shall be a Special Officer for linguistic minorities to be appointed by the President;

(ii) It shall be the duty of the special officer to investigate all matters relating to the safeguards provided for linguistic minorities under this Constitution and report to the President upon those matters at such intervals as the President may direct, and the President shall cause all such reports to be laid before each House of

Parliament, and sent to the Governments of the States concerned.

These constitutional provisions constitute "magnacarta" or "Charter of Rights" for the religious and linguistic minorities. They are intended for the well-being and all round development of the minority communities. The government at the Centre, State and Local levels are to comply with them in letter and spirit. Any law made by them in contravention of these provisions can be challenged in the course of law and declared ultravires of the constitution. The aggrieved minority individuals and organisations have approached the Supreme Court and High Courts whenever any Act against their interest has been passed by the legislature and injustice done to them has been undone by the judiciary. The government has constituted the Minorities Commission who inter-alia ensures that the Constitutional provisions and the laws made by the governments for the welfare of the minority are properly implemented. The government takes necessary action on the findings of the Minorities Commission.

MINORITY COMMISSION

The Minorities Commission was set up by the Government of India, Resolution in 1978. Resolution provides that the Commission shall consist of a Chairman and two other Members. However, subsequently its strength was increased from three to five. The Commission now consists of the Chairman and four Members. The Resolution also provides that the Officer appointed as Special Officer in terms of Article 350-B of the Constitution will function as the Secretary of the Commission but has not been given effect to as the proposed Constitutional amendment to confer statutory status on the Commission and to merge the duties of the Special Officer for Linguistic Minorities in India with those of the Commission, under a Constitutional provision, have not yet materialised. Consequently, the Commission has been looking into specific grievances of the linguistic minorities quite apart provisions of Article 350-B of the Constitution.

Functions: The Commission was established out of concern for secular traditions and to promote national integration. Effective enforcement and implementation of safeguards provided for religious and linguistic minorities in the Constitution, in Central and State laws and in Governmental policies and administrative schemes, enunciated from time to time were intended so that feelings of inequality and discrimination prevalent amongst minorities, whether based on religion or language, are removed. To carry out these objects, the Commission was entrusted with the following functions:

(i) to evaluate the working of the various safeguards provided in the constitution for the protection of minorities and in laws passed by the Union and State Governments;

(ii) to make recommendations with a view to ensuring effective implementation and enforcement of all the safeguards and the laws;

(iii) to undertake a review of the implementation of the policies pursued by the Union and State Government with respect to minorities;

(iv) to look into specific complaints regarding deprivation of rights and safeguards of minorities;

(v) to conduct studies, research and analyses on the question of avoidance of discrimination against minorities;

(vi) to suggest appropriate legal and welfare measures in respect of any minorities to be undertaken by the Central or the State Governments;

(vii) to serve as a national clearing house for information in respect of the conditions of minorities; and

(viii) to make periodical reports at prescribed intervals to the Government.

The Commission considers various complaints received by it from aggrieved individuals and associations of minority communities or which come to its notice through any other source. It also gives hearings to individually or collectively visit various States to investigate important general and specific issues relating to minorities. The Commission also entrusts studies on identified subjects to persons having expertise in the matter. It also gives detailed opinions on matters referred to it.

The Commission has been considering various grievances of minorities and making recommendations for appropriate action to redress them. For example, the Commission looked into the grievances of Muslims regarding demolition of Muslim graveyards in Mirzauddin area, Delhi for the construction of a fly-over, creation of the post of Urdu Officer in Delhi Administration for development of Urdu, problems of Urdu medium schools in Delhi, conversion of Harijan to Islam in Meenakshipuram, Tiruniveli, Tamil Nadu etc; investigating into the grievances of Sikhs regarding the status of Punjabi language in the Union Territory of Delhi, threatened eviction of Punjabi settlers in Terai region of Uttar Pradesh, permanent settlement rights of ex-serviceman of Indian Army in districts Kurukshetra, Karnal, Haryana.

The Commission had also considered the issue of "Khalistan" raised by some members of the Sikh Community in August, 1981. It had felt that the grievances of Sikhs if any, should be examined with a view to finding constructive solutions for them. Gyani Sujan Singh accompanied by the Secretary of the Council had visited Punjab to assess the feelings of the Sikhs in general about their grievances and the Khalistan issue in particular. In the meantime, the Government had decided to study the demands and grievances of the Sikh community and opened a dialogue with leaders of the Sikh community and others. The Commission decided that before taking any further action in the matter, it may be ascertained from the Home Ministry whether it would like the Minorities Commission to go ahead with the study of the grievances with a view to suggesting constructive solutions for them. The Ministry of Home Affairs informed the Commission that since the grievances of the Sikhs already being considered by the government, it was not necessary for the Commission to take up the matter. The Commission had therefore not taken any further action in the matter.

Similarly, the Commission had gone into the complaints of alleged atrocities against Buddhists in Hupari district Kolahpur, and the request of the Trustees of Parsis Panchayat Fund and properties for exemption of their properties from the operation of Bombay Rent Act.

The Commission has been receiving representations from various religious minorities that they have been under represented in the State and Central Services and that they have also been excluded from the benefits of higher technical education in Engineering, Medical, and other disciplines, causing strong resentment and frustration among the minorities. In fact, this is one of the main grievances of minorities in general and of Muslims in particular.

The Commission noted that an inter—Ministerial Committee had already made certain recommendations with regard to sponsoring of candidates belonging to the minorities for Government employment by the Employment Exchanges. The Commission is ascertaining the action taken by the Ministry of Labour on the various recommendations made in this regard. However, it was felt that, for a more purposeful consideration of the matter, it would be necessary to make a detailed study of the problem with a view to evolve measures to ensure adequate representation of the minorities in Government employment in general and for the provision of educational and professional training facilities to the deserving candidates of minority communities. A change in the recruitment policy is urgently called for so that, other things being equal, preference may be given to candidates from minority communities to make up for the backlog whatever may be the reasons for an increasing drop in the proportion of members of minority communities in Government services so that this situation could be remedied; In the selection bodies, too, there should be adequate representation of minorities.

In addition to the Annual Report, the Commission has been submitting separate reports on various subjects such as dispute over Jama Masjid at Sidhpur, District Mehsana, Gujarat; its opinion on Mandal Commission Report; Religious Freedom as adopted to conditions in India; Demands from a section of the Parsis for exclusion of the Parsi community from the purview of the adoption of children Bill, 1970, grievances of St. John's Medical college, Bangalore, proposed amendments to the Central Wakf Act of 1954, matters connected with National Integration etc. .

Annual Reports: The Commission had submitted ten Annual Reports during the Congress (l) rule. The Tenth Report for the period April 1, 1987 to March 31,1988 was submitted to Dr. (Smt.) Rajendra Kumari Bajpai, Minister of State for Welfare on March 30,1989 containing various activities of the Commission, studies undertaken by it arid action taken on representations received by it as well as review of the implementation of 15-Point programme and other schemes for the welfare of minorities and suitable recommendations to the Government.

It is regrettable that out of the ten reports presented to the government only four reports were laid in Parliament. That reflects the casual concern of the Congress governments at the centre towards the problems facing the minorities. The 11th report of the Commission was presented to the Government on January 31,1990 and it was proposed to place four reports in Parliament during the Budget session 1990.

As an evidence of its concern for the welfare of minorities, the National Front Government has set up a Cabinet committee, under the Chairmanship of former Prime Minister V.P. Singh to give a new thrust to the 15- Point programme for the welfare of the "Minorities and to ensure its effective implementation. The Committee at its first meeting on January 12, 1990 had decided to have a concrete programme of action comprising specific projects covering various aspects of the 15-point programme. The projects were to be taken up by different Ministries in 41 minority concentration districts.

It had also taken a number of other decisions, including better representation of the minorities in services especially in the police and creation of composite police battalions consisting of members of minority and majority communities in the States for law and order duty;

(i) Special courts would be set up exclusively to try communal offences in places where large scale riots break out. While special courts in Delhi and Meerut had already been constituted, a court at Bhagalpur in Bihar is being set up shortly and the progress in the disposal of cases would be closely monitored;

(ii) The amount of ex-gratia relief granted for cases of death or permanent incapacitation fixed at Rs 20,000 per case is being revised upwards to Rs 50,000 for every case;

(iii) A pension of Rs 500 per month would also be given to widows and riot victims with low income. These would become effective for case occurring from April 1990 onwards; and

(iv) A special programme for the rehabilitation of weavers, most of whom belonged to minorities and who have been affected by Communal riots in Bhagalpur and Meerut was being taken up.

LINGUISTIC MINORITIES' COMMISSION

Article 350 B of the Constitution provided for the office of the Special Officer for Linguistic Minorities (CLM) designated as Commissioner for Linguistic Minorities in pursuance of the recommendations of States Reorganisation Commission. Accordingly it was created in July 1957. At present the CLM Organisation consists of the Headquarters Office at Allahabad and the three Regional Offices at Calcutta, Madras and Belgaum. The post of the Commissioner for Linguistic Minorities has not been filled since the last incumbent left it in May 1977. The Deputy Commissioner for Linguistic Minorities is overall administrative incharge of the Headquarters office and the Regional Offices.

The office of the Commissioner for Linguistic Minorities investigates all matters relating to safeguards provided for linguistic minorities under the constitution as also those agreed to at the national level. It also looks into the representations and complaints received from various institutions, bodies and individuals belonging to linguistic Minorities for redressal of their grievances. It submits its reports annually to the Government. So far it has submitted 27 reports out of which 26 have been laid before the Parliament.

Irregularities : The Deputy Commissioner for Linguistic Minorities also acts as the Deputy Secretary of the Minorities Commission. He is not responsible for his work in the former capacity to the Minorities Commission and reports directly to the President. This position is very anomalous, and needs to be rectified either by filling up the post of Commissioner for Linguistic Minorities or by transferring his functions to the Minorities Commission itself and merging his duties with those of the Minorities Commission as already suggested to the Government by the Commission.

This will bring the position in consonance with the Government Resolution creating the Commission making the whole Commission responsible to look after the interests of both religious and linguistic minorities. The amalgamation of the two institutions as envisaged above will also result in economy and efficiency as it would enable investigations into the conditions of religious and linguistic minorities simultaneously.

Structural and Administrative Format of the Commission : The Commission suffers from certain weaknesses and shortcomings in its organisation and administrative set up and therefore is unable to discharge its functions to achieve its laudable objectives in an efficient and effective manner:

(i) It has not been granted constitutional status so far. The constitutional (Forty sixth) Amendment Bill, 1978 was introduced in the Parliament to this effect but had failed to be carried through due to lack of prescribed quorum during the budget session of 1979. Since then, no fresh constitution amendment bill has been introduced on this subject. Lack of constitutional status to the Commission has hampered its working. The Government should therefore take necessary steps in the matter without any further delay.

(ii) The Commission does not enjoy any statutory investigative powers. The government is under the impression that not only would all government agencies reasonably and effectively but all other management bodies or private citizens whose help is often indispensable, will voluntarily come forward to give information whenever required by the Commission. But it has not happened. The commission therefore needs to be equipped with adequate powers of enquiry under the Commission of Enquiry Act, 1952.

(iii) The post of the Commissioner of Linguistic Minorities should be filled up or his powers transferred constitutionally to the Minorities Commission for removing the existing anomaly and fulfilling the obligations of the two institutions.

(iv) Some of the State governments have appointed State

Minorities Commission/Committee/Cell to look into the problems of religious and linguistic minorities in their respective jurisdiction. It is desirable that every state should have an institution to look into specific grievances of the members of minority communities. Arrangements for coordination of activities of state commissions or Panels with those of the Central Minorities Commission are also imperative,

(v) The restructuring of the Secretariat of the Commission is desired by the establishment of Research and Studies Division, Legal Division, Information and Publications Division, and Establishment of Regional Offices.

(vi) The administrative infrastructure available to the Commission for the discharge of its functions is quite unequal to its task both quantitatively and qualitatively. Staffed as it is at present, it has been able to do precious little to carry out its numerous functions assigned to it in its terms of reference. The staffing pattern therefore needs to be reviewed and the Commission requirement for adequately qualified staff of its choice to be met with.

(vii) References made to state/central government by the Commission are not attended to promptly and the reports received from them are found to be routine, sometimes perfunctory and sketchy. Some cases remain pending for years together. The instructions issued by the Ministry of Home Affairs to the Chief Secretaries/ U.T. Administrations seem to be of little avail. This not only delays redressal of grievances but also lowers the image of the Commission.

Minorities Commissions/Boards on State Level : State Minorities Commissions/Boards exist in some states also. These are Andhra Pradesh Minorities Commission, Assam Minorities Development Board, Bihar Religious and Linguistic Minorities Commission, Gujarat Minorities Board, Madhya Pradesh

Minorities Commission and Uttar Pradesh Minorities Commission. Other state government has also been requested to set up minority Commission/Boards.

In addition, separate Development/Financial Corporations have also been set up for the economic upliftment of minorities. These are Andhra Pradesh State Minorities Financial Corporation, Assam Minorities Development Corporation, Bihar State Minorities Financial Corporation, Karnataka Minorities Development Corporation, U.P. Minorities Financial Development Corporation. In Tamil Nadu, the Backward Classes Economic Development Corporation provides assistance to the minorities as a special case, while in Haryana, the Mewat Development Board has been set up for the welfare of the Muslim community inhabiting this area.

An annual conference of the Chairman and members of the Central and State Minorities Commission/Boards which is also attended by the representatives of the State Minorities Development/Finance Corporations, the representatives of the concerned Ministries of the Government of India and Reserve Bank of India is held to discuss the problems of the minorities. At the conference held in 1988, the Chairman of the Central Minorities Commission had highlighted the fact "that even amongst the religious and linguistic minorities there were some sections which could be regarded as the poorest of the poor.

To them, economic development seemed distant, social equality a dream, education advancement an illusion and alienation a constant fear. It was decided at the conference inter-alia that the Central and a State Minorities Commission should be vested with statutory powers of investigation as contained in Section 5 of the Commission of Enquiry Act, socio-economic survey of minorities be conducted by the State Minorities Commission with the assistance of the state governments as was done by Andhra Pradesh State Minorities Commission, the Planning Commission be requested to set up a working group on the welfare of minorities, and to prepare a separate component plan for the welfare of minorities as is being done for the Scheduled castes/tribes, and State Minorities Commission should be involved in the review of the implementation of 15-Point Programme at the State level and also at the District level etc.

Prime Minister's Fifteen Point Programme : The 15-Point Programme for the welfare of the minorities was formulated by Late Prime Minister Smt. Indira Gandhi as a result of the deliberations of the National Integration Council. It is intended to ensure fuller participation of the minorities in all aspects of national life. These points are:

Communal Harmony

(1) The State governments are advised that in the areas which have been identified as communally sensitive and riot prone, District and Police Officials of the highest known efficiency, impartiality and secular record must be posted. In such areas and even elsewhere, the prevention of communal tension should be one of the primary duties of DM and SP. Their performances in this regard should be an important factor in determining their promotion prospects.

(2) Good work done in this regard by District and Police officials should be rewarded.

(3) Severe action should be taken against all those who incite communal tensions or take part in violence.

(4) Special Court or Courts specifically earmarked to try communal offences should be set up so that offenders are brought to book speedily.

(5) Victims of communal riots should be given immediate rehabilitation prompt and adequate financial assistance for their rehabilitation.

(6) Radio and TV must also help in restoring confidence, communal harmony and peace in such affected areas.

(7) It is unfortunate that certain sections of the press some times indulge in tendentious reporting and publication of objectionable and inflammatory material which may incite communal tension. It is hoped that editors, printers, publishers and other concerned wilt cooperate in finding a way to avoid publication of such material.

Recruitment in Services

(8) In the recruitment of police personnel, state government should be advised to give special consideration to minorities. For this purpose, the composition of Selection Committees should be representative.

(9) The Central Government should take similar action in the recruitment of personnel to the Central Police Forces.

(10) Large scale employment opportunities are provided by the Railways, Nationalised banks and Public sector Enterprises. In these cases also the concerned departments should ensure that special consideration is given to recruitment from minority communities.

(11) In many areas recruitment is done through competitive examinations. Often minority groups have been handicapped in taking advantage of the educational system to compete on equal terms in such examinations. To help them to overcome these handicaps, steps should be taken to encourage the starting of coaching classes in minority educational institutions to train persons to compete successfully in these examinations.

(12) The acquisition of technical skills by those minorities who are today lagging behind would also help in national development. Arrangements should be made to set up ITIs and Polytechnics by Government or

private agencies in predominantly minority areas to encourage admission in such institutions of adequate number of persons belonging to these communities.

Other Important Measures

(13) In various development programmes, including the 20 Point Programme, care should be taken to see that minorities secure a fair and adequate measure the benefits flowing there from. In the various committees which are set up to oversee the implementation of such programmes, members of those communities should be actively involved.

(14) Apart from the general issues to which reference has been made, there are various local problems which develop into needless irritants to minorities. For instance encroachment of Wakf properties and on grave yards have led to protests and grievances in some places. Suitable steps should be taken to deal with such problems on an expeditious and satisfactory basis.

(15) Problems relating to minorities need to be attended to on a continuing basis so that apprehensions are allayed and genuine grievances redressed. To facilitate this, a special cell will be created in the Ministry of Home Affairs to deal with matters relating to minorities.

Implementing Tools : The Progress of the implementation of the programme is monitored by the Minorities Cell in the Ministry of Welfare headed by an Additional Secretary. The Minorities Cell obtains quarterly reports on progress of the implementation of the programme from State governments, Union Territory Administrations and Central Ministries/ Departments. The quarterly reports are analysed and reviewed and the deficiency noticed in the implementation of the programme are brought to the notice of the authorities concerned through meetings, discussions and field visits etc.

The concerned Central Ministries/Departments and the

state governments, have nominated Nodal Officers to coordinate the implementation of the activities connected with the programme. All State and Union Territories, with very few exceptions, have also set up Minorities Cells to oversee implementation of the programme. A few State governments have also set up Research Units to take up random sample surveys to assess the benefits of development programme reaching the minorities.

The States of Uttar Pradesh, Bihar, Madhya Pradesh and Andhra Pradesh have State Minorities Commissions whereas the States of Gujarat and Assam have Minority Welfare Boards to deal with minority grievances and minority welfare measures. States of Uttar Pradesh, Bihar, Andhra Pradesh and Karnataka have also established State Minorities Financial Corporations to help promote economic development of minorities.

Programme Implementation Review : The implementation of the 15 Point Programme was earlier reviewed in a Conference of the State Nodal Officers in June 1986 it was, felt that the programme required a further review at a higher level. The Ministry of Welfare accordingly organised a conference of Chief Ministers/State Ministers in charge of 15 Point Programme on 19 June 1987 at New Delhi to review implementation of the Programme.

The Conference was attended by the Chief Ministers of Uttar Pradesh, Sikkim and Pondicherry and Ministers incharge of Minorities Welfare in the States of Andhra Pradesh, Assam, Bihar, Gujarat, Himachal Pradesh, Jammu and Kashmir, Karnataka, Kerala, Maharashtra, Mizoram, Tamil Nadu and West Bengal. The remaining States and Union Territories were represented by the Secretaries to respective Government/Nodal Officers. The representative of the concerned Central Ministries/Departments as well as chairman and members and Secretary of the Minorities Commission also attended the conference.

In his message to the conference, then Prime Minister Shri Rajiv Gandhi had emphasized the need for ensuring a fair deal to minorities in term of opportunities for employment and economic betterment and protection from any kind of discrimination.

Following were the important action points which had emanated as a result of the discussions in the aforesaid conference:

(i) Quarterly review meetings shall be held at the level of Chief Minister and also at the level of Chief Secretary in each state on a regular basis;

(ii) Monthly review meetings to be held at Divisional Commissioner/District Collector's level;

(iii) State Minorities Commissions/Boards in the respective States would be associated with the review at the state level;

(iv) Quarterly review meetings would be held at the State level with Nationalised Banks and Financial Corporations to review the processing of applications for financial assistance;

(v) Orientation courses for improving awareness of development schemes amongst minorities would be organised at the field level involving District Collector to create awareness of various developmental schemes in which minorities are largely employed;

(vi) Measures would be taken to improve registration of minority candidates in employment exchanges to minority educational institutions and minority concentration areas;

(vii) Reviews at State level regarding credit flow and credit plan evolved by the State Lead Banks;

(viii) In the context of Programme of Action under the National Policy on Education, 1986 relating to the educationally backward minority groups, State government will draw up a time bound action plan for implementation;

(ix) Selection Committees for recruitment to various posts to Include a representative of minority community;

(x) Minorities Cell would be set up in those States which have not yet set up;

(xi) Random sample surveys to be carried out by the States in selected areas for assessing the extent to which benefits of developmental programme reach the minority communities; and

(xii) Special stress on orientation training of officers at various levels to deal with problems of minorities and minorities welfare.

Reporting Format: In order to make the quarterly reports more result oriented with emphasis on physical progress achieved and to monitor the progress of implementation of Programme in qualitative terms, wherever possible, the conference adopted a format suggested by the Ministry of Welfare for the submission of the Information every quarter by the State Governments and Union Territory Administrations. Likewise, the concerned Central Ministries/Departments were asked to finalise formats for reporting on action taken in implementing the points in the Programme.

Though it is not possible to indicate the progress achieved in qualitative terms, the analysis of the information received does indicate that programme is being taken very seriously and the same has generated fair amount of awareness about the problems of minorities amongst officers not only at the State or District levels but also at the Block and village levels.

Communal Harmony Measures and Relief to Communal Riots Victims : State Government which have riot prone areas have shown positive response to the measures for prevention and control of communal violence and promotion of communal harmony. Most states have accepted the Central guidelines on relief to communal riot victims.

Recruitment in State Police : Some states have taken action or making selection committees for recruitment to State police representative but some of the States are yet to do so. None of the states have provided for nominating non-official members on the Committee in case of non-availability of suitable minority officials.

Recruitment in Central Police : Selection Committees for recruitment to Group C and D categories have been made representative in five Central Police organisations namely Central Reserve Police Force, Border Security Force, Central Industrial Security Force, Assam Rifles and Indo-Tibetan Border Police.

Selection Committee Representation : The ministry of Personnel, Public Grievances and Pension have issued instructions to all Central Ministries/Departments to enure that the selection committee for Group C and D posts comprise representatives from minority community. Some of the State governments and Union Territory Administrations have also issued orders making the selection committees for recruitment to various posts and particularly police service broad- based by inclusion of representatives of minority communities.

Employment Exchanges Directions : Director General Employment and Training (DGE & T), New Delhi has issued detailed instructions to State Governments to ensure that there is no discrimination against minorities in registering names and in sponsoring names to recruitment agencies by the employment exchanges. Instructions have also been issued by the DGE & T for conducting special registration drives in minority concentration areas and in minority educational institutions. The State Governments have been requested to review the arrangements for monitoring effective implementation of these instructions. The States of Assam,

Gujarat, Kerala, Madhya Pradesh, Orissa, Rajasthan, Sikkim and Delhi Administration have set up Monitoring Cells for the purpose. The State of Uttar Pradesh has set up a Coaching Centre together with an Inspection Cell to help larger number of minority candidates to obtain jobs.

Scheme for Coaching : University Grants Commission operates the scheme for coaching of weaker sections amongst minority communities through 20 universities and 14 coaching centers. The monitoring of the results of this scheme is done by the Department of Education of the Ministry of Human Resource Development, Analysis conducted by the UGC of the reports received, however, showed that the scheme had been rather ineffective and there were very few successful minority community candidates. The entire scheme is therefore being reviewed by the Standing Committee of the UGC.

Ministry of Welfare also grants 100% financial assistance to the minorities institutions to set up coaching centres exclusively for minorities to prepare them for All India and State Competitions for entry into IAS and other allied services as also the State services.

NATIONAL EDUCATION POLICY

Programme of Action under the National Policy for Education, 1986 contains an exclusive chapter on the education of the educationally backward minorities. The programme of action contains concrete measures to raise the literacy standard of the minorities. It provides for the drawing up a time bound action plan for implementation of the progress on items contained in the Programme of Action and also for setting up a Monitoring Cell in the State Education Departments to monitor the programme of educationally backward minority groups. It lays emphasis on in service training for teachers from educationally backward minority managed institutions in Science, Maths, English and provision of career guidance through National Council of Educational Research and Training, State Educational Research and Training and other resource centres.

It also provides for adequate representation of minority educational institutions in computer literacy scheme, vocational education at higher secondary levels in minority managed institutions, adequate thrust to adult education and early childhood education programme in minority concentration areas, survey of available facilities for girls' education and for setting up girls' institutions/hostels in minority concentration areas wherever necessary.

The Programme also provides for ensuring minority representation in all educational advisory committees/bodies at the Central/State level. The Programme also provides for drawing up clear guidelines for recognition of minority educational institutions and for timely disposal of pending applications.

The Programme of Action also requires introducing Maths, Science and English in Madrasas on voluntary basis and also setting up of early childhood centres and introducing socially useful productive work in these institutions besides provision for drawing up schemes for scholarships for weaker sections on merit-cum-means-basis, inbuilt system of placement in good institutions, fee exemption/fee concession compensation for opportunities lost for artisans and other weaker sections and formulation of a scheme for remedial coaching in minority managed educational institutions.

The Programme of Action also provides for setting up craft training institute in identified minority artisans concentration blocks with 80 per cent seats for artisans' children. The Programme of Action is being monitored by the Department of Education in the Ministry of Human Resource Development which has devised a format collecting information from State Governments and Union Territory Administrations.

MONETARY STRENGTH

The State Government and Union Territory Administrations are urged to organise quarterly review meetings by Secretary in-charge of institutional Finance with Commercial Banks at the State level to review flow of credit in minority concentration areas and to discuss the progress on flow of credit in minority concentration areas in the District Consultative Committee meetings. The States/Union Territories are also advised to take action on the following issues:

(i) Implementation of time bound action by the Lead Banks for setting up officers pre-recruitment centres for minority candidates at the State capitals;

(ii) Holding quarterly review meetings at state level with commercial banks and the state financial institutions to monitor progress in processing of applications sponsored by Minorities Financial Corporation for financial assistance;

(iii) Drawing up phased programme on research studies to identify sectors in industries, crafts and trades where minority communities are largely employed and on flow of credit to Minority artisan areas by State Government and Nationalised Banks; and

(iv) Drawing up a phased programme for organising orientation courses on creating awareness of schemes of financial assistance by banks and other financial institutions in minority artisan concentration blocks and in minority educational institutions.

Minorities Days : The Ministry celebrates "Welfare of the Minorities Day" every year as it did on 20th November 1987 as part of celebration of "Quami Ekta Week". The Day is celebrated highlighting the implementation of Prime Minister's 15 Point Programme for Minorities Welfare. The State government and Union Territory Administrations are also advised to celebrate this day in the following manner:

(i) Organisation of orientation courses at field levels involving District Collectors for creating awareness amongst minority groups of various development programmes undertaken by Central and State governments and by Financial institutions, with special focus on schemes involving community participation and voluntary organisations in the field of education, health, women and children's welfare;

(ii) To give adequate publicity the progress made in implementation of Prime Minister's 15 Point Programme; and

(iii) Publication of articles through newspaper etc. highlighting progress made in implementation of various aspects of Prime Minister's 15 Point Programme in local languages.

POLICE FOR RIOT CONTROL

According to Union Minister of State for Home, Mr. Subodh Kant Sahay the Centre has decided to raise a special task force to deal with communal riots and terrorism. The force shall be raised on the pattern of National Security Guards (NSG) and trained to strike at short notice at trouble spots. It will be equipped with sophisticated weapons. The Chief Ministers of all the states would raise similar task forces in their states to deal with emergencies. The rationale for creating the task force was:

(1) The Centre was deeply concerned about the flare-up of communal riots and growth of terrorism in various parts of the country. The governments did not consider it advisable to summon army to handle disturbances. The deployment of army had been so frequent in recent years that there were apprehensions that the armed forces might also become controversial;

(2) The need of the hour was therefore to have a task force,

which should inspire confidence among the people and cause terror among the troublemakers;

(3) The state police forces have been found to be inadequately trained and equipped to handle such situations;

(4) The army, in any case, was not trained to handle civil disturbances.

A cell had been created in the Home Ministry to monitor communal flare-ups in the country. It has also been assigned the task of keeping in touch with the social and voluntary organisations at the grassroots level which could be used to create communal harmony. The Home Ministry has identified sensitive areas and prepared guidelines for the states on how to handle communal flare-ups. The Government also proposes to set up a core group of media persons to evolve a mutually acceptable code for reporting communal riots and-terrorists activities. The role of the electronic media in this context is also being assessed and film and TV personalities will be asked to chalk out a strategy for using the electronic media to effectively spread the message of communal harmony and amity.

Deficiencies in the Riot Task Force Proposal : The proposal for Riot Task Force has been criticised among others by Bharatiya Janata Party. It suffers from certain deficiencies some of which are as follows:

Absence of Political Will: It was when Indira Gandhi was Prime Minister that the suggestion for the creation of a task force to deal with communal riots was first made. Though communal riots ravaged the country during Mr. Rajiv Gandhi's regime the idea was not pursued seriously. The V.P. Singh government did not last long enough to be able to consider various aspects of the suggestion. Now the Union Minister of State for Home of JD (S) government has announced that his government has decided to set up a "special task force" to deal with communal riots and terrorism and he has written to the state Chief Ministers also to set up similar task forces. Accordingly Mr. Chimanbhai Patel, Chief Minister of Gujarat decided to establish a special riot police force and asked top officials of his government to work out the details and submit a report in ten days. The report was not in evidence by the stipulated deadline. The reason obviously is weakness of political will.

Action Against Politicians Engineering Riots: It is common knowledge that most communal cases are engineered by politicians or their supporters. To give a specific instance when Mr. Patel was heading a coalition government a few months ago, there were communal riots in Baroda and according to an intelligence report he had received one of his cabinet colleagues was camping in the city and instigating the riots. Yet the Chief Minister did not take any action against him for fear of Bhartiaya Janata Party withdrawing from the government leading to his fall. It has not been spelt out clearly if the proposed task force will have power to round up politicians instigating communal riots or its jobs will be fire-fighting.

The Conception and Tasks of the Force Unclear: It appears that the centre does not have a comprehensive conception of what the force should be like and what tasks it should perform. It is expected to deal with both communal riots and acts of terrorism. The two are totally different from each other and any force saddled with the twin responsibility of a dealing with both must necessarily find itself less than equal to the tasks. For instance, the recent communal trouble in Hyderabad was immediately preceded by acts of terrorism by Naxalities- A task force cannot cope with both, the time gap between which was so small as to be almost negligible.

Difficulty of Coordination between Central and State Task Forces: As stated earlier the Centre is to have a task force and every state has to set up one of its own. That will create the problem of coordination of activities between the two. It has been an-accepted convention that the Centre can send reinforcements only on the specific request of the state government whose police force is unable to face a situation. Since the proposed task force will be a paramilitary organisation, it is not clear if the centre will decide suo moto to despatch it to a riot-torn state.

Nature of Composition of the Task Force: The Parliament had been told on August 21, 1987 that the states had been advised to have "mixed riot squads". Considering the proven communalisation of Uttar Pradesh's PAC and to a lesser extent, that of Bihar Police, the advice was sound but no state has acted on it so far.

Unless the above mentioned lacunae are removed, it would be desirable to streamline the existing police and paramilitary forces and continue the practice of deploying CRPF and Army in an area rocked by communal riots as these provide a sigh of relief to the peace (loving and law abiding members of both the communities).

NATIONAL UNITY

One of the main objectives of the Minorities Commission has been the promotion of national integration and secular outlook which is also one the goals provided in the Preamble and the Chapters on Fundamental Rights, the Directive Principles of State Policy and Duties of citizens in our Constitution. We had built a powerful psychological bond in the course of a common struggle for freedom against exploiting imperialism which had tried to defend themselves by the use of traditional divisions, economic or religious, cultural or regional to prolong their rule.

They had adopted a policy of 'divide and rule', hence we could not throw off the foreign yoke without experiencing the trauma of a rather distressing and disastrous partition which resulted primarily from the manipulations of the foreign ruler who exploited all our weaknesses. Now our country is politically free. But both internal and external forces of exploitation still try to use the same weaknesses and fissiparous tendencies whether they be based on religion, culture or region, to serve their own supposed interests. Even the struggle of political parties for power is not free from exploitation of caste, language and region for obtaining votes in an unscrupulous fashion. In this context, national integration has a relevance and importance in our national life which is perhaps unprecedented.

National Integration can only take place satisfactorily if there is a cooperation both from minorities as well as majorities in every part of the country to secure this objective. The Minorities Commission has been trying to explore means of promoting national recommendations. Such as:

> Establishment of an institute of National Integration with departments for study as well as of teaching of every aspect of national integration under a highly qualified director helped by experts formulating schemes of education for national, and coordination of all the agencies of national integration both voluntary and official; A national integration week should be observed every year commencing with the observance of communal harmony day; Citizens belonging to the religious minorities should be encouraged to participate in each others religious festivals and social and cultural festivities like Holi, Id, Dashehera, Milad, Guru Nanak Day, Christmas, etc.; 'Teachers and students' camps from national to regional at university, college and school levels; It may also the desirable, where feasible, to introduce non-denominational students hostels and to encourage willing young people to marry according to their free choice

irrespective of creed, caste or community; Persons who exploit communal and caste sentiments should be dealt with firmly; Special programmes for the education of women to bring about a genuine understanding and synthesis of the Indian culture should be undertaken.

The women, as mothers, wives, teachers and influential citizens, set best examples of human understanding, tolerance and respect for different religious beliefs, cultures and customs and can built the strongest bridges in their homes conducive to children intermingling without differences of religion, castes or creed; No particular caste or community should be allowed to have a dominant position in the paramilitary and police organisations; special forces should be created to combat riots; and Administrators have an important role to play in maintaining communal harmony and peace. In sensitive areas, specially trained senior officers with broad cultural outlook should be posted.

The most revolutionary recommendation was however, the formulation of a very comprehensive scheme for the promotion of National Integration and secular traditions and protection of human rights of all sections including minorities such a scheme involved the setting up of appropriate institutional machinery such as National Integration cum Human Rights Institute to help a National Integration-cum-Human Rights Commission to be provided for by the Constitution itself in place of multiplicity of Commission and panels looking after the interests of the minorities, Scheduled castes/tribes and backward classes as naming Commissions as those meant for minority communities or Scheduled castes etc. was by itself misleading and encouraged decisiveness.

The proposed Commission could have sub-commissions or sections separately with the problems of Minorities and those of Scheduled castes and Scheduled tribes and a Human

Rights sub- commission as a part of it could cover cases of all citizens alleging discrimination against them on any illegal grounds.

While all the suggestions except the last one are being implemented, the Government would do well in giving serious consideration to the establishment of National integration-cum-Human Rights Commission to obliterate the concept of exclusiveness among different segments of our society and welding them into one nation.

The Assessment : Minorities in our country have been disadvantaged by educational backwardness or other social and economic disabilities. The constitution has therefore provided certain protection and safeguards for them to secure social justice to them and to achieve national integration. Multi-social, multi-culture, multi- lingual and multi-religious societies all over the world have enacted legislations to safeguard the interests of minorities and protect them against discrimination on the basis of religion, caste, creed or colour.

In USA there is Civil Rights Commission to enforce the increasing number of statutory provisions meant to counteract and combat discrimination in every form and in every sphere of life and to achieve a new form of national integration, so is the Human Rights Commission and the Ministry of Multiculturalism, in Canada. In Britain, there is an elaborate legal machinery provided by the Race Relations Act. In USSR there is more comprehensively and strictly controlled socio-economic and legal framework as to attain a powerful form of integration between those who are culturally and racially so disparate as to be conceived of separate nationalities (though a move of disintegration has swept the country as a result of the twin policies of "Glasnost" and "Perestrioka" initiated by President Mikhail Gorbachov leading to the demand of independence by the constituent Republics of the USSR. The measures taken by our government in pursuance of the provisions of the constitution for the welfare of minorities have contributed substantially in raising their living standards but much more needs to be done to ameliorate their lot by floating new programmes and schemes to meet their special needs which have been thoroughly looked into and for meeting which a very comprehensive report has been submitted by High Power Panel headed by Dr. Gopal Singh.

The whole hearted implementation of the Prime- Minister's 15- Point Programme for the welfare of minorities is a high national priority. Its review from time to time by the centre and state nodal officers and the National Integration Council has impelled the governments to initiate more effective measures for their educational, economic and employment development and promotion of communal harmony but the achievements made so far in these fields leave much to be desired.

The Minorities Commission claims to have done whatever could be possible under the existing organisational structure and administrative set up and the resources made available to it. To make the commission to perform its function more effectively, it deserves to be granted constitutional status, statutory powers of investigation and the appointment of Commissioner for Linguistic Minorities or its integration with the Minorities Commission, appointment of State level minorities commission etc.

The suggestions made by the Minorities Commission in respect of national integration and secular values though commendable have not been able to yield the desired results. As a matter of fact, communalism has aggravated with the announcement of the implementation of Mandal Commission's Report and Babri Masjid-Ram Janambhoomi controversy by the vested interests with a view to create favourable vote banks, and in the process our ideas of national integration, communal harmony, casteless society, social justice etc. have become the first causalities-Communal riots have occurred on an unprecedented scale in the recent past.

Communalism is not of recent origin in India. It has been allowed to be exploited for too long in the calculated and pernancies pursuit of power by almost all politicians. No leader on either side of the fence hesitates to put self before countrymen and play communal politics at some time or the other. In fact, politics has come to be based practically on caste, religion and language and few leaders are willing to break the vicious circle. The generality of politicians are power hungry and are unwilling to shed communalism. Consequently one sees daily the debris of secularism in one city or another.

Gandhiji saw religion as a strong unifying force. He told the contending religious groups that "true religion should have nothing to do with activities such as riots or territorial divisions of the country". Nehru regarded as dangerous the alliance of religion and politics in the shape of communalism. But there is no going away from the fact that secularism is what holds the variety of religious, cultures and traditions India together. Thus for our survival as a nation we must take courage in both hands. This calls for concerted and sincere efforts by the leaders of all political parties to promote a secular way of life and shed the hangover (divide and rule) policy of the British rule. All the political parties should be unanimous in condemning those who let the country drift into recurrent communal disasters. They should whole heartily support the efforts aimed at curbing the menace which is eating into the vitals of our democratic secular fabric.

EVILS OF COMMUNALISM, CASTEISM AND REGIONALISM

National Integration Council was set up in 1961 by Pt. Jawaharlal Nehru to "find ways and means of combating the evils of communalism, casteism, regionalism etc. which were working against the unity and integrity of the nation. It has been reconstituted several times after its birth- as a rule with the change of regime in Delhi. It has been unable to achieve its objectives. New dimensions have been added to communalism in Punjab where efforts have been made to create ill-will between Hindus and Sikhs and thank God that these have not yet succeeded in causing Hindu-Sikh riots on communal lines. Casteism has been encouraged by the Janata Dal's passionate backing of the Mandal Commission's Report and regionalism has taken a highly dangerous form in certain states and is the very antithesis of national integration as manifested in Kashmir's demand for independence, the campaign for Sikh Homeland and insurgency in Assam founded on the premise for an independent state.

We have thus moved to national disruption rather than integration. A ritualistic approach to national integration will not do any more. Enough speeches, worded in holy phrases have been made by our leaders in the past. Dissatisfaction among the sections of populations in the concerned states would have to be removed by taking appropriate concrete steps to guard the country against separatists and secessionists.

It is alleged that the minorities are being appeased, they have been given more than equal rights and privileges in the Constitution, the majority are not getting their due, the minorities are being given more than their share and perhaps pampered in the bargain. On the other hand it is contended that the Muslims are more badly off than most other communities, around 3 per cent of them are to be found in the All India services, their representation in the army, police and other services, is much lower than their proportion in the population. When the 1986 policy on education was being formulated, it was discovered that they were educationally the most backward in he country.

Bharatiya Janata Party stands for the abolition of the Minorities' Commission and its substitution by Human Rights

Commission for all citizens of India irrespective of their religion, caste or creed, scrapping of Article 370 granting special status to Kashmir to bring back the state to the Indian mainstream, adoption of uniform civil code for all Indians irrespective of their religion, caste or creed, promotion of all languages and repeal of Muslim Women's Act to restore to Muslim women their dignity and right to justice that other Indian women have. The solution lies in appreciating the selfless struggle of Mahatma Gandhi to bring love among Hindus and Muslims. Symbolically, the thought of Rama of the Hindus to be the same as Rahim of the Muslims and never accepted the separation of Hindus and Muslims and became a martyr to this cause. We may rescue from the fratricidal quarrel the harmonious co-existence of the faiths by adhering to traditions of tolerance and togetherness emphasized by Gandhi.

9

NON-GOVERNMENTAL AGENCIES

SOCIAL WELFARE

Social welfare has its roots in voluntary action and had been sustained by it from several centuries in the past upto the present. India has a glorious tradition of organising voluntary work for social good. The term, 'Voluntarism' is derived from latin word 'Voluntas' which means "will" or "freedom". Harold Laski an eminent British political scientist defined "Freedom of association" as a recognised legal right on the part of all persons to combine for the promotion of purposes in which they are interested. Article 19 (1) (c) of the Constitution of India confers on the Indian citizens the right 'to form association'. Freedom of association is rightly regarded as taking high rank among the liberties of man. It is the liberty of the widest scope for men may wish to associate for any purpose which two or more of them may have in common.

They may wish to associate to do something together, or to get something done to further their own or other people's interest, to resist oppression or injustice or to practise either to pursue great or small, general or public object. In the U.N.

terminology voluntary organisations are called non-governmental organisation (NGOs). These are also identified as Volags (Voluntary agencies) and AGs (Action groups). The term voluntary association is variously defined. According to Lord Beveridge, 'A voluntary organisation, properly speaking, is an organisation which whether its workers are paid or unpaid, is initiated and governed by its own members without external control. Definitions given by Mary Morris and Modeline Roff are also similar. The only addition that Modeline Roff makes is that these voluntary organisations should depend in part at least, upon finding support from voluntary resources.

Michali Banton defines it as a group organised for the pursuit of one interest or of several interests in common. In the words of David L. Sills, Voluntary organisation is a group of persons organised on the basis of voluntary membership without state control for the furtherance of some common interests of its members. Norman Johnson in his examination of the various definitions of voluntary social services points out their four main characteristics: (i) Method of formation, which is voluntary on the part of a group of people, (ii) Method of government, with self-governing organisation to decide on its constitution, its servicing, its policy and its clients; (iii) Method of financing, with at least some of its revenues drawn from voluntary sources; and (iv) Motives with the pursuit of profit included.

To some writers like Sills legal status of voluntary organisations is not of much consequence for its activities. But in the Indian context, it is of special significance for their financial accountability it is clearly stipulated that only those voluntary associations would be considered for grants-in-aid which are incorporated and have been existing for at least three years; Smith and Freedman considered voluntary association as a structure formally organised, relatively permanent, secondary grouping as opposed to less structural, informal, ephoneral or primary grouping. Formal organisation is reflected in the presence of offices which are filled through some established procedures, scheduled meetings, qualifying criteria for membership and some formalised division and specialisation of labour, although the organisations do not exhibit all these characteristics to the same degree; voluntary organisation have to sacrifice substantially their autonomy as there are quite a few restrictions (though regulatory in character) which they have to accept if they expect public grant. In India, for example, religion besides politics is the other social sphere from which they have to keep themselves away if they wish to seek public money for participation in nation building activities. This is in consonance with Indian secularism which prohibits use of public money for propagation of any religion; finally in India, they must be committed to national objectives namely socialism, secularism, democracy national unity and integrity.

Attempting a comprehensive definition of voluntary organisation Prof. M.R. Inamdar observes, "A voluntary organisation in development to be of durable use to the community has to nurse a strong desire and impulse for community development among its members, to be economically viable to possess dedicated and hard working leadership and command resources of expertise in the functions undertaken."

MAIN CHARACTERISTICS

The definitions of a voluntary organisation given above bring out its following main characteristics:

(i) It is registered under the Societies Registration Act, 1880, the Indian Trusts Act, 1882; the Cooperative Societies Act, 1904 or the Joint Stock Companies Act, 1959 depending upon the nature and scope of its activities to give it a legal status;

(ii) It has definite aims and objectives and programmes for their fulfilment and achievement;

(iii) It has an administrative structure and a duly constituted management and executive committee;

(iv) It is an organisation initiated and governed by its own members on democratic principles without any external control and

(v) It raises funds for its activities partly from the exchequer in the form of grants-in-aid and partly in the form of the contributions or subscription from the members of the local community and/or the beneficiaries of the programmes.

Motivating Factors of Voluntary Action : The factors which motivate people take to voluntary action or the sources of voluntarism may be identified as religion, government, business, philanthrophy and mutual aid. The missionary zeal of religious organisations, the commitments of government organisation to the public interest, the profit making urge in business, the altruism of the 'social superiors' and the motive of self-help among fellowmen all are reflected in voluntarism. At the operational level, the above mentioned components may not differ much from one another but each of them is moved by an impulse with service as the common motivation.

Bouradillon and William Beveridge viewed mutual aid and philanthrophy as two main sources from which voluntary social service organisations would have developed. They spring from individual and social conscience respectively. The other factors motivating voluntary action could be cited as personal interest, seeking benefit such as experience, recognition, knowledge and prestige, commitment to certain values etc.

Further, impulses of a great variety move men for their grouping or forming voluntary associations to serve themselves, their fellowmen or the unfortunate lot of the society. These are idealistic, educative, psychological and social in character operating separately or on varying combination. Idealistically voluntary associations preserve democracy and the individuals' personality and contribute to the general health of the society.

They are a strong agent of political socialisation in a democracy and educate their members about the social norms and values and help combat loneliness. Psychological impulses lead people to join voluntary associations for security, self expression and for satisfaction of their interests with the decaying of social institutions like family, church and community.

Sociologists have studied the psychology of membership with the motivating interests in view namely, community, class, ethnic, religious, sex, age etc. and they have found that the association gives the individual a feeling of community with his fellowmen-membership has class bias where socio-economic interest has motivated the joining of association, membership of a given group has been found to be largely homogenous in terms of class, ethnicity and religion, membership is directly related to socio- economic status, as measured by level of income, occupation, house ownership, level of living and education, greater interest is evinced in joining voluntary association in urban areas than rural; men dominate the direction boards of most agencies; women join organisation depending upon their family status and the stage they occupy in the family cycle, participation in voluntary association declines as people grow old and so on, thus the psychology of joining voluntary association is a complex phenomenon. It may vary from one individual to another and one group of individuals to another depending on their culture, social milieu and political environment.

THE ROLE

In a democratic, socialistic and welfare society, voluntary organisations are indispensable and they perform a number of functions for the welfare of its members, the development of the country and integration and solidarity of the society and nation. Some of these objectives and functions may be discussed as follows:

(i) Man is by nature gregarious. The urge to act in groups is fundamental in him. People therefore form groups and associations voluntarily for their benefit as also of others with a view to lead a full and richer life as is reflected in voluntary associations formed for promotion of recreational and cultural activities, social services, professional interests etc.

(ii) A pluralistic society with a democratic system requires multitude of independent, voluntary non-government associations as buffer between the individual and the state preventing the government from developing monopoly in various fields. Voluntary organisation involve citizens in noble affairs and avoid concentration of powers in the hands of government and thus serve as power breakers. Sharing of power by voluntary groups restrain government from developing monopolistic approach to organisation of services.

(iii) They enable the individuals to learn the fundamentals of groups and political action through participation in the governing of their private organisations.

(iv) Organised voluntary, action helps groups and individuals with diverse political and other interests, contributes to strengthening of feeling of national solidarity and promotes participative character of democracy.

(v) The state does not have the requisite financial resources and manpower to meet all the needs of its citizens. It can therefore have the responsibility of providing them minimum needs. The voluntary organisations by raising additional resources locally can meet uncovered needs and enrich local life.

(vi) Voluntary organisations also help the state in the areas which are its exclusive responsibility but for which it has limited sources and perform such functions in much better way as compared to the state organisations. Education for example is the responsibility of the state but the educational institutions being run and managed by voluntary organisation far outnumber the government institutions and excel the latter in quality of service also in view of the flexibility, ability at experimentation, pioneering spirit and other virtues. Same is the case in respect of the provision of health services which is again the responsibility of the state. But the hospitals sponsored by philanthropic and charitable institutions are well known for better care and concern in comparison to government owned hospitals. Maharaj Sawan Singh Charitable Hospital at Beas is a unique modern institution giving free treatment and food to thousands of patients without any distinction of caste and creed.

(vii) Voluntary organisations thus have not only a role to play even in the accepted state responsibilities but they can also venture into new needs, work in new areas, unveil social evils and give attention to hitherto unattended and unmet needs. They can act as sappers and miners of unfolding development revolution. They can function as recognisance squades. They can be fore runners of change and anticipate and take action to make it less painful. They can work for progress, development and consequently in course of time they can help the state in extending its activities over wider areas, thus raising the national minimum.

(viii) They provide avenues for activities to those persons who do not relish participation in the activities of the state through politics and government, but organise into voluntary groups thus making their talent, experience and spirit of service available to society in bringing about changes in it with a view to meeting the needs and aspirations of the people concerned and enriching their lives.

(ix) They act as a stabilising force by welding together people with such groups as are not politically motivated and are not concerned about the fortunes of one or the other political party in capturing government power but are above party politics and are interested in other areas of nation building and thus contribute to national integration and concentration on non- political issues.

(x) They also perform the functions of educating their members and the public at large about the policies and programmes of the government about their welfare, their rights and obligations and also are in a position to offer constructive criticism in respect of wrong policies and activities of government without any fear and with courage of conviction obliging the government to make necessary adjustments to accommodate the viewpoints of the public likely to be affected by such policies and actions as has been the experience in the case of programme concerning schedule tribes and environment conservation and preservation.

(xi) The endeavour to meet the special requirements of specialised interests and special groups such as the aged, the handicapped, women, children, etc. which cannot be adequately met by the state for reasons of financial scarcity. Age-India, and Help age are voluntary organisations engaged in the welfare programmes of aged, Indian Council of Child Welfare is engaged in the promotion of child welfare. All India Ex-servicemen Welfare Association is concerned with the welfare of the ex-servicemen. Similarly thousands of voluntary associations exist to look after the interests of the groups they represent.

(xii) They are in a better position to function to their own satisfaction as also to that of their clientele for the reason that they can identify the needs of individuals, groups and community being close to them and formulate appropriate programmes to meet them, make necessary changes and modification in them in the light of the experiences gained in their implementation processes, involve people's participation, raise necessary funds and win public confidence and cooperation by human touch, human warmth and sympathy which the bureaucrats in governmental organisation are not capable of.

In sum, voluntary organisations' main functions comprise giving concrete expression to the fundamental right of freedom of association, identifying the needs of individuals, groups and communities and initiating projects and programmes to meet them on their own or with the grant-in-aid of the government, sharing the responsibility of the state in providing minimum needs of the citizens, covering the areas of uncovered and unmet needs, preventing the monopolistic tendencies of the government, providing opportunities to people imbued with the spirit of service and dedication to organise themselves to promote public welfare, educating citizens about their rights and obligations and informing them about the policies and programmes of the government contemplated and initiated for their welfare, mobilising public support through publicity campaigns, raising functional resources through contributions and donations and finally organising activities of non-partisan and non-political nature for wellbeing of the society, enriching the lives of citizens and progress of the nation.

Weaknesses and Deficiencies of Voluntary Organisation: Despite the achievements and success of voluntary organisations in various fields and the excellent work done by them in specific areas, the inherent defects and weaknesses which if overcome would equip them to function move effectively in the formulation of implementation of numerous programmes intended for the welfare of the concerned clientele. Numerous weaknesses afflicting voluntary organisations may be discussed as follows:

No Dedicated Leadership : In the post-independence era, the voluntary organisations faced the crisis of leadership as the leaders who pioneered voluntary action and worked for it with spirit of devotion and dedication chose to enter politics to find berths in legislatures and parliament thus creating a vacuum for leadership in voluntary organisations.

No Young Leadership : The leadership with some exceptions is concentrated in the hands of elderly people. Their style of functioning exhibits auhoritarianism and frustrates the younger people who are embodiments of new ideas, initiatives and innovation which are not allowed to be expressed and practiced.

Leadership Monopolisation and Interlocking : It has been observed that there is a tendency towards monopolisation and interlocking of leadership at the top level of voluntary action groups and organisations as is reflected in the same person being the President in one organisation, Secretary in the other , Treasurer in the third and a member of the executive in the fourth. This interlocking of leadership can be advantageous in formulating coordinated policies, programmes and activities, facilitating exchange of technical know-how and experience and mobilising people for a common goal.

But the greatest disadvantage of such leadership is that fresh blood is not allowed to flow into the organisation and leadership. Leaders in most of the groups would like to perpetuate themselves rather than allow the second rank leadership to grow. Instances of occupying positions of importance by the same persons for decades are numerous. The continuation of elected or nominated members for very long tenures in any group or agency makes them so powerful that they prove to be counter democratic.

Service Deterioration : The voluntary organisations had to engage themselves in social welfare services in many areas after independence to meet the aspirations and hopes of people and accept all available programmes whether they had the requisite resources in men or material or not. With this sudden expansion of their activities without adequate preparation the quality of their service was inevitably to deteriorate and was bound to be below the expected standards.

No Popular Participation : Voluntary organisations are meant to provide opportunities to the citizens for democratic participation but they have not been able to fulfil this obligation due to the method and manner in which they function, and failed to attract people interested in constructive work and develop channels for peoples' enthusiastic participation. Some of the factors responsible for such a state of affairs are general backwardness of the people, absence of and adequate number of dedicated persons, over emphasis on targets and time bound programmes, political interference and vested interests, easy availability of funds without proper planning and assessment of felt needs and safeguards for the community, distrust of agencies and workers who do not have a base in the community and are unable to win its support and lack of decentralisation which could give a feeling of being partners in development rather than development being thrust from above.

Isolation of Voluntary Agencies : Thousands of voluntary organisations functioning at local level throughout the length and breadth of the country, though doing appreciable work have no links among themselves and therefore feel isolated and their workers lonely and depressed, consequently they have little influence on the policies and programmes formulated by the government. Moreover since their actions are fragmented and spread over a variety of fields, they do not seem to meet needs in a sizeable way and make visible impact on the life of the community.

VOLUNTARY ORGANISATIONS

The voluntary organisations have played magnificent role in rendering services to different section of society and they have bright prospects to continue with their present programmes and extend them to the areas where they are not existing with the support of the government of which they are partners and not contenders in the service of people. If their weaknesses, draw- backs, deficiencies and disabilities as delineated above are removed and their organisation and structure are streamlined and strengthened especially in the matter of periodical enrolment of fresh members, democratic election of office bearers, provision of right type of leadership, decentralisation and delegation of authority, qualified and trained personnel, people's participation in the formulation and execution of programmes, proper use of funds, forum for discussions of common problems, mechanism of coordination, non-interference of politicians, abolition of vested interests, the enlistment of dedicated and devoted workers, social accountability and self-evaluation etc., they are bound to recapture their old pioneering spirit and serve the society with greater vigour earning the gratitude and appreciation of both the government and the society.

Voluntary Organisations : Aid by State Governments : In addition to the Central Ministries of Welfare, Health and Family Welfare, Human Resource Development, Rural Development, Environment and Forests etc. various Departments of State governments especially their Department of Social Welfare provide grants-in-aid to voluntary organisation catering to the welfare programmes of various-sections of society. But the Departments of social Welfare need to be toned up to improve their efficiency to serve better the interests of their beneficiaries. The Department of Social Welfare of Haryana Government had allotted budget of Rs 141.47 crores for 1988-89 for the implementation of number of welfare schemes for the destitute women and widows, old and aged and handicapped persons in the state but it had spent only 46 per cent of the total budget allocation on the various schemes till January 1989.

The Estimates Committee of Haryana Vidhan Sabha has made various recommendations and suggestions for streamlining the working of the Department of Social Welfare in general and that of the voluntary organisations in particular:

(i) With a view to checking the misutilisation of funds, the Department should spend amount on various schemes proportionately as provided in the budget so that amount may not be spent at the fag end of the year, indiscriminately,

(ii) The Department should also pursue the matter with the Finance Department vigorously and get the pending schemes sanctioned and funds released well in time so that the purpose of the schemes for which they are meant could be achieved,

(iii) Most of the important posts in the Department were lying vacant since 1987. The vacant posts should be filled up immediately to improve the efficiency of the department or abolished if not required or converted and filled up at the earliest,

(iv) The present procedure of routing the applications for grants-in-aid to voluntary organisations through the Deputy Commissioner is very much time-consuming. All such applications should be forwarded by the District Social Welfare Officer with his inspection reports so that grants be issued by the Department well in time,

(v) The question of releasing grants in time may be reviewed in depth by the Government and a clear time schedule be laid down to avoid hardship and difficulties to the voluntary organisations,

(vi) All Voluntary organisations should maintain record of all assets acquired wholly or substantially out of government grant and should not be disposed off, embezzled or utilised for purposes other than those for which grant-in-aid was given without the prior sanction of the government,

(vii) Voluntary organisation should be encouraged through financial assistance to promote needed welfare services in the areas where they do not exist and also to initiate new welfare services not hitherto undertaken.

Voluntary Organisations : Aid by Foreign Countries: Voluntary organisations in India like their counterparts in developing countries receive aid from international voluntary agencies (non- government organisations).

BIBLIOGRAPHY

Alderson, J. : *Social Classes : an Introduction,* Hamish Hamilton, London, 1984.

Berhard, Davies : *The Use of Groups in Social Work Practice,* Routledge and Kegan Paul, London, 1975.

Burns, M. : *Social Security and Public Policy,* Macgraw Hill, New York, 1956.

Burton, F. : *The Politics of Legitimacy: Struggles in a Belfast Community,* Routledge and Kegan Paul, London, 1978.

Clarke, R. V. and Hough, J. M. : *The Effectiveness of Policing,* Gower Publications, Farnborough, 1980.

Critchley, T. A. : *The Conquest of Violence: Order and Liberty in Britain,* Constable, London, 1970.

Dubey, S.N. : *Administration of Social Welfare Programmes in India,* Somaliya, Bombay, 1973.

Friedlander, W.A. : *Concepts and Methods of Social Classes,* Prentice Hall New Delhi, 1960.

Gangrade, K.D. : *Community Organisation in India,* Popular Prakashan, Bombay, 1973.

Gisela, Knopka : *Group Work: A Heritage and a Challenge,* National Association of Social Welfare, New York, 1960.

Gore, M.S. : *The Beggar Problem in Metropolitan Delhi,* Delhi School of Social Work, Delhi, 1959.

Honderich, T. : *Problems of Social Classes in India,* Penguin, London, 1980.

Jocob, K. K. : *Methods and Field of Social Work in India*, Asia Publication, Bombay, 1965.

Kulkarni, P.D. : *Social Policy and Social Development in India*, Association of Schools of Social Work in India, Madras, 1979.

Mamoria C.A. : *Labour Welfare, Social Security and Industrial Peace in India*, Kitab Mahal, Allahabad, 1983.

Mathur, A.S. and Gupta, A.S. : *Social Classes and Social Change*, Ram Prasad and Sons, Agra, 1965.

McMillan, Wayne : *Community Organisation for Social Welfare*, University of Chicago Press, Chicago, 1951.

Minhas, B. S. : *Planning and the Poor*, S. Chand & Co, New Delhi, 1974.

Norton, P. : *Law and Order and British Politics*, Gower Publications, Farnborough, 1984.

Pankar, S.P. and Rao, Kamala : *A Study of Prostitutes in Bombay*, Lalwani Publishing Houses, Bombay, 1962.

Pennock, J. R. and Chapman, J. W. : *The Limits of Law*, Leiber-Atherton, New York, 1974.

Reddi G.Narayana, and Reddi Soma Narayan : *Women and Child Development: Some Contemporary Issues*, Chugh Publications, Allahabad, 1987.

Shklar, J. N. : *Encyclopaedia of Social Classes*, Harvard University Press, Cambridge, 1964.

Skolnick, J. H. : *Justice Without Trial: Law Enforcement in Democratic Society*, John Wiley, New York, 1967.

Srivastavia, S.P. : *Public Participation in Social Defence*, Lucknow University, Lucknow, 1978.

Taylor, I. : *Law and Order : Arguments for Socialism*, Macmillan, London, 1981.

Taylor, I. P. Walton and J. Young : *The New Criminology: for a Social Theory of Defiance*, Routledge and Kegan Paul, London, 1973.

Zaidi, M. : *Social Classes*, Basic Books, New Delhi, 2000.

INDEX

P

R

S

T

U

V

W

❑❑❑